1988

Securing the Future for Americans Over Sixty-Five

Contemporary Issues Series

Securing the Future for Americans Over Sixty-Five

An Overview of the Issues Surrounding the Quality of Life for Aging U.S. Citizens

Carl Flaningam

National Textbook Company
a division of *NTC Publishing Group* • Lincolnwood, Illinois USA

Published by National Textbook Company, a division of NTC Publishing Group.
© 1988 by NTC Publishing Group, 4255 West Touhy Avenue,
Lincolnwood (Chicago), Illinois 60646-1975 U.S.A.
Manufactured in the United States of America.
8 9 0 ML 9 8 7 6 5 4 3 2

362.6042
7585

Contents

129,647

Preface

In addressing the problems of aging, the high school debate community breaks new ground but also returns to some familiar ground. Although the problems of the elderly have never been the basis for a topic before, medical care has been a topic on several occasions and a number of case areas subsumed (e.g., generic name drugs, nursing home regulation) have been debated before.

The three topic options parallel growing areas of social concern. Growing numbers of persons over age 65, especially those over age 75, have sparked interest in assessing the long-range health of the Social Security trust funds. Providing for retirement security has been the subject of several pieces of legislation, including amendments to the Social Security Act, the Employee Retirement Income Security Act, and the Age Discrimination in Employment Act. Within the past few years, both federal and state governments have acted to curb rapidly increasing health care costs affecting the fiscal solvency of the Medicare and Medicaid programs. And Congress has become increasingly attentive to problems of quality of care in nursing homes.

Chapters One and Two attempt to provide an overview of the topics, providing definitions of key terms and laying out argumentative ground on the three topics. Chapters Three, Four, and Five examine core issues on the different topics: the economic status of the elderly under current legislation, health care and health care cost containment strategies under federal and state law, and factors affecting the provision and quality of nursing home care. Chapter Six discusses four different services of importance to the elderly: home health care, prescription medication, mental health care, and transportation services. Finally Chapter Seven addresses three special concerns: elder abuse, age discrimination in employment, and housing problems of the elderly.

1 Topic Definitions and Affirmative Ground

TOPIC: That the federal government should implement a comprehensive program to guarantee retirement security for United States citizens over age 65.

TERMS

"federal government"

Corpus Juris Secundum ("CJS") defines "Federal": "(i)n American law, belonging to the general government or union of the States, founded on or organized under the Constitution or laws of the United States."[1] *Black's Law Dictionary ("Black's")* defines "Federal" as "(p)ertaining to the national government of the United States."[2]

All three topics make the federal government the agent of action. This is not a significant departure from current systems dealing with the elderly. Old Age and Survivor's Insurance ("OASI") under Title II of the Social Security Act is exclusively federal in funding and administration, while Medicare is federally funded and operated by the Health Care Financing Administration. Particular exceptions are Medicaid, which is funded by both the federal government and the states, and persons who receive Supplemental Security Income ("SSI") under Title XVI of the Social Security Act also receive supplementary state funds in some states.

"implement"

This term, the verb in the topic sentence, means "to put into effect," as in "we implemented the plan," according to the *Oxford American Dictionary ("Oxford")*.[3] In the context of the topic sentence, "implemented" means that the agent of action is required to put into effect mandates of the affirmative resolution, i.e., the interpretation given "comprehensive program to guarantee retirement security."

"a comprehensive program"

"Program" as defined by the *Oxford American Dictionary* is "a plan of intended procedure"[4]; "comprehensive", an adjective, means "inclusive, including much or all."[5] "A" is defined by the same source as an "indefinite article: one person or thing, but not any specific one," as in "I need a knife."[6] *Black's* further comments that "(t)he article 'a' is not necessarily a singular term: it is often used in the sense of 'any' and is then applied to more than one individual object," although meaning is dependent on context, "a" also being synonymous with "the" where a particular item is referred to.[7]

"A comprehensive program" is language which has been used on other topics in the past. The issues created are ones of the reasonableness of affirmative interpretations which seem limited to a narrow subset of the class of persons addressed by the topics, or to only one of the concerns of those persons, as well as the reasonableness of negative topicality arguments which argue that the affirmative interpretation fails because it excludes some portion of the population addressed by the topic, or some issue of concern to them. "A" in the sense of "any" means that the affirmative proposal is not the sole or exclusive program or plan to ensure retirement security; it is logically possible for other comprehensive programs to exist, the affirmative's proposal is simply the one under discussion. While it can be argued that "a" in the sense of "the" means that the affirmative plan is the single comprehensive program to guarantee retirement security, the better view is that "a" in its "the" sense, in context, would refer to a particular program, in this case "the" affirmative program. The question of whether the affirmative interpretation is a reasonable one must be answered by considering whether it meets the "inclusive, including much or all" standard. The affirmative need only "include much" in the scope of its program. As will be discussed later, it should be noted that neither this topic nor the other two topics use the word "all" before "United States citizens over age 65." Hence, limitations on the population within persons over age 65 appear permissible under any of the topics.

"guarantee"

In the context of this topic, this term means "to promise" or "to state with certainty." *(Oxford)*[8] CJS is in accord, commenting that "guarantee" "may be used, not in a technical legal sense, but as synonymous with 'agree', 'assume liability' ... 'insure', 'promise', 'secure' or 'warrant'."[9] "Guarantee," as used on this and on the other two topic choices, refers to the degree of assurance of solvency of the affirmative plan, i.e., the likelihood that "retirement security" will be attained.

"retirement security"

This is the key phrase in the topic: affirmative mandates must be synonymous with "measures to attain retirement security." As is discussed later, "retirement security" is not a phrase with a well-defined meaning, nor is it a phrase used with any frequency in the literature on transfer payments to the aged or on care for the aged. *Oxford* defines "retire" as "to give up one's regular work because of advancing age" or "to cause (an employee) to do this."[10] The same source pertinently defines "security" as "safe, certain not to slip or fail, reliable."[11] Therefore, any measure or set of measures guaranteeing safety, certainty or reliability for persons in the state of retirement appears to fit within the confines of this topic. An arguable point is about the measurement of whether "retirement security" has been attained, whether this is to be measured objectively and externally or subjectively and internally. The former view would posit that assurances meeting objective standards, e.g., guaranteeing an income above the poverty line would be sufficient; the later view is that whether persons age 65 or older are secure in their retirement is subjectively determined: do they feel safe or certain or can they rely on the affirmative's program? At most, this is productive of a solvency argument that retirees will not "feel" secure in the promises of the affirmative plan.

Although the interpretation given above of "retirement" is the standard one, there are alternative views. The economist Michael Boskin argues that cessation of working activities altogether is only one of several possible interpretations of retirement: he would, for example, add a shift to part-time work, cessation of work for a period of time, or shifts to voluntary activities.[12]

"United States citizens"

As *Black's* notes, under the Fourteenth Amendment, this term refers to all persons born or naturalized in the United States.[13] The obvious limiting factor is to exclude legal and illegal aliens in the United States, as well as to avoid plans affecting retirement security outside the United States.

"over age 65"

All three topics use this phrase as the operational definition for "aging" or "aged." A chronological figure is a clearer definitional point than such alternative phrases as "elderly," or "senior citizens," or "aged," although literature referring to those terms generally indicates a reference to age 65 and older.[14] It should be noted, however, that persons age 65 and older are hardly homogeneous as to income, health status, or a variety of other factors.[15] A recurrent topic in literature on the elderly is the emerging subgroups of persons age 75 and older (as well as age 85 and older) and the effects of having a sizeable number of "very elderly" on social services.[16] Although "over age 65" appears to be an extremely precise term, a technical argument can be made that this wording excludes persons who are 65 from the scope of the affirmative mandates. More precise wording of this topic (and the other topics as well) would be "age 65 and older." To use a legal example, the phrase "exceeds the sum or value of $10,000" is interpreted to mean "at least $10,000.01."[17] Thus, it could be argued "over age 65" does not include persons who are age 65. A reasonable response to this argument is that everyone who has attained the age of 65 is "over age 65," by at least a minute, hour, day, etc.

COMMENTS ABOUT THIS TOPIC WORDING

This topic wording is easily the most inclusive and far reaching of the three topics, largely because of the choice of the phrase "retirement security" as the focus of the resolution. While this wording may have been intended to separate this topic as a transfer payments-focused topic from the topics on custodial care and long-term health care, "retirement security" as a phrase is a poor choice to accomplish this aim. "Retirement security" is not a term with a settled definition: it is not used to refer to a set of approaches, programs, or objectives by writers in the field. Hence, "retirement security" programs can be reasonably interpreted to include any plans which guarantee assurances of safety, certainty, reliability, etc. of retirement for persons 65 or older. While this would certainly include modification or wholesale change of Social Security, private pensions, or Supplemental Security Income, "retirement security" plans may encompass a great deal more. A strong argument can be made that "retirement security" encompasses the other two topic choices, nursing home care and medical care for the elderly: both have significant impacts on the degree of assurance of quality of life in retirement. Additionally, such issues as age discrimination in employment and the availability of quality services to the elderly (e.g. housing, adult protective services, home health care) would have a similar impact and come under programs to guarantee "retirement security." From this perspective, topical mandates include all comprehensive programs (those which include or respond to much or all of a particular age-based concern) which can be established to enhance assurances of safety, certainty, or reliability of the retirement life styles of persons 65 or older.

As was mentioned above, none of the topics include the word "all" before "United States citizens over age 65." Hence, coverage of such citizens by program mandates need not be universal for this population: affirmative plans need only be restricted to persons who are United States citizens and who are over age 65. Decisions as to what portion of this population is to be focused on by the affirmative is a matter of judgment by the affirmative. Therefore, affirmative plans dealing with, for example, services to American Indian elderly would fit the topic just as reasonably as overhauling Social

Security. The rebuttal to this position is that it implies that this topic (as well as the other two) refers to "some United States citizens over age 65," which they clearly do not. The reasoning behind this argument is that no modifiers were used before or after "United States citizens over age 65," when such modifiers could have been included: "low-income," "in poverty," etc. Absent the placement of modifying language before or after these phrases, the argument proceeds, the topics should be presumed to refer to all such persons. There are two rebuttals to this position. First, it unreasonably restricts debate. Under this interpretation, only plan mandates which can be established to apply to each and every United States citizen over age 65 fit the resolution and are topical.

A second response has been used on other topics in the past, particularly those involving "comprehensive programs" and the provision of medical care to United States citizens. The approach is to argue that the affirmative mandate is available and applicable to all United States Citizens over age 65 and therefore typical, even though the services of the affirmative plan may in fact only be used by some proportion of that population. This would be the case, for example, where the affirmative sought to reduce abuse and neglect of persons over age 65 ("elder abuse"), an example which would apply to at least the retirement security and the custodial care topics. The guarantees of the affirmative plan would apply to all persons over age 65, although it is estimated that four percent of the elderly are abused.[18] A slightly more problematic case would be one where the affirmative guaranteed a type of service or level of health care (e.g., nursing home care, home health care) excluded at present from low or moderate income elderly persons but enjoyed by persons age 65 or older with private health insurance or who are otherwise able to pay for such services. While a weak argument could be made that the affirmative extends the guarantee only to persons under a certain income level, the affirmative can argue that the plan makes the service available to all of the elderly, regardless of income. A content-specific factor helps affirmatives in this regard: nursing home care is so expensive that all but persons with considerable assets or very generous private health insurance soon "spend down" their assets and become eligible for Medicaid.[19] High cost custodial care and acute health care services are inclusive in potential scope as to most, if not all, persons over age 65.

The retirement security topic, as well as the other two topics, are worded in such a fashion as to virtually require "topicality by effect" approaches by affirmatives. This is because none of the topics specify even in general the form of action to be taken. For example, the custodial care topic could have been phrased, "Resolved: that the federal government should provide nursing home care for United States citizens over age 65" or "Resolved: that the system of regulations for nursing homes in the United States." Instead, all three topics, especially the retirement security topic, are written in a "guarantee of results" format. One can read the custodial care and long-term health care topics as requiring affirmatives to enact programs which will in turn produce the result of guaranteeing adequate custodial care or long-term health care. While one could also read these topics as only asking for the provision of adequate custodial care or long-term health care, the retirement security topic is not susceptible of such an interpretation. This is because it uses the language, "implement a comprehensive program to guarantee" the results of the resolution, retirement security. Affirmatives are hence required to propose programs which will have the effect of producing retirement security.

The effect of this wording is a broadening of affirmative ground, particularly on the retirement security topic. This is because the scope of possible affirmative mandates is not limited by the language of these topics: limitations of affirmative proposed courses of action comes only from the putative results to be achieved by the adoption of courses of action, i.e., can the affirmative prove that its plan mandates will result in retirement security. To pick what is probably an unlikely example, an affirmative could argue that eliminating the budget deficit (through defense spending cuts and corporate tax increases) would have the effect of guaranteeing retirement security because of the economic consequences of balancing the budget. "Topicality" would not be determined on the basis of whether the affirmative plan is linguistically synonymous with the resolution: it should pass this test, as it would be a comprehensive program intended to guarantee retirement security. Rather, "topicality" would be a function of whether the affirmative could establish that the economic effect of balancing the budget would in fact be that of guaranteeing retirement security. Topics limited in scope by language are usually more restrictive than those limited only by the solvency evidence of the affirmative.

The effects nature of the topics means three things. First, although mandates can be directly related to retirement security, custodial care, or long-term health care, they need not necessarily be so related. So long as a non-custodial care related program had the result of guaranteeing adequate custodial care (e.g., changed Medicare or Medicaid funding or reimbursement), it would fit within the topic. Second, affirmatives can attempt to claim add-on advantages from the method used to guarantee retirement security, custodial care, or long-term health care. In the budget-balancing example given above, add-ons could be claimed for decreasing defense spending, balancing the budget, etc., completely apart from the retirement security effects advantages. Therefore, the scope of both possible mandates and the possible justifications for such mandates is broadened by the "guarantee of results" language.

A third and important consequence of the effects nature of the three topics is that the scope of actions adopted by the affirmative need not be confined to persons over age 65, so long as the effect of such actions is to guarantee retirement security, adequate custodial care, or long-term health care. While the most direct approach for affirmatives will be to limit plans or proposals to persons over age 65, the language of the resolutions does not restrict them to this. Several examples pertinent to the retirement security topic clarify this.

A first example is age discrimination in employment, discussed in Chapter Seven. As was discussed above, "retirement" need not necessarily mean "complete cessation of work." Even for those who have ceased work, however, an affirmative could argue that by preventing age discrimination in employment against persons 45 to 65 years of age, retirement security has been guaranteed because of the substantially altered economic situation of the retiree. By preventing discrimination, the retiree will have earned more, been less prone to layoffs or terminations, and less likely to be forced to take early retirement (with reduced Social Security benefits) at age 62. All of these factors would increase the retiree's Social Security benefit amount and his or her likelihood of receiving private pension payment, as well as eligibility for private health insurance on reaching 65. Hence, although plan mandates (modified approaches to age discrimination) directly affect only persons under age 65 (employees and employers, except for persons over age 65 and still working), affirmatives could argue that retirement security for persons over age 65 is guaranteed by plan mandates and is therefore topical.

Two related examples would be private and public employee health insurance benefits and pension plans. Here the focus of the affirmative plan mandates would be protection of employee rights to build up post-retirement benefits in the form of health insurance after retirement and the payment of monthly pension amounts (which can be though of as salary or wages after retirement). Retirement security for persons over age 65 would be guaranteed by ensuring that persons under age 65 could build up such rights and that employers not be able to infringe on them or retract their obligations to help fund such programs. In addition, such plans could also limit or curtail the ability of employers to abridge such rights after the employee has reached 65 (this is currently taking place where "rust belt" industries announce they are no longer able to fund pension and medical plans for present retirees). The point to be made is that retirement security can be argued to be guaranteed through measures aimed at persons primarily, if not exclusively, under age 65.

TOPIC: That the federal government should guarantee adequate custodial care for United States citizens over age 65.

TERMS

"federal government"
See comments above.

"guarantee"
See comments above.

"adequate custodial care"
This is the key phrase in the topic, and it is a curious choice. The more direct term, "nursing home care" was not used. Nursing homes are generally maintenance or post-acute care facilities: if this topic is meant to be distinct from "long-term health care" (which also has its problems), "nursing home care" vs. "hospital care" phrasings could have been used. Nursing homes are generally divided into two categories for care purposes: skilled nursing facilities (SNFs) and intermediate care facilities (ICFs). Again, "custodial care" is not a phrase used by literature in the field as regards care of the elderly in nursing homes, this topic does include other forms of 24-hour care facilities for the elderly, such as mental institutions.

Definitions of "custodial" are, of course, derivative of "custody." The *Oxford English Dictionary* defines "custody" as "the right or duty of taking care of something, guardianship, in safe custody, safely guarded imprisonment."[20] Legal definitions are probably not appropriate: in a criminal justice sense, "custody" refers to restrictions on the freedom of movement of individuals, i.e., they have been placed under arrest or placed in confinement. *CJS* even defines "custodial" as distinct from care: "(t)he term is defined as being related to watching and protecting rather than seeking to care."[21]

Of course, one probably unanticipated affirmative case under this topic could be adequacy of care for elderly prisoners. This seems dubious as an affirmative option: the elderly tend to be arrested for misdemeanors (e.g., shoplifting), not felonies, and generally are not confined.[22] The advantages from better care for the few over-65 residents of federal and state prisons (generally, organized crime figures and persons convicted of capital crimes who have not been paroled for health reasons) would be overwhelmed by counterplans correcting conditions for under-65 convicts.

"Care" is defined by the *Oxford* dictionary as "protection, charge, or supervision."[23] *CJS* defines "care" as "(a) relative term and one of broad comprehension and flexibility of meaning, which has been generally defined or employed as meaning attention or management, charge or oversight, responsibility, or watchful regard and attention; also preservation, safekeeping, or security."[24] "Adequate" is defined by the *Oxford* dictionary as "sufficient, satisfactory, passable but not outstandingly good."[25]

The phrase "adequate custodial care," therefore, surrounds a not very precise term (custodial) with a very broad term (care) and one with a minimal threshold for attainment (adequate). In practice, affirmatives would presumably attempt to attain something more than mere adequacy for solvency purposes. The breadth of what can be included under "care" probably expands the topic only in terms of the kinds of activities in long-term care institutions relevant to the topic.

"United States citizens"
See comments above.

"over age 65"
See comments above.

COMMENTS ABOUT THIS TOPIC WORDING

The scope of this topic is probably not likely to be the source of great controversy. The topic covers primarily long-term care institutions, i.e., nursing homes, plus a limited number of other 24-hour care institutions containing elderly residents. The topic appears to exclude two types of entities dealing with the maintenance or care of the elderly: acute care hospitals and home health care services. "Custodial care" in the sense of maintenance or guardianship is distinct from the type of care dispensed by acute care facilities to the elderly, which is typified by brief length of stay, intense medical or surgical services, followed by release and after-care services. There is a possible blurring in that some hospitals have started converting some of their space to nursing home, post-medical care purposes.[26] Home health care by definition involves services to the elderly in a non-custodial setting.

The topic appears to permit two general types of directions in which affirmative case analysis can be directed. First, cases can focus on funding or reimbursement considerations. Such cases would be directed at the availability or accessibility of custodial care to the elderly. Implicitly, these cases would interpret this topic as emphasizing the guarantee of custodial care to citizens over age 65. Second, cases can focus on the quality of custodial care. This would follow an interpretation of this topic as emphasizing the adequacy of custodial care provided. Such cases would focus on current state regulation and monitoring of the nursing home industry. There can also be considerable overlap between the two approaches, as nursing home quality is of course a function of the level of funds made available through Medicaid or private payment, and accessibility of adequate care facilities as determined in part by reimbursement levels.

This topic specifies no mechanism for implementation. In general terms, the federal government is the agent of action, and the object of the resolution is adequate custodial care. However, how this is to be achieved is not constrained, even in general terms, by topic wording. Therefore, use of types of inspectional services or independent ombudsmen to insure quality of care, or modification of reimbursement formulas or even nationalization of long-term care facilities all could fit within topical action as means of guaranteeing adequate custodial care.

TOPIC: That the federal government should guarantee long-term health care for United States citizens over age 65.

TERMS

"federal government"
See comments above.

"Guarantee""
See comments above.

"long term health care"
This is the key phrase in this topic and, as was the case for "adequate custodial care," it is an odd choice for wording. As mentioned above, "long-term care" generally refers to nursing home, non-health-care-related settings. Related issues which may be included under this heading would include both care for chronic conditions (e.g., hypertension, arthritis) to which the elderly are prone: care for such conditions is generally not in-patient care, focussing more on preventive measures, medication, and therapy. In addition, acute care treatment would probably be relevant here, assuming the care provided would fit the definition of long-term. Not all catastrophic illnesses are long-term in duration: myocardial infarctions and lung cancer (oat-cell carcinoma) can be very brief in duration.[27]

The terms of importance in this phrase are "long-term" and health care." There seems to be no agreed-upon chronological point at which care becomes long-term. The *Oxford* dictionary defines "long-term," not very helpfully, as "of or for a long period."[28] It further defines "health" as "the state of being well and free from illness."[29] Definitions of "care" were provided in the preceding section.

COMMENTS ABOUT THIS TOPIC WORDING

The intention of this topic appears to be that of separating "long-term" from "short-term" health care. As was commented above, this does not necessarily mean that catastrophic health care costs are included within this topic, as very serious illnesses for which high medical care costs can be incurred may be of relatively brief duration. The topic may have in mind extending provisions of Medicare past current limitations on days of hospitalization covered: this is discussed in detail in Chapter Four.

It is arguable whether this topic includes nursing home or convalescent care, as such facilities normally conceive of themselves as post-acute care institutions, geared toward maintenance or rehabilitation, not health care. Affirmatives would need to interpret "health care" very broadly to include other than medical care providers.

The topic probably does include two other types of services for the elderly other than hospitals: home health care and hospices. These are more fully discussed in Chapter Six. Home health care consists of a variety of services which provide after-care for persons previously hospitalized, as well as continuing care services in lieu of either hospitalization or institutionalization. Hospices are alternative care services for the terminally ill emphasizing reduction of pain and other symptoms of mental and physical distress of terminal illness, as well as meeting the emotional needs of the terminally ill and their families. Hospice care can be provided in the person's home or in an intermediate or skilled care facility. Hospice care is meant to be an alternative to the "terminal wards" of hospitals.

As is true of the custodial care topic, the long-term health care topic specifies an agent, a mandate, and a target population but is devoid of any language on implementation mechanisms. How long-term health care is to be guaranteed, in other words, is at the option of the affirmative. Narrow approaches would include extending the length of current Medicare coverage, broadening such coverage, reducing or eliminating patient copayment and deductibles, or replacing Medicare with insurance coverage or medical vouchers for persons over age 65. Technical approaches could also be adopted as means of guaranteeing health care: this could include, for example, government-funded health maintenance organizations for the elderly. This approach could overlap with preventive care services, especially locating such services in long-term care or continuous care living centers.

Another way of viewing this topic has to do with the "citizens over age 65" portion of the topic. As is discussed further in Chapter Four, Medicare and Medicaid by no means provide a guarantee of health care services to all of the elderly. The affirmative may choose to play with the absence of the word "all" in the topic, described above. This topic may be thought of as proposing "filling the gaps" of coverage left by current government medical services and private health insurance carriers. As opposed to broadening the quantative coverage of Medicare for current recipients, this approach would broaden the scope of who is eligible for such assistance.

NOTES TO CHAPTER ONE

1. *Corpus Juris Secundum* (*"CJS"*), v. 35, p. 965.
2. *Black's Law Dictionary*, 5th ed. (*"Black's"*) (St. Paul: West Publishing Company, 1979), p. 549.
3. *Oxford American Dictionary* (*"Oxford"*) (New York: Oxford University Press, 1980), p. 329.
4. *Oxford*, p. 534.
5. *Oxford*, p. 130.
6. *Oxford*, p. 3.
7. *Black's*, p. 1.
8. *Oxford*, p. 288.
9. *CJS*, v.38, p. 1125.
10. *Oxford*, p. 578
11. *Oxford*, p. 612.
12. Michael J. Boskin, *Too Many Promises: The Uncertain Future of Social Security* (Homewood: Dow-Jones Irwin, 1986), p. 47.
13. *Black's*, p. 221.
14. While this is generally the case, "elderly" sometimes means 60 or older or 55 or older. "Elder abuse" statutes sometimes use age 60 as a benchmark: see Dyana Lee, "Mandatory Reporting of Elder Abuse: A Cheap But Ineffective Solution to the Problem," *Fordham Law Review*, (1986), v. 12, p.735, n.60. Boskin notes a drift toward a retirement age of 62 instead of 65. Boskin, p. 46.
15. Bostin, pp. 38-43, 114.
16. See, for instance, Charles Brecher and James Knickman, "A Reconsideration of Long-Term Care Policy," *Journal of Health Politics, Policy and Law* (1985), v. 10, pp. 254-256.
17. This is the "jurisdictional amount" needed for state diversity claims to be heard in federal district courts. See 28 U.S.C. Sec. 1332(a).
18. This was the estimate of the Senate Select Committee on Aging in 1981, based on data from 10 states. See Dyana Lee, "Mandatory Reporting of Elder Abuse: A Cheap But Ineffective Solution to the Problem," *Fordham Law Review* (1986), v. 14, pp. 727-28.
19. Brecher and Knickman, p. 248.
20. *Oxford*, p. 156.
21. *CJS*, v. 25, p. 4.
22. Gary Feinberg and Dinesh Khosla, "Sanctioning Elderly Delinquents: Judicial Response to Misdemeanors Committed by Senior Citizens," *Trial* (Sept. 1985), pp. 46-50. In 1981, 213,000 persons 60 years old and older were arrested, 36,000 of which were felony arrests, 56,000 for drunkenness, 49,000 for driving while intoxicated, and 15,000 for disorderly conduct, about two percent of total arrests.
23. *Oxford*, p. 93
24. *CJS*, v. 12A, pp. 922-23.
25. *Oxford*, p. 9.
26. Robert Newcomer, Juanita Wood, and Andrea Sankar, "Medicare Prospective Payment: Anticipated Effect on Hospitals, Other Community Agencies, and Families," *Journal of Health Politics, Policy and Law* (1985), v. 10, pp. 276-77.
27. Noralou Roos, Patrick Montgomery, and Leslie L. Roos, "Health Care Utilization in the Years Prior to Death," *The Milbank Quarterly* (1987), v. 65, pp. 231, 235.
28. *Oxford*, p. 390.
29. *Oxford*, p. 30.

2 Negative Ground: Alternatives and Counterpositions

This chapter outlines generic positions available to negatives on each of the three resolutions, as well as basic solvency and disadvantage positions. Most of these positions are common to the three resolutions. Analysis begins with the broadest topic, retirement security, but a great deal of the materials discussed there apply to the other topics as well.

TOPIC: That the federal government should implement a comprehensive program to guarantee retirement security for United States citizens over age 65.

A. NEGATIVE GROUND ON THIS TOPIC

An initial consideration is the nature of negative ground, i.e., that which the negative can defend. Negative ground can be conceived of as: 1) non-federal efforts to achieve retirement security, however defined; 2) competitive counterplans achieving benefits through measures other than efforts aimed at retirement security; and 3) current programs and policies relevant to affirmative advantage areas.

As was discussed in Chapter One, "retirement security" is a vague and inclusive term. This creates problems for the second approach above. For example, consider the following situation: the affirmative proposes guaranteed annual income for persons over age 65, while the negative presents a counterplan in which the budget deficit is eliminated through a combination of defense spending cuts and reducing social security benefits. The negative could argue that the counterplan is competitive because it is the antithesis

13

of the affirmative (it reduces the guarantee of retirement security) and because it would not be fiscally possible to provide a guaranteed annual income to all persons over age 65 and to simultaneously reduce social security benefits. The counterplan could be argued to be nontopical for much the same reason: it weakens the guarantee of retirement security.

The affirmative could respond, however, that by eliminating the budget deficit, the negative would, indirectly, guarantee retirement security. This would require an interpretation of "retirement security" not limited to assurances of transfer payments to the elderly. The alternative view, that "retirement security" is the result of forces creating changed employment conditions, rates of inflation, or private savings which alter the retiree's economic status, could be argued to include balancing the budget. Since this topic permits, even requires, effects topicality, the affirmative can argue that so long as the counterplan had the effect of creating assurances of retirement security, it would be topical. This example used a counterplan which explicitly reduced social security benefits. If the negative were not that explicit, the affirmative could argue that the results of the counterplan actions would be to make it more fiscally or politically feasible to increase transfer payments or enhance benefits, making the counterplan "a comprehensive program to guarantee retirement security" and hence topical.

The nature of this topic wording also could create problems for the negative team whose approach to inherency is that of "minor repair" or "expansion of current programs." "Repairing" current federal regulations, to for example, provide a separate cost-of-living index for the elderly on which social security adjustments would be based could be argued to have the effect of guaranteeing retirement security. "Expanding" efforts against age discrimination in employment or senior citizen housing could be said to have the same result. Such inherency approaches[1] would thus become topical counterplans.

Whichever of the three types of positions described above is taken by the negative, negative analysis begins with the type of "present system" being attacked by the affirmative. Again, given the amorphous nature of "retirement security," the focus for discussion can vary wildly from debate to debate. However, the negative should be analyzing the following set of programs: 1) transfer payments to the elderly; 2) private, employment-based pensions; 3) in-kind assistance programs, including subsidized housing; 4) medical programs for the edlerly (really a type of in-kind assistance), primarily Medicare, Medicaid, and Veteran's Assistance; and 5) efforts to reduce discrimination against the aged, primarily in employment, but in public accommodations as well. Transfer payments can be broken down into Old Age and Survivor's Assistance ("OASI") and Supplemental Security Income ("SSI"), and are discussed in Chapter Three. Medicare is discussed in Chapter Four. Medicaid has more relevance to long-term care and is discussed in Chapter Five. Age discrimination in employment is discussed in Chapter Seven.

Negatives defending on the basis of current programs will experience limitations based on their inadequacies, as described in the chapters listed above. Assuming that affirmative proposals expand benefits and increase program costs, there are a variety of disadvantage arguments available, which are discussed below. There are also a variety of counterplan positions available. Before turning to a discussion of those positions, one additional feature of the retirement security topic should be noted which could possible affect negative ground. That feature is that the topic does not expressly require an increase in assistance to the elderly.

Although it might be inferred that implementing a comprehensive program to guarantee retirement security would require increased assistance to persons over age 65 (through increased transfer payments, broadened coverage of the elderly population, or its expenses), no such stipulation is included. Affirmatives, therefore, could argue that decreased federal efforts would guarantee retirement security. The affirmative comprehensive program could, in other words, eliminate some programs, require cost-sharing by the elderly, or reduce benefit levels.

This is perhaps an unlikely approach, but it would permit affirmatives to avoid disadvantages linked to increased federal spending. What would be critical to the affirmative's cause would be being able to establish that the program being eliminated or pared back is the source of insecurity on the part of the elderly: topicality (and solvency) would be dependent on showing that the affirmative cutbacks would increase assurances of security for persons over age 65. For example, the affirmative could argue that deficits from Medicare hospital insurance ("HI") and supplementary medical insurance ("SMI") are what joepardize the financial health of the overall Social Security program. By reducing these programs (or increasing insurance premiums by the elderly) the affirmative would increase the security of retirement benefits.

The above approach may not in fact generate any viable case options. However, the point to be made is that the retirement security topic is not directional insofar as quality of services is concerned. The same is true of the custodial care and long-term health care topics. Although most affirmatives will probably augment current services for persons over age 65, none of these topics compels them to do so. Hence, negatives cannot automatically premise generic positions on increased federal spending on expanded transfer payments or in-kind benefits to the elderly.

B. GENERIC COUNTERPLAN POSITIONS

There are three fundamental types of counterplan positions which may be presented by negatives on this topic: 1) state counterplans; 2) nongovernmental approaches; and 3) federal programs distinct from those dealing exclusively with persons over age 65. The first has limited viability on this topic: the other two may be of great utility, depending to some degree on the specifics of the affirmative case.

1. State Counterplans

The traditional state counterplan consists of doing everything the affirmative plan does, but at a state level. The chief problem for this type of counterplan on this topic is state-to-state variations in the ability to fund programs dealing with the elderly. This is combined with the "clustering" of the elderly in disproportionate numbers in some states (Florida, Arizona, Arkansas). Case areas in which significant amounts of funds must be spent would not be viable in low-income states or states with a small industrial base. Essentially, such a counterplan would transfer current Social Security contributions to state treasuries: since the amount deducted from employer payrolls and employee paychecks in a given state is not proportional to the amounts of transfer payments received by the elderly within that state, problems in funding would be created. A state with a small economic base or a very disproportionate share of retirees would be forced to increase its taxes on the non-elderly. Hence, tax rates on individuals and businesses would vary from state to state, with the largest burden placed on states with little income or large numbers of the elderly. Besides creating an equitable treatment disadvantage, there could be some degree of business migration produced.

When the affirmative plans do not focus on Social Security benefits, state counterplans become somewhat more viable. For example, consider an affirmative plan which broadened laws against age discrimination in employment. The counterplan approach would be to adopt similar edicts on a state-by-state basis. As is discussed further in Chapter Seven, there currently is dual antidiscrimination machinery in nearly all states. A person who seeks redress for age discrimination can do so in federal court under the Age Discrimination in Employment Act ("ADEA"). He or she can also do so under state laws proscribing discrimination.[2] The negative can utilize most of the traditional arguments for state counterplans: that states are closer to and more sensitive to regional and localized concerns; that there are variations in the intensity and frequency as well as character of problems on a state-by-state or regional basis; and that it is easier to adjust or tailor responses to particular problems on a state-by-state basis than on a national basis.

The flip side of this is that individual state governments are more vulnerable to co-option and to motives for weak regulation of industries. This is arguably true in the case of the nursing home industry, for example, which is concentrated in a number of states. Counterplans which do not involve taking over transfer payment functions do not face the problem of disproportions between state income and retirement benefit requirements. However, they could potentially face problems of industry migration (e.g., nursing homes or long-term care centers) should they permit state-by-state variations in regulation.

2. Nongovernmental Approaches

Should affirmatives attempt to reform or modify Old Age and Survivor's Insurance, private approaches could be a competitive response. The basis concept is that of contrasting government transfer payments to the elderly with the private retirement annuity approaches. Such approaches are currently a topic of much interest in conservative economic circles. However, they may actually have somewhat greater viability as an affirmative approach on this topic than as a counterplan. As is discussed further in the next chapter, Social Security-OASI describes itself as an insurance program for largely political reasons. Conservative critics charge that instead OASI is largely made up of "intergenerational transfers" and in effect is a welfare program for the elderly, poor, and wealthy alike.[3] One proposal is to make OASI payments strictly tied to contributions plus interest, like a private pension annuity program, with the proviso of a minimum-figure transfer payment for persons whose contributions would entitle them to a lesser figure (due to unemployment or underemployment).[4]

The problem for negatives adopting this as a counterplan approach is that they are excluded from federal efforts having the effect of guaranteeing retirement security. This would present no problem insofar as the privatization of pensions and conversion of OASI to an annuity formula would be concerned. However, guaranteeing minimum payments to the elderly poor would be virtually impossible for a private fund or corporation from a financial standpoint. Using the federal government for this purpose would, of course, be topical. One possible answer would be that the elderly which did not generate sufficient annuity income could instead collect benefits under the Supplemental Security Income ("SSI") program. However, an "annuities" approach, ironically, seems to fit more easily within the affirmative and federal government action than within actions by non-governmental entities.

A different "privatization" technique would be to counterplan in much the same fashion as state counterplans, adopting affirmative mandates, but using private agents of action instead of the federal government. For example, if the affirmative case area was housing for the elderly, a privatization counterplan could be just as effective, if not more effective, than state or federal action. Instead of countering federal efforts to build or otherwise improve housing for the elderly with similar state efforts, the negative would use private sector initiatives. This would involve relying on private lending institution fund pooling arrangements, low interest loans, mortgage repayment adjustments, and other measures to maintain and improve housing for the elderly.

Private sector actions raise a fiat power question: can the negative fiat guarantee uniform courses of action by private, nongovernmental actors? The author views fiat's function as one of removing from policy proposition debates consideration of what "will" happen (will legislation be passed, will funds be appropriated, etc.), permitting debate to focus on what "should" happen. From this perspective, fiat power is just as applicable to counterplans as it is to affirmative plans. Affirmatives are articulating the merits of resolution action, while negatives are articulating the merits of opposing, competing, non-resolutional action. There is no reason for imposing on negatives a burden of showing that its counterplan "will" be adopted.

Private sector initiatives present a different sort of fiat power problem, precisely because they deal with non-governmental entities. The issue is one of whether questions of adoption and implementation which are waived with regard to governmental units specified in the policy proposition for fiat reasons are also waived with regard to non-governmental institutions (e.g., all home mortgage lending institutions). A broad view would be that the distinction between type of agent of action makes no difference. Although policy propositions used in high school and college debate characteristically involve governmental actions, there is nothing in the nature of policy propositions which creates such a restriction. The essence of policy resolutions is their discussion of the merits of a course of conduct. For reasons of convenience, it is preferable to specify governmental agents of action in resolutions used by scholastic debating organizations.[5] However, since one can phrase policy propositions which can specify non-governmental agents of action, fiat power can therefore be applied to the agents of action in such topics: if that is true, fiat power can be applied in equal terms to counterplans which adopt a "non-resolution" which has as its agent of action a non-governmental entity.

A more narrow view of this issue is that by their own terms, counterplans such as the housing one described above imply governmental action. In other words, government would have to require ceilings on interest rates for home repair loans to the elderly, or provide tax incentives for the housing industry or financial lending institutions to deal with the elderly on preferential terms. Hence, while private institutions are involved in the implementation of the counterplan (or an affirmative plan), the agent of action remains a governmental entity: for reasons of nontopicality, the negative should use state governments as their agent. This approach dodges the thorny issue of whether a negative can really fiat that all private lenders will adopt a set of mandates. Implicitly, though, most state counterplans imply that fiat power removes as an issue whether all states will adopt the counterplan mandates, and do so simultaneously. The author, it should be made clear, is not advocating debates about that question: the whole point of fiat is avoiding such debates. The author prefers the broader view articulated above. The narrower approach probably is more prudent as it avoids creating a controversy where one need not be created.

3. Other Federal Proposals

This counterplan approach would, like the affirmative, use the federal government as the agent of action, but would be nontopical by mandating action other than programs aimed at retirement security for the elderly. The fundamental approach here is one of fiscal competitiveness: adopting the affirmative precludes the spending required for the nontopical and more net-beneficial counterplan.

The chief problems for the negatives will be supporting the position that the counterplan has a superior level of benefits than does the affirmative plan and demonstrating that there is no fiscal room for simultaneous adoption of both proposals. Affirmatives should be able to claim substantial benefits in terms of reduced death and suffering among the elderly, although at a substantial cost as well. Negatives must propose counterplans which are also relatively expensive, in order to win the ·budgetary competitiveness argument. At the same time, such proposals must produce dramatic and sweeping benefits to outweigh the affirmative. Negatives utilizing this approach should be prepared for affirmatives which attempt to preempt them by proposing plans with minimal costs or through funding proposals through cuts in defense spending: both would defeat the negative competitiveness position. A creative negative approach, viable on several of the examples below, would be to argue that the counterplan should be adopted first, as it would produce a situation in which the affirmative proposal would be rendered unnecessary.

Examples of this type of counterplan are briefly described below. The only real limitations on what would fit this category are those of staying away from programs which could be argued to be aimed at the elderly, plus the limitations noted above: only programs which would cost a great deal and generate large advantages are worth proposing. This type of counterplan would also be useful with regard to the other two topics, so long as the "fiscal room" competitiveness argument can be alleged: this is more likely to be true of the long-term health care topic than of the custodial care topic.

a. National Health Insurance

The argument for this counterplan would be that it would create greater net health benefits than the affirmative by not restricting itself to the elderly, and that the health benefits of the counterplan outweigh any economic benefits of the affirmative. The negative should have no difficulty in arguing that the federal government could either institute national health insurance or expand transfer payments to the elderly, but not both. This is also a good candidate for an argument by the negative that the counterplan should be adopted first. The health care needs of the elderly could be argued to demand priority over their financial needs, and, if the health care needs of the elderly were met, it could be contended that the financial problems of the elderly would also be resolved in large part. The "ageism" disadvantage could be alleged as a reason not to focus exclusively on the health problems of the aged if this counterplan example is used on the custodial care and long-term health care topics.

b. Job Creation and Job Training Programs

This is an idea which has gotten some amount of discussion by several of the Democratic Presidential hopefuls, Jesse Jackson and Paul Simon in particular. The chief criticism of these proposals is their requirement of large federal expenditures, which would aid the negative in arguing competitiveness. Outside of the direct benefits to be obtained through employment, the negative can argue that it would render at least parts of the affirmative advantages non-unique. This would be easier to do with the retirement security topic, where it could be contended that larger numbers of persons making contributions in larger amounts to the Social Security Trust Fund would get at affirmative advantages. To the degree that employment is connected with insurance coverage (as well as eligibility for Medicare) increased employment could be contended to get at some benefits claimed under the custodial care and long-term health care topics. A central point of this counterplan is that the gloomy predictions for both OASI and Medicare funds, discussed in the next two chapters, in part reflect the degree of stagnation in the economy over the past decade. Extensive benefits for the elderly have tended to have been proposed, and are budgetarily palatable, when the economy is healthy and expanding. That, of course, is also the key defect of this counterplan: it exposes negatives to a growth disadvantage.

c. National Day Care

This is another proposal which has generated much discussion and several Congressional proposals. Like job creation programs, the chief criticism of day care proposals, their large cost, aids with regard to establishing competitiveness. The key problem for negatives is the character of the advantages which can be claimed. The benefits to be claimed are in terms of freeing up parents, particularly female heads of household, for more productive employment. There are also advantages claimable in terms of greater educational attainment and socialization benefits to children. While these are of considerable worth and importance, these are not of the dramatic character negatives might need to set off against increased death and suffering advantages alleged by affirmatives on the custodial care and long-term health care topics. The economic benefits argued might be more appropriate on the retirement security topic.

d. Balancing the Budget[6]

This option was mentioned in a different context in Chapter One. The counterplan could take several forms but all would involve eliminating substantial portions of federal social spending, transferring them to state and private entities (or raising taxes). Probably the simplest would involve shifting OASI to a basis tying benefits strictly to annuities plus interest, transferring the operation to a non-governmental or quasi-governmental consortium, set up along the lines of the Federal National Mortgage Agency (Fannie Mae). With reference to the long-term health care topic, the same thing could be done with regard to Medicare, shifting it to a private or not-for-profit, quasi-governmental insurance pool. Depending on the affirmative funding technique, the negative could also propose decreased defense spending.

The negative could argue fiscal competitiveness on any of the three topics. Of course, how the plan is funded is critical, as is the amount of spending by the affirmative. The negative which is determined about running this approach will have to argue preemptions to affirmative positions on no net increase in spending being required, and on whether the affirmative can really generate substantial savings from defense cuts, for example. However, the negative will probably create a bias against this approach if it is used against affirmatives in fact spending very little beyond administrative costs.

Benefits can be claimed for this counterplan both in the areas of reduced harms to the economy (money being diverted to paying interest on the debt) and in superior ways of dealing with the financial and health care problems of the elderly.

C. GENERIC DISADVANTAGES ON THIS TOPIC

1. Economic Growth

The link between this disadvantage and the affirmative is the connection between the Social Security tax and rates of private saving. While there is some dispute about the degree of the effect, a number of conservative economists, led by Martin Feldstein, have published studies establishing that the Social Security tax depresses private saving.[7]

Options for the negative depend on the effect of the affirmative plan on the form and amount of taxation. A decrease in the Social Security tax because of decreased spending could be argued to increase the rate of private saving and therefore the rate of growth. An alteration in the form of taxation (e.g., a shift to progressive taxes on income, replacement of a portion of the Social Security tax with decreased defense spending or "sin" taxes on liquor and cigarettes) would require different link evidence than the studies referred to above. However, the idea would remain the same, showing that the net effect of the affirmative plan would be to remove an impediment to economic growth, then argue negative effects of growth. Alternatively, if the affirmative plan causes net increases in federal spending, the negative can argue (depending on the funding source) that there will be decreased private savings and investment. This would then be linked to a "growth is good" disadvantage.

2. Ageism

This argument is described in greater detail in the sections in Chapter Seven on elder abuse and age discrimination. This is an argument which applies to all three of the topics. The fundamental concept is that laws and programs which identify the elderly as requiring special treatment reinforce stereotypic notions about them. These include views of the elderly as incompetent and incapable of conducting their own affairs; it also includes a view of the elderly as a politically well-organized lobby, selfishly accumulating benefits and special considerations under the law at the expense of the rest of the nation. Ageism can also apply to how the elderly view themselves: if social welfare legislation treats them as unable to deal with their own problems, it encourages the elderly to adopt that view as a self-image.

Ageism is a dangerous precedent or snowball argument. The disadvantage comes not so much from the mandates of the affirmative plan as from its reinforcement of a view of some elderly as infantile and others as politically grasping, coloring how the elderly will be treated in other regards. The disadvantage has uniqueness problems in that a great deal of social welfare legislation already treats the elderly separately and makes presumptions about their capabilities. The task for the negative is to identify features of the affirmative program which serve to sharpen the stereotype or at least to reinforce it. As was mentioned with regard to the national health insurance counterplan, ageism can be used as an additive advantage for negative approaches which are not limited to the elderly. The argument would be that the negative at least avoids if not ameliorates the stereotype by treating the elderly on the basis of individual conditions, not age.

3. Crisis in Confidence

This disadvantage stems from some of the same material as described in the ageism disadvantage. The elderly do have organizations, such as the American Association of Retired Persons, which lobby very effectively on their behalf. The disadvantage argument would be that the elderly would perceive the affirmative as anti-elderly, and take action accordingly. The disadvantage would appear to apply most directly to the retirement security topic, although it could be applied to the other topics as well. On its face, the retirement security topic (and the custodial care and long-term health care topics, too) appears to be pro-elderly. The negative could argue one or all of three things: 1) specific elements of the affirmative mandates would be perceived as anti-elderly; 2) even though incorrect in their perceptions, the elderly would view the affirmative as anti-elderly; and 3) related to the second, groups which are advocates for the elderly view federal "reforms" of benefits to the elderly with deep suspicion, no matter how innocuously they are labelled.

Some negatives undoubtedly would run this disadvantage as a repeal argument. The scenario would be that the elderly will oppose the plan's enforcement after enactment through fiat, and will then lobby successfully to have the plan repealed. The author's opinion is that this is a "should-would" argument and is of no relevance on a policy proposition. In essence, the argument says that the plan should not be adopted because it will be repealed in short order. This diverts attention from debate about the merits (and demerits) of the affirmative. In other words, the focus should be on why the elderly might oppose the affirmative, not on what they might do as a consequence. It should be noted that the negative is not arguing that the plan will not be adopted, but that it will be adopted and then repealed. This is an attempted dodge around fiat considerations. A response to this is that the decision-maker is only concerned with whether the plan ought to be adopted at this point in time: while the effects of adoption are legitimate concerns, later legislative action is not relevant to the merits of the affirmative.

Argued properly as a disadvantage, the negative would contend that the result of the affirmative would be decreased confidence in government social welfare programs on the part of the elderly. The consequences of this would include opposition or resistance to other legislation on the part of the elderly, nonuse and avoidance of other government programs, and distortions in individual decision-making by the elderly (e.g., purchase of unnecessary or duplicative insurance or disability plans out of fear of government fund cutbacks).

As mentioned above, the key item in this disadvantage is establishing some basis for the perceiving of the affirmative as anti-elderly. This would be less of a problem for affirmatives using this argument as a disadvantage to a negative counterplan. The concept would be one of turning negative prioritization of other social concerns over those of the elderly into a causal link to the disadvantage. Clearly, counterplans on the retirement security topic which decreased benefits or transferred programs to private or quasi-private institutions would cause suspicion on the parts of advocates for the elderly, triggering the disadvantage.

4. Squeezing Out Other Social Spending

This is a venerable argument which could have added forces on any of the three topics for debate in 1988-89. The link to the affirmative is increased spending by the plan, resulting in compensating cutbacks in other domestic spending. The Reagan Administration and the Gramm-Rudman-Hollings law have changed the details of this argument. First, a number of social programs have been jettisoned over the past few years. Conversely, some programs have been retained within the budget and seem likely to continue except under extraordinary fiscal pressures, chiefly through vigorous lobbying of groups affected by these programs. Second, Gramm-Rudman-Hollings makes some domestic programs off-limits to cuts (although Congress has managed, through creative accounting, to avoid "sequestration" of funds).

The added wrinkle on the 1988-89 topic is that there is evidence that funds for health care of the elderly and poor compete with each other. As is discussed further in Chapter Five, a large portion of Medicaid funds go for nursing home care of the elderly poor. This has resulted in a reduction of funds available for services to the non-elderly poor, who for the most part are single mothers and their children. A key concern has been funds made available for pre- and post-natal care, although funding has recently been increased for this purpose.[8]

As funding for health care services for the poor has become scarce under the Reagan Administration, private hospitals have engaged in "dumping" of indigent patients (whose health care costs would not be reimbursed) on public hospitals, increasing pressures on those institutions.[9] Hospitals have also attempted to engage in "cost-shifting," covering unreimbursed expenses for Medicare, Medicaid, and charity care patients through higher rates for insured patients, something which private health insurers are resisting.[10] Hence, affirmative mandates increasing care for the elderly may have "squeeze out" effects on other patient care.

Increased spending for the elderly, through funds for custodial care, long-term health care, and, to a lesser degree, on social welfare spending for this group generally, can therefore be argued to diminish health care for the non-elderly poor. This, of course, is an incremental disadvantage: its impact is tied to the degree of increase in spending, especially health care spending for the elderly.

Another set of competitive pressures can be argued to exist between programs specifically for the elderly. This is more a social budgetary "cost" argument. The idea is that there is only so much political "capital" available to a particular constituency: when programs are approved for that class of persons in one regard, the chances of additional programs being approved within the same area are diminished. An example of this type of effect is discussed in Chapter Seven with reference to laws making reporting of elder abuse mandatory.

The utility of this argument is that negatives can argue that among the universe of things which would be of value to the elderly, the affirmative plan is of relatively slight importance. However, by adopting the affirmative, the chances of the other legislation being passed are reduced. This argument is probably relevant on all three topics. It is probably most relevant on the retirement security topic. This is because of the breadth of proposals which could fit within this rubric, and because retirement-related proposals are more susceptible to squeezing each other out, given their potentially large cost and political reluctance to deal with retirement-related issues more than absolutely necessary.

TOPIC: That the federal government should guarantee adequate custodial care for United States citizens over age 65.

A. NEGATIVE GROUND ON THIS TOPIC

Negative ground can be comceptualized as: 1) non-federal efforts to guarantee custodial care to the elderly; 2) competitive counterplans achieving benefits through measures unrelated to custodial care for the elderly; 3) current programs and policies related to custodial care for the elderly; and 4) counterplans obtaining affirmative advantages, but not through guarantees of custodial care for the elderly.

The "present system" can be divided into several sections on this topic. First, there are the current purveyors of custodial care: government-operated institutions, private but non-profit nursing homes, and private proprietary nursing homes. Second, there are regulatory agencies enforcing nursing home standards. These operate at a state level. In addition, Medicaid provides "regulation" through its reimbursement and related procedures for nursing homes. Congress has recently acted to attempt to improve nursing home quality for Medicaid beneficiaries through participation requirements, survey and certification procedures and enforcement remedies.[11] Private groups which are advocates for the elderly also provide some element of "regulation," defined broadly, as do private attorneys representing nursing home residents neglected or abused by staff members. Both of these latter "regulators" are constrained by the laws of their states with regard to nursing homes.

129,647

Second, the present system consists of different forms of long-term care. These include skilled nursing facilities ("SNFs") and intermediate care facilities ("ICFs"). SNFs are post-acute care facilities, while ICFs are essentially residential, maintenance facilities. Alternately, there is the program of home health care services, meant to provide services necessary for activities of daily living, as well as some outpatient and post-acute care services.

Since this topic says "custodial care," not "nursing homes," negative ground also includes other institutions providing care to the elderly in a residential setting. This would primarily include mental institutions, both private and public. Although states have attempted to "deinstitutionalize" the mentally ill to the greatest extent possible, populations in public institutions have decreased markedly. However, there are both mentally ill and mentally retarded older adults residing in state institutions, as well as some elderly in private institutions. Such facilities are regulated by state law. While conditions in surviving state hospitals, particularly those for the mentally retarded, are generally regarded as deplorable,[12] this is probably not a productive area for affirmative cases. This is because of the same reasoning described in Chapter One with regard to older adults in correctional facilities: state counterplans dealing with state institutions (and claiming advantages from dealing with under-65 retarded and mentally ill residents) would outweigh whatever significance affirmatives would be able to claim.

Third, the present system includes different forms of payment for nursing home care. The major method of reimbursement at present is through the government, in the form of government Medicaid reimbursement. Much smaller but growing in significance is private insurance for nursing home care. Third, there is private payment by nursing home residents and their families. Medicare provides relatively little nursing home care assistance. The form of payment also sets out a dichotomy discussed further in Chapter Five: nursing homes can be divided into those which accept and rely on Medicaid-reimbursed patients for the bulk of their business and those which attempt to screen out Medicaid-reimbursed patients, relying on private-pay residents. In nursing homes which accept both, there can also be a division in the types of care received by patients, according to the level of reimbursement provided the nursing home.

B. GENERIC COUNTERPLAN POSITIONS

The same general counterplan options exist on this topic as on the retirement security topic. Most of the same considerations apply to them, with the few exceptions described below.

1. State Counterplans

As mentioned above, arguments can be made in favor and against state regulation of nursing homes. Traditionally, nursing homes have been licensed and regulated by the states. In addition, nursing homes are concentrated more heavily in some states. There are strong arguments against this, however. In addition to the co-option argument discussed above, it is not entirely true that nursing homes have been solely regulated by the states. Given the expanding role of Medicaid in funding nursing home care, the federal government does have an interest in the quality and provision of nursing home care. Medicaid is funded by the federal government with state matching grants, so there is a combined financial interest. However, it would be difficult to support an argument that nursing home regulation has been the exclusive province of the states.

An additional argument is that federal administration is warranted because of the national scope of the problem: proprietary nursing homes often are run by corporations operating in multiple states; federal regulation would provide uniform standards for nursing homes in all states. Finally, the state counterplan option is probably most viable with regard to "regulation" cases: where the affirmative proposes payment for care or construction, state disparities in finances and the number of elderly make state administration less viable.

2. Nongovernmental Approaches

Nongovernmental options are not especially attractive on this topic, although two possible approaches can be offered by negatives: 1) self-regulation by the nursing home industry; and 2) regulation by the insurance industry.

Self-regulation is to a certain extent what occurs at present, given relatively weak state controls on nursing home operations. The argument is that nursing homes, particularly for-profit enterprises, will regulate health and safety matters out of economic self-interest. For example, nursing homes have an economic incentive to avoid lawsuits charging abuse or neglect of residents. The form of the counterplan would be to require nursing homes to be members of an industry association, and to mandate standards to be met by member institutions. The principal advantage to such an approach would be that it would avoid the expense and administrative delays associated with federal regulation. What is described below is a generic disadvantage on this topic driving nursing home operators out through excessive regulation, becomes the additive advantage to this counterplan.

There are some weaknesses and limitations to this approach. First, it does not appear responsive to arguments that private nursing homes seek to avoid low-income or "heavy care" prospective clients. It could be argued that nursing homes have economic incentives to avoid admitting such persons. Second, there is empirical evidence that the primary effect of economic self-interest on nursing home operations is that they tend to cut corners on labor costs. This can be tied to a position that abuse and neglect in nursing homes is associated with having poorly trained, low-paid staff. Finally, by analogy, industry organizations and trade associations tend to generate rules for self-conduct which are relatively lenient: such groups tend to be more lobbying and public relations-oriented than substantive in focus.

A second type of nongovernmental approach is insurance industry regulation. As is discussed in Chapter Five, insurance policies for nursing home care are just now beginning to be written in any appreciable numbers. The concept of the counterplan is that insurance companies would operate as a third-party provider of funds for nursing home care. As is the case with insurance coverage of hospital and physician expenses, insurers (e.g., Blue Cross-Blue Shield) would reach agreements with nursing home operators as to services provided and standards to be met. Private insurers, rather than the government, would therefore have an interest in enforcing quality of care in nursing homes, as well as in making sure that care facilities were available in adequate quantities for policyholders.

There are conceptual problems with this approach as well. The primary problem is universality of coverage. Unless coverage were universal, the counterplan would simply reinforce the current tendency toward two-tiered care for those with assets and those on Medicaid described earlier. The counterplan might deal with they by operating in conjunction with state agencies, or through offering policies on a sliding scale according to income.

Another problem is cost-shifting: based on the past history of hospitals dealing with charity or unreimbursed care, private insurers would be a convenient "deep pocket" for nursing home operators to utilize in meeting their expenses. Again, it should be remembered that most nursing homes, unlike hospitals, are for-profit operations. Two extreme reactions could occur. First, the expenses of nursing home care could skyrocket, in that nursing homes could look to large insurance companies for reimbursement, as opposed to Medicaid and the resources for the individual resident and his or her family. Second, insurance companies, in an effort to control expenses, could place restrictive regulations on nursing home services, which would have an adverse effect on the care to be received by older adults. And, if coverage was not universal, there might be a tendency to foist costs off on the state and federal agencies, or on private-pay individuals.

3. Other Federal Proposals

Whether this counterplan approach can be followed on this topic will be determined by the selection of affirmative basic approach to this topic.

Affirmative plans which are regulatory in nature (e.g., a prospective payment system for nursing homes or federal standards for nursing home care) would not be susceptible to this counterplan, since their costs would be administrative in nature. Affirmative plans which were funding-oriented, such as providing for the construction of nursing homes on a Hill-Burton basis (federal loans in return for a percentage of free care for low-income elderly) or direct assistance to the elderly to pay for nursing home care (grants to low-income persons) would be susceptible, as they would require sufficient expenditures to compete directly with the counterplan examples listed in the retirement security section.

The counterplan examples listed for the retirement security topic would all work here as well. A different type of federal government counterplan appropriate only on this topic would be mandating home health care for the elderly and other persons who are disabled or convalescent.[13] The argument would be that home health care is the antithesis of custodial care, so the mandates of the affirmative and negative would be mutually exclusive.

The tricky question for this counterplan is the nature of the advantages claimed. If the negative argued that home health care resulted in a net cost savings, the affirmative could argue that both the affirmative plan and the counterplan should be adopted, home health care to be used where appropriate and custodial care where appropriate. If there was a net savings from home health care, there would be no fiscal barrier to adopting both approaches. Hence, the negative would have to claim benefits in terms of quality of care and emotional well-being of the elderly, not cost savings.

The other problem for this counterplan (if argued as a federal option) would be dealing with those elderly persons who require 24-hour care, i.e., need to be in a nursing home. Providing for adequate custodial care under a federally administered counterplan would be topical. One way of finessing this would be to argue that the counterplan would provide custodial care only for "some" persons over age 65, whereas the affirmative presumably would be more all-inclusive. This would be unlikely to be persuasive, since the topic does not create an "all" versus "some" distinction: in addition, 24-hour care would have to be available potentially to all persons using home health care, in the event of need on their part. Another approach would be to argue that persons requiring 24-hour care could also be cared for in an acute-care institution, as opposed to a skilled nursing facility.

C. GENERIC DISADVANTAGES ON THIS TOPIC

Of the generic disadvantages discussed on the retirement security topic, all but the crisis in confidence disadvantage would also apply to this topic. The viability of the economic growth disadvantage and squeezing out other social spending would be determined by the amount of spending of the affirmative, i.e., whether the affirmative plan is regulatory or expenditure-based in its mandates. Ageism on this topic would require arguing that the affirmative would heighten the associations between aging, infirmity, and incompetence. However, the crisis in confidence disadvantage would be difficult to argue on this topic, because it requires a showing that the elderly would perceive the affirmative mandates as anti-elderly.

One generic disadvantage is unique to this topic: driving nursing homes out of providing care. This argument would focus on the financial nature of nursing home operations, which are either for-profit corporations seeking to maximize revenues or not-for-profit arrangements (e.g., established by a church or fraternal order) with a limited ability to sustain debt or unreimbursed care. In either case, being forced to accept low-income residents would be unattractive. Where the affirmative plan stiffened regulations, causing an increase in costs, (e.g., in labor) the safe effect would occur: it would be rational for nursing home operators to cease business. For a diversified corporation with activities outside of nursing home operations, it would be a better use of investment funds to place them in other areas. For a church or fraternal order unable to sustain additional costs without increasing costs beyond the reach of its members, it would make sense to get out of nursing home management altogether. Negatives could also analogize to disadvantages on other topics (e.g., exporting hazardous waste or industries seeking to avoid environmental or safety regulations) in that nursing home operations could easily be transferred to Canada or (for much wealthier persons) assorted islands in the Caribbean.[14] If affirmatives attempt to pre-empt this by providing subsidies to nursing home operators, it feeds the disadvantages described above, particularly the social spending argument.

TOPIC: That the federal government should guarantee long-term health care for United States citizens over age 65.

A. NEGATIVE GROUND ON THIS TOPIC

Negative options on this topic can be conceptualized along two lines: first, there are current instrumentalities for providing long-term or acute-catastrophic care; and second, there are health care approaches which are alternatives to the provision of such care.

Current providers of long-term health care can be further broken down in two ways: form of health care providers and form of health care financing. Health care providers include hospitals providing long-term acute care, skilled nursing facilities, and hospices. Funding instrumentalities include Medicare (both hospitalization insurance and supplemental medical insurance), private health insurance ("Medigap"), and, to a lesser extent, health maintenance organizations ("HMOs").

Health care approaches which are alternatives to long-term care are trickier to identify. The basic concept is that of non-traditional sources of care for long-term illnesses and chronic conditions being used as an alternative to acute care hospitalization. Hence, home health care would fit this category, since it reduces the reliance of persons with chronic conditions on hospitalization for care. The preventive care measures emphasized by HMOs would fit this category for the same reason, as they reduce the average length of hospital stay of HMO members. Hospices could also fit into this category, because they are less a facility than an approach to care for the terminally ill. The idea behind a hospice is that of providing an alternative to acute care facilities for persons who will no longer benefit from the services of those facilities.

B. GENERIC COUNTERPLANS ON THIS TOPIC

With regard to the counterplan options for this topic, the following comments are distinct from the discussions of the first two topics.

1. State Counterplans

This would be a relatively weak approach on this topic, given the health care financing nature of this topic. The amount of funding which would need to be undertaken, plus variations in funding capacity among the states, make federal approaches to long-term health care superior to state initiatives.

2. Nongovernmental Approaches

The basic debate on this topic is between government funding of long-term health care and private health insurance reimbursement of long-term health care providers. The form of the counterplan would be that of insurance industry risk-pooling to cover catastrophic health costs.

3. Other Federal Proposals

This could be an extremely potent approach on this topic, since the nature of this topic virtually commits the affirmative to significant federal budget outlays. The only real question is the balance between benefits claimed by the affirmative and those claimable for the counterplan.

C. GENERIC DISADVANTAGES ON THIS TOPIC

All of the disadvantages described in the first section of this chapter apply here, with the possible exception of the crisis in confidence argument. The negative could argue that the affirmative resolution would be seen as a tacit admission that Medicare had failed to provide for all contingencies. However, it is difficult to see how providing additional funding for health care for the elderly could be construed as an attack on the aged.

NOTES TO CHAPTER TWO

1. This author is dubious as to whether these approaches are inherency arguments in any event. Instead of opposing the resolution (i.e., arguing that affirmative benefits are not unique to the resolution), the negative is really arguing that resolutional action can be taken without adopting the resolution.

2. For example, Illinois has a Human Rights Act, under which age discrimination is prohibited. Persons subject to discrimination can file complaints with either the state Human Rights Commission or with the federal Equal Employment Opportunity Commission. As is discussed in Chapter Seven, there is wide variation in the effectiveness of such state remedies.

3. Michael J. Boskin, *Too Many Promises: The Uncertain Future of Social Security* (Homewood: Dow Jones-Irwin, 1986) pp. 35-36, 38.

4. Boskin, pp. 116-118.

5. Policy propositions using government as agents of action permit national and global topics, provide more resources for research, provide more alternative case options, and are more "value-free" as to notions about the agents of action. For example, it would be theoretically and logically possible to have a policy resolution, "Resolved: that parents of children under age 18 should engage in programs of sex education with their children." However, for the reasons given above, it would make more sense as a scholastic debate to phrase a resolution as "Resolved: that public secondary and/or elementary schools should engage in programs of sex education for students." However, a negative option (the "non-resolution") would be to defend use of nongovernmental entities to accomplish the same purpose, i.e., parents, religious institutions. The author would not care to defend that as a counterplan, but it illustrates the point.

6. "Balancing the budget" is closer to a political icon than to a discrete proposal. To obtain the types of economic benefits which can be claimed for "balancing the budget," the negative need not show a net surplus: it need only get budget deficits down to manageable amounts, as opposed to the large and rising figures of the 1980s.

7. Boskin, pp. 76-78.

8. National Health Law Program, "The Omnibus Budget Reconciliation Act of 1987: Legislative Changes in Medicaid, Medicare, and Related Programs," *Health Advocate* (February, 1988), pp. 1-2.

9. Kenneth E. Thorpe and Charles Brecher, "Improved Access for the Uninsured Poor in Large Cities: Do Public Hospitals Make a Difference?" *Journal of Health Politics, Policy, and Law* (Summer 1987), v. 12, no. 2, pp. 313-314, 318-320.

10. Jane Perkins, "The Effects of Health Care Cost Containment on the Poor: An Overview," *Clearinghouse review* (December 1985), v. 19, p. 832.

11. Roger Schwartz and Jane Perkins, "The Omnibus Budget Reconciliation Act of 1987: Legislative Changes in Medicaid," *Clearinghouse Review* (April, 1988), v. 21, pp. 1301-1302.

12. One state hospital which was the subject of litigation which went to the Supreme Court has been referred to as "Dachau without ovens." See McCoy, "Due Process and Judicial Deference to Professional Decision-makers in Human Service Agencies," *Syracuse Law Review*, 35 (1984), pp. 1299-1301, 1315-18.

13. For reasons described in the section on state counterplans on this topic, this counterplan would probably be more successful if argued as federal rather than state government action. Negatives would certainly avoid counterplan topicality arguments if this option were presented as a state counterplan. However, they would also have problems with variations in state ability to fund programs. The best argument for presenting this as a state counterplan is that negatives could then preserve the option of having nursing home care for persons who need 24-hour care, an optio which would be topical if not administered by an agency other than the federal government. If argued as a state counterplan, benefits could be claimed in terms of reduced costs, although, as discussed in Chapter Six, there is some question as to how much money home health care actually saves.

14. A number of nursing home corporations are multinational and headquartered in Canada already running nursing homes in both Canada and the United States. See "Profits in Health Care," *Mclean's*, June 8, 1987, pp. 26-27.

3 Economic Security and the Elderly

The economic status of the elderly in the United States has changed dramatically over the past 50 years, in large part due to "Social Security," the Old Age Survivors Insurance ("OASI") program. In the Great Depression era which gave rise to the program, about 50 percent of the elderly population was considered poor; between 1959 and 1970, the proportion of the elderly below poverty dropped from 35.2 percent to 24.6 percent.[1] By the 1980s, this figure had almost been cut in half: while the poverty rate for the population as a whole increased from 11.7 percent to 15 percent between 1979 and 1982, the proportion of the elderly in poverty declined from 15.2 percent to 14.6 percent.[2] And, if one counts non-cash benefits in food, housing, and medical care received by the elderly as income, the U.S. Census Bureau lowered the number of elderly in poverty in 1982 from 14.6 percent to 3.5 percent.[3]

At present, over 36 million people, most of them elderly, receive benefits from the Social Security Administration.[4] In addition, there has been tremendous growth in the number of persons covered by private pension plans: approximately one-half of the U.S. labor force has such plans, two-and-one-half times the percentage only 30 years ago.[5] Correspondingly, the proportion of U.S. citizens past the age of 65 still working has declined greatly. According to census data, the proportion of men over the age of 65 in the labor force declined from 55.6 percent in 1920, to 42.2 percent in 1940, 28.9 percent in 1960, 23.9 percent in 1970, and 18.4 percent in 1981: although more than 50 percent of all women over 18 were gainfully employed in 1981, only 8 percent of women over 65 were in the labor force.[6] And half of the men and three-fifths of the women over age 65 who were working in 1981 were working part-time.[7] As of 1981, Social Security benefits accounted for 37 percent of money income for elderly households, while earnings accounted for 25 percent, property income for 23 percent, and pension 13 percent.[8]

As much as the economic condition of the elderly has been improved upon over the past 50 years, future progress is running a collision course with demographic factors. First, the proportion of the population over age 65 will increase substantially in the next century. Gradually increasing from 11.3 percent in 1980 to a projected 13.9 percent by 2010, the percentage of the population over 65 will then increase to 17.3 percent by 2020, and 21.1 percent by 2030, as the baby boomers retire.[9] Simultaneously, the life expectancy rates of persons over age 65 will increase. Currently, the life expectancy of persons age 65 is 14 years for men and 18 years for women, but the Social Security Administration forecasts that this will increase by 3 years for men and 4 years for women by the time the baby boom generation retires.[10] Hence, in the next century, a work force smaller in proportion to the number of retirees than is currently the case will be asked to provide benefits for longer periods of time per retiree.

This chapter addresses the methods of providing for the economic well-being of the elderly: the transfer payments of the Social Security programs, work, and private pensions. Employment among the elderly is discussed concurrently with Social Security in this chapter, as well as in connection with age discrimination in Chapter Seven. Supplemental Security Income is discussed separately, for reasons of its method of funding and level of benefits, as well as the population served. The focus is on the ability of these modalities to provide for the economic security of the elderly and on proposed adjustments and their likely impact.

A. SOCIAL SECURITY AND GOVERNMENT TRANSFER PAYMENTS

1. Social Security, 1935-1983

Social Security is the legacy of the Roosevelt New Deal. Yet in key respects, the current system of retirement benefits differs from that envisioned by New Deal planners in the 1930s. In addition, several programs have been added to Social Security, in particular, disability benefits and Medicare (discussed in Chapter Four).

The two key features of the Old Age and Survivors' Insurance ("OASI") program under Title II of the Social Security Act are as much perceptual and ideological as they are substantive: these are, first, that the program is an "insurance" or "annuities" program, not a welfare program; and, second, that it is separate and distinct from assistance for the non-elderly, Title VII of the Act, Aid to Families with Dependent Children ("AFDC") in particular. Initially, old-age insurance was conceived of by social reformers as part of a comprehensive social welfare package, including public assistance for the non-elderly and unemployment compensation.[11] While assistance to the aged and the disabled is now administered by the federal government according to uniform standards, public aid remains the creature of state agencies, with varying standards of eligibility and benefit levels.[12] And while the public views Social Security as social insurance, based on workers' contributions, public aid is associated with negative stereotypes about the work effort and morality of its recipient, together with no small amount of racial stereotypes as well.[13]

The "insurance" feature of Social Security is open to debate. While one's Title II benefit amount is tied to income level and level of contributions (is is based on an average of the three years with the highest earnings in the ten years preceding retirement,[14]) it can also be argued that the "insurance" label was used largely for political purposes in the early years of the program. Arthur Altmeyer, the first chairman of the Social Security Board, stressed an analogy between Social Security and private savings and insurance, describing the payments received as contractually determined, being based on the "fair return" to each individual according to his or her relative income standing during working years.[15] In fact, Social Security has always paid proportionately higher pensions to poorer beneficiaries, and payments of benefits were speeded up and coverage made more generous during the early years of the program in order to beat back efforts to repeal the program.[16] The idea of the trust fund was used to describe the program as the building up of individual future benefits through contributions, rather than a payroll tax in which current workers subsidized earlier retirees; the trust fund also insulated Social Security money from other government activities.[17]

The "insurance" feature has survived to this date and characterizes the differential treatment of Social Security and AFDC. That the earnings on which the Social Security tax are levied determine the taxpayer's future benefits creates a link between the financing and benefit sides of the program, which greatly reinforces the security of future benefit payments.[18] The perception that Social Security benefits are annuities, tied to past contributions, makes changes in benefits extremely difficult to enact: as is discussed later in this chapter, the 1983 reforms required lengthy phase-in times to secure political approval.[19] In contrast, AFDC benefits come from general revenue, must compete with other spending priorities, and are viewed by the public as largesse on the part of the federal government: significant cuts were made in AFDC funding in 1981 with relatively little advance planning, and took effect immediately.[20]

The different attitudes toward and treatment of Social Security and "welfare" should be kept in mind in evaluating reform proposals with regard to Social Security. Some critics would replace the current program with a means-tested welfare program for the elderly, or combine such a program with limiting Social Security payments to annuities based on actual contributions. The "insurance" image of Social Security, together with its limitation to the elderly, has been responsible for a separation in the minds of most Americans between Social Security and "welfare" programs. Of course, Social Security is almost as much a pure transfer payment as AFDC, at least for current recipients. For current retirees, approximately 80 percent of receipts are in excess of past contributions and interest.[21] That Social Security tax revenues are earmarked for distribution as benefits gives the program a high degree of predictability, which is important to the degree of confidence its recipients may have in its continued operation.[22]

Treating Social Security as welfare, subjecting it to competition with other social programs for general revenue would greatly alter the public's perception of the program. It would blur the distinction between old age assistance and welfare which, as Munnell notes, grows out of the different traditions for the programs: Social Security is based on a tradition of self-help, contributory financing, and benefits provided as an earned right, while public assistance grows out of the paternalistic and punitive tradition of the English poor laws.[23] Even though the differences between the programs in funding are more perceptual than substantive, they are reflected in the manner in which recipients are treated by the government. "Welfare-izing" Social Security would do its recipients no favor.

A number of important changes have occurred in Social Security since its inception in 1935. Additional programs provided old age insurance for survivors in 1939, for disabled workers in 1956, and, importantly, for retirees in need of medical care in 1965 (Medicare).[24] The Supplemental Security Income (Title XVI of the Act) was brought fully within the aegis of the Social Security Administration in the 1972 Amendments. Prior to that time, federal aid to the aged who did not qualify for benefits under Title II of the Act (either for their own past work or as survivors), as well as to the blind and the permanently disabled was administered much as AFDC is administered today: the federal government provided matching grants to the states, who ran the programs through public aid offices, and who set eligibility and benefit levels.[25] After the 1972 Amendments, these programs were merged under SSI, funding became exclusively federal, and one nationwide set of eligibility standards and benefit levels was imposed.[26]

The 1939 Amendments, which made the first Title II benefits payable in 1940, two years earlier than originally scheduled, covered beneficiaries whose earnings in covered employment were $15 per month or less.[27] The initial Title II minimum benefit in the 1935 Act was $10 per month.[28] By 1949, the average Title II retirement check was $25 per month, less than the $42 per month provided by Old Age Assistance.[29] In 1950, 56.7 percent of the civilian labor force contributed to the program: nearly one million persons received benefits under Title II.[30] All of this was prefatory to dramatic growth in both coverage and the amount of benefits over the next few decades. In September, 1950, benefit levels were increased 77 percent over their 1939 levels. They were increased another 12.5 percent in 1952, 7 percent in January, 1954 and 13 percent in September, 1954.[31] By 1972, minimum and maximum monthly benefits for a single retiree were $66 and $259, for a couple, $270 and $389; 1972 also saw the introduction of cost-of-living adjustments in benefits, which took effect in 1975.[32] The 1950 Amendments brought an additional 8 million workers under the goverage of the system; by 1977, 88.7 percent of the civilian labor force was covered.[33]

The 1935 Act funded future Title II benefits by placing a 1 percent tax on the employee's wage up to $3,000, with the same amount to come from the employer: revenues collected went to an Old Age Reserve Account.[34] The OASI trust fund was not created until 1940.[35] By 1985, the tax had increased to 14.1 percent of the first $39,600 on income, split between employer and employee, and is scheduled to increase to 15.3 percent in 1990.[36] Expenditures under Title II rose from $40.4 million in 1940 to $784.1 million by 1950.[37] The sum of $258.4 billion was authorized for the Social Security Budget for fiscal 1988, with an additional $92.8 billion authorized for Medicare.[38]

Two trends characterize the history of Social Security during its first 50 years; one political, one demographic. The political trend has been to increase benefits, widen coverage, and add new types of benefits to the program. As Achenbaum has noted, "(i)t is probably not accidental" that the major increases in Social Security benefits usually occurred shortly before elections.[39] Hence, whenever the OASI trust fund has generated a surplus, Congress has found new use for excess revenues: projected surpluses have nearly always proved illusory.[40] Social Security in its early years was not always so attractive: the 1939 Amendments can be argued to have been designed to blunt political opposition to the program.[41] Conservative opposition to Social Security remained until the 1950s, when the U.S. Chamber of Commerce proposed Social Security's replacement by a universal flat-pension system, under which all citizens over age 65 would be given a minimum benefit of $25 per month, underwritten on a pay-as-you-go basis.[42]

The demographic trend is reflected in the numbers cited at the start of this chapter, detailing the increasing percentage of the edlerly in the United States, as well as the decrease in the percentage of persons over age 65 (and persons over age 50 as well) to be active members of the labor force. As a result, the ratio of beneficiaries to contributors to the program has dropped steadily, from 1:45 in 1940, to 1:16.5 in 1950, and to 1:3.3 in 1980.[43] This has unfortunately coincided with a stagnant period in economic growth, periods of high unemployment (decreasing contributions), and high inflation.[44] By 1983, the trust fund had only 8 weeks' worth of reserves: conservative critics argued that over the next 75 years, Social Security would need about $25 billion (in 1983 dollars) over and above anticipated revenues, meaning that the discounted present value of the deficit would be at least $1.6 billion by 2058.[45]

The demographic trend, as well as the renewal of conservative opposition to Social Security in its current form, set the stage for the 1983 Amendments. Beginning in the 1970s, a series of dire predictions began appearing about the future of the Social Security fund.[46] This coincided with high rates of inflation, which affected benefit levels, as well as stagnation in economic growth, which affected the political as well as the fiscal climate. During the Carter Administration, four blue-ribbon panels were appointed to study specific aspects of Social Security, and reforms were recommended.[47] While the Carter Administration succeeded in raising the Federal Insurance Contributions Act ("FICA") tax rate and wage base, as well as reforming disability insurance, it engaged in no comprehensive reform of benefits.[48] After Health, Education, and Welfare Secretary Joseph Califano's 1978 proposal to cut Social Security expenditures by $600 million resulted in strong criticism, President Carter was reluctant to deal with Social Security in any substantive way: Califano's replacement, Patricia Roberts Harris, hestiated to recommend major charges.[49]

The first two years of the Reagan Administration also produced no results, although not for lack of effort on the part of the Administration. In May, 1981, the Administration proposed a 250 percent point reduction in early retirement benefits effective January, 1982: a three-month delay in the COLA scheduled for July, 1982, with later adjustments to be made in October, 1982; and tightened disability benefits under SSI.[50] 1981-1982 also was a period of intensive efforts by the Reagan Administration to reduce the numbers of persons currently receiving disability benefits under SSI through "Continuing Disability Investigations," under which current beneficiaries were scheduled for review and re-review of their status.[51] Although several hundred thousand recipients had their benefits terminated (and the rate of new applicants for benefits approved declined as well), two-thirds of the decisions which were appealed were reversed.[52] The broader proposals of the Administration were rejected as hasty and having significant impacts on retirees without giving them an opportunity to adjust retirement plans accordingly: e.g., changing the reduction formula for early retirement only seven months before implementation.[53]

2. The 1983 Amendments

In 1983, Congress passed amendments to the Social Security Act in an effort to deal with both short-term and long-term fiscal problems affecting the trust fund. In doing so, it in large part followed the recommendations of the National Commission Social Security Reform ("NCSSR"). The NCSSR was a fifteen-member, bipartisan (eight Republicans, seven Democrats) panel of experts, both in and out of government.[54] It was established in December, 1981, by President Reagan, with a mandate to review the current and long-term financial condition of the trust funds, identify problems jeopardizing

Social Security's solvency, and to analyze solutions to the problems faced by the program: the NCSSR was to report its recommendations by December 31, 1982.[55] Of course, the NCSSR has no authorization to promulgate any legislation or regulations, only to make recommendations, which could be ignored or denounced if unattractive.[56] In reality, the NCSSR functioned as both a study group and as a team of negotiators between Democrats in the Congress (especially the Speaker of the House, Thomas "Tip" O'Neill) and the White House (the President, but also then-Chief of Staff James Baker, aides Richard Darman and Kenneth Duberstein, and then-Director of the Office of Management and Budget David Stockman).[57]

The NCSSR produced its recommendations within a highly charged political atmosphere. The 1982 off-year elections featured political campaign efforts by both Republicans and Democrats seeking to make Social Security an issue.[58] Meanwhile, on November 5, 1982, the Social Security old-age trust fund was forced to borrow over half a billion dollars from the disability trust fund to meet current expenses.[59] On November 11, the NCSSR voted unanimously to accept the analysis of its Executive Director that the combined trust funds faced a current funds shortage of $150-200 billion between 1983 and 1989 and a projected deficit of $1.6 trillion in 1982 dollars over the next 75 years.[60] After intense negotiations with Speaker O'Neill and White House Staff members, the NCSSR eventually arrived at a compromise package which was projected to generate an additional $168 billion in revenues during the 1980s and to eliminate two-thirds of the long-range deficit.[61] The short-term savings were to be achieved by delaying the COLA on benefits for six months and by revising the tax-rate schedule for 1984-1990, taxing 50 percent of benefits for Social Security recipients with income over $20,000 for single taxpayers and $25,000 for couples, and through imposing greater uniformity in Social Security coverage and financing.[62] Long-term savings were to be produced through the continuation of the measures above: the NCSSR could not agree on whether to eliminate the remaining one-third of the projected deficit through a gradual raising of the retirement age or another round of increases in tax rates in 2010.[63]

The 1983 Social Security Act Amendments largely parallel the NCSSR's recommendations. Congress added a provision (after much debate) to raise the age of eligibility for full benefits to 66 by 2009 and 67 by 2027. In addition, workers retiring at age 62, who currently have their benefits reduced by 20 percent, would have them decreased by 25 percent in 2005 and 30 percent in 2022. Greater incentives for delayed retirement and continued work past age 65 were provided: the current 3 percent increase in benefits per year delayed would be increased to 8 percent in 1980, and benefits would be reduced by only $1 for every $3, instead of $2, that was earned over prescribed limits.[64] Congress rejected efforts to amend proposed compromise legislation in any significant way, recognizing it as imperfect but the product of negotiations, the only package acceptable to competing factions.[65] As Representative Barber Conable, a key NCSSR member, commented, "(t)he conference report may not be a work of art, but it is artful work ... It will do what it is supposed to do. It will save the nation's basic social insurance system from imminent disaster."[66]

What is the legacy of the 1983 Amendments? First, it should be noted that dealing with the Medicare trust fund (Hospital Insurance) was beyond the mandate of the NCSSR, and Congress attempted no basic reform in providing for the health care costs of older Americans. As is discussed in the next Chapter, tremendous growth in expenditures in Medicare threaten the stability of the trust funds as a whole: before 1983, the projected deficit in the Medicare trust fund over the next 75 years was projected to be three times as large as that for the Title II programs.[67] What Congress did do in 1983 was to authorize a new form of Medicare hospital reimbursement, the Prospective Payment System ("PPS"). The effect of PPS on Medicare costs is discussed in Chapter Four.

Second, the 1983 Amendments did avert the short-term crisis in Social Security funding. One question to be asked is whether there really was a short-term crisis: an argument could be made that while the long-term problems of Social Security appear to be real, the short-term problems of the trust funds needed to be played up to force Congress to act.[68] On a politically sensitive issue such as Social Security, Congress appears willing to act only as disaster looms.[69] Yet Social Security, by its nature, requires lead time of several decades to adjust for major changes in the amount and level of benefits of prospective retirees. Hence, the best thing about averting the short-term crisis, real, illusory, or somewhere in between, was that it also permitted progress to be made in dealing with the long-term problems of Social Security.

Third, it should be remembered that the "savings" produced by the 1983 Amendments are projected to occur between roughly 1990 and 2020: during that period, the trust funds are to run a surplus, which will cover the deficits which are projected to occur thereafter.[70] And, as noted above, the changes in age of retirement on full benefits and in percentage of reduction from full benefits for persons who retire early are not scheduled to go into effect until the next century. A plausible argument can be made that the projected savings from the 1983 Amendments will never take place. In the past, surpluses have always been eaten up by increased benefit levels.[71] And, as is discussed in the next Chapter, major increases in Medicare will make it tempting for Congress to use up the pre-2020 "surpluses" to be able to pay for Medicare without raising taxes. As for the increases in retirement age, AFL-CIO President Land Kirkland (a NCSSR member) considers this measure a mirage that can be rescinded before it actually goes into effect.[72]

Munnell has argued that the accumulation of a large trust fund surplus during the years 1990-2020 is not necessarily a desirable policy goal. If no surpluses were developed before 2020, Congress would then be forced to increase the FICA tax rate. However, Munnell calculates that the increases required to cover post-2020 fund deficits would be fairly modest, the equivalent of slightly more than 1 percent each for employer and employee.[73] On the other hand, development of surpluses would have interim negative effects. Formation of a surplus would come at the expense of lowered consumption for the generation working during the period of accumulation, 1990-2020.[74] Since the United States' economy's recent experience has been one of limited growth anyway, the benefits of further reduced consumer spending are dubious. In addition, Munnell contends that the build-up of Social Security trust fund reserves will be an ineffective mechanism for increasing saving and capital accumulation, based on the experiences of Sweden, Canada, and Japan. In those three countries, large trust funds were accumulated and invested; Munnell's conclusion is that trust fund activity has a beneficial impact on saving only in a centrally planned economy, but would cause distortions and logistical problems in a non-planned economy like that of the United States.[75] Trust fund reserves, therefore, need only be large enough to provide a buffer against brief, unanticipated fluctuations in the economy; amounts above and beyond that would be political, not economic, in nature, providing paper assurances that future commitments would be fulfilled.[76]

3. Future Courses of Action for Social Security

This section examines proposals for changes in Social Security. There are two broad purposes for these changes: improved adequacy of funding the program and greater equity of the program. "Adequacy" of funding means several different things. First, it can mean simply that the 1983 changes are inadequate, and additional monies must be found. As discussed previously, this may be more politics than economics. Despite pretensions that it is an insurance system, Social Security functions as a "pay as you go" system, with current transfer payments to the elderly coming primarily from current FICA collections, not from interest on past collections. However, it is argued that there will be a substantial increase in Title II outlays after 2010, when baby boomers start retiring, and only through advanced fund accumulation can this eventually be met.[77] The second and more common meaning of "adequacy" of the trust funds is an "adequacy to do what" meaning, i.e., more funds need to be raised to add a program, or provide greater funding for an existent program. So, for example, the funds as constituted presently are not adequate to bring SSI payments up to the poverty level, as discussed in the next section.

"Equity" also has a variety of meanings, depending on the political perspective and goals of the person or groups advocating the change. To liberal critics of the system, equity means increasing benefits for women and blacks and other minorities. Social Security's retirement payments, although replacing income at a higher rate for low income retirees, tends to perpetuate wage and salary discrimination against women and racial minorities. Social Security's methods of determining eligibility militate against the interests of those whose employment and earnings histories differ from those of "average" white males.[78] Since women, until recently, differed in their work experiences (type and length of employment, average size of covered earnings, and age at retirement) they were less likely to be found eligible than men, and for lower benefit amounts.[79] Nevertheless, Social Security has been more responsive to women's demands for equity in benefits than it has to those of minorities: for them, formula changes would have to be more complex, possible race-based, while benefits have never been race-based (although they have been gender-based).[80]

Equity, to conservative critics, means something quite different, and conflicts with the liberal agenda. Equity from this perspective means linking benefits received to contributions made. Amounts received in excess of what are "pure" transfer payments, i.e., Title II is a welfare program. These transfers can be intergenerational, from current taxpayers to current retirees: they can also be intragenerational, from two-earner families to one-earner families and from single parents to multi-person families within the same generation.[81] The latter in particular refers to surviving spouse benefits, where the survivor takes benefits at the rate of his or her deceased, if larger than his or her own entitlement. Given that women have had greater longevity than men and that women have had lower benefit amounts, based on earnings history, Survivor's Insurance has worked to the benefit of women. Hence, improved equity in a conservative sense would conflict with liberal equity goals.

Intergenerational equity refers to the degree to which benefit levels are not supported by contributions. Only about one-fifth of the benefits received by current retirees are supported by their lifetime contributions.[82] The purpose of establishing intergenerational equity is to avoid the projected fund crisis after 2012 when, given presently-provided for rates of funding, the transfer will be negative, i.e., retirees will receive lifetime benefits lower than their lifetime contributions.[83] This gives rise to proposals that there be a shift from present FICA contribution to "Personal Security Accounts," where retirement payments are annuities, not transfers.[84]

A conservative view of equity also refers to the extent to which Social Security is "welfare for the rich." From this perspective, Social Security was intended originally only to provide minimum protection from poverty for the elderly, but has gone beyond that.[85] While it is true that Social Security benefits provide the greatest proportion of income received and provide an amount proportionally closer to preretirement earnings for the low and low-middle income groups, in absolute amounts, most Social Security payments go to persons not in poverty.[86] Hence, if the purpose of Social Security is to avoid poverty among the elderly, it spends much of its money superfluously.

Another way to classify the following changes is between "incremental" and "radical." The history of Social Security reform, including the 1983 Amendments, has been that of incremental change, fine-tuning, minor adjustments, rather than sweeping change. Some of the proposals below are in keeping with this tradition: others are for fundamental changes in the system, arguing that major course corrections are now needed.

a. Expanded Coverage

As has been described above, Social Security has expanded greatly in the occupations it covers since it was originally enacted in 1935. Expanded coverage, at this point, is not so much a matter of guaranteeing adequacy of retirement benefits to newly covered employees as it is a way of increasing contribution amounts. A major battle in passing the 1983 Amendments was in securing expanded coverage to new federal civil service employees, which was resisted by organized labor.[88] Older federal workers who were "grandfathered" by the 1983 law and state and municipal employees remain the most significant exception to Social Security coverage (and FICA taxation).

Congress has attempted to expand coverage to increase the revenue base for Social Security. In 1987, Congress proposed taxing the earnings of armed forces reservists, 18-21 year olds working for their parents, and people employed by their spouses, which would add $148 million per year in revenue.[89] The step to expand coverage to all government workers would far outshadow this. Writing in 1985, Munnell estimated that coercing all state and local employees would have provided $1.4 billion in 1985 and $11.0 billion over the period 1985-1989.[90] However, this would be a short-term benefit to the system which would create long-term costs. Adding government workers would provide a one-shot increase in FICA revenues. But if these employees were brought in on an actuarially fair basis, they would simply add to the future benefits to be paid out by Social Security, and would provide no net help.[91] The argument for including government workers in Social Security is an equity or fairness argument, that pensions to government workers are provided at taxpayers' expense, yet government workers do not contribute to the retirement scheme affecting the population as a whole.[92]

A related proposal is expanded immigration. This is based on the theory that this would expand the ratio of contributors to recipients. The effect would ultimately be the same as that of expanding coverage to government workers: a one-shot increase in contributions but long-term costs in benefits paid. If new immigrants were brought in on the same basis as current workers in terms of eligibility for benefits and formulas for the calculation of benefits, the net effect on the contributions: benefits ratio might be negative. This is because most immigrants tend to fall in the low to low-middle income range, and the benefit formula is tilted in favor of such groups, providing a proportionally greater return on contributions than for higher income groups.[93]

b. Taxing New Income Sources

FICA has always been a flat rate based on income up to a certain level. Both the percentage tax paid by employers and employees and the level of income subject to taxation has been steadily increased, as described above. An incremental change would be to collect Social Security funds from alternative sources, using this revenue to fund Medicare. As is discussed in Chapter Four, part of Medicare (Supplemental Medical Insurance) is already funded through insurance premiums paid by recipients, with the balance paid out of general federal revenues.

The new sources of revenue are more innovative. One idea is to consider fringe benefits as taxable income for Social Security purposes. Munnell estimates that had the major statutory fringe benefits—pensions, group life insurance, and group health—been taxed at the same rate as wages and salaries in 1985, it would have added $28 billion, and $192 billion over the period 1985-1989.[94] There would also be an equity argument for such taxation, as fringe benefits are concentrated among higher-paid employees, while all taxpayers must pay higher taxes (or receive fewer benefits) to compensate for the favorable tax treatment accorded employee benefits.[95] In addition, the highest paid employees pay a smaller percentage of their income to Social Security, since amounts in excess of $39,600 are not taxed.

A related proposal would be to tax Medicare and Social Security benefits. Under the 1983 Amendments, as described above, one-half of benefits above relatively high levels are already taxes.[96] This was to reduce the pre-1983 projected deficit by one-third.[97] One proposal would be to fully tax these benefits as income.[98] Of course, the amounts at which taxation begins could be lowered as well. A similar proposal would be to tax the value of Medicare benefits. If one considers Medicare to be a benefit, it, like other fringe benefits, could be taxes as part of a comprehensive proposal. To be consistent with the above Social Security tax provisions, one-half the average value of Medicare protection for beneficiaries whose incomes exceed the same income thresholds: had this been implemented in 1985, it would have raised $800 million, and $5.6 billion over the 1985-1989 period.[99]

The point to increasing these taxes would be that of enhancing revenues, with some equity-fairness effects taking place as well. The principal argument for revenue enhancement would be meeting short-term funding deficits, principally in Medicare. This could have negative effects in two respects. First, as long as revenues are available without facing general revenue taxes, there may be less incentive to reform Medicare and make Medicare expenditures more efficient. Second, especially for lower paid employees in smaller workplaces, taxation of fringe benefits might induce employers to cut or eliminate benefits. Fringe benefits provide tax advantages to employers, so long as they are not considered income: their classification as income, added to the uncertainty of health care costs, could cause employers to drop benefits. Even if employees received the same amount in salaries as they would have in fringe benefits, they would be able to buy less health care if not members of groups, and would also be less attractive to pension plans if not part of an employer-wide package.

c. Changes in the Age of Retirement and in Work Incentives

As noted above, the 1983 Amendments encouraged persons to work past age 65 through increasing (at a future date) the percentage credit a worker receives for working past 65 once he or she does retire, and through reducing taxation on earnings above a minimum amount for persons working past age 65 from 50 percent, dollar-for-dollar, to 33 percent. The stick to go along with this carrot was to (again, at a future date) lower percentages of full benefits received on earlier retirement. As difficult politically as it was to achieve the changes in early retirement benefits, raising the age at which full retirement benefits begin was even more difficult. These changes were intended to enhance revenues and reduce claims, including those by persons attempting retirement before age 65.

As is discussed in Chapter Seven, these changes are all in contrast to the trend in employment, which is to encourage early retirement. If one wished to enhance revenue further, all of these changes could be expanded upon. For example, the tax rate could be reduced still further from one-third, early retirement benefit percentages could be cut even more, and the age of retirement could be raised to 70.

Proposals to encourage postponement of retirement or work after age 65 encounter two problems. First, they run into a fairness problem. To the extent that they penalize persons who wish to retire at age 65 (or age 62 or 60), they engage in disparate treatment of persons according to their retirement decisions. Decisions about the age of retirement correlate roughly with the physical demands of the job.[100] In addition, as Achenbaum has commented, policymakers who press for raising the retirement age to permit persons to work past age 65 forget that "few derive the same satisfaction from work as they."[101] And, despite the Age Discrimination in Employment Act, workers over the age of 55 do experience high rates of underemployment and unemployment.[102] To postpone the date at which these persons may achieve full benefits or decrease the amount of benefits they receive at age 62 seems particularly harsh if they effectively have been involuntarily retired.

The second problem faced by such proposals is whether they actually work, i.e., do they really add to contributions and subtract from benefits claimed. As was noted earlier, there is some question whether the higher retirement ages will be repealed before they become effective. However, leaving that aside, there are good reasons to believe that Americans will continue to retire before age 65 anyway. While a person who retires at age 62 receives only 80 percent of full benefits, the retiree can replace years in which he or she would have had low or no earnings with years in which they had greater earnings, negating the loss of benefits.[103] Early retirement decisions are based on factors which may vary from case to case: the decision may be based on estimates of when the retiree thinks he or she can get the best return on contributions to Social Security, other retirement programs, or savings, as well as market calculations and flexible benefit provisions of their employer.[104] Most older people currently appear to believe that retiring early makes sense, even if they will receive lower benefits at retirement.[105] In addition, persons wishing to retire for health reasons but below the age for full benefits can apply for disability status under Title II of the Social Security Act.[106] If the retirement age is raised to 66 in 2009 and 67 in 2027, the number of persons applying for disability at age 65 can be expected to increase as well.

d. Changes in the Replacement Formula

The "replacement formula" is the means by which Title II amounts are calculated. The retirement rate is inversely related to income, so persons with a preretirement income of under $7,500 get benefits which "replace" slightly more than 90 percent of that income, while persons whose preretirement income was between $7,500 and $12,499 on an average had only 54.5 percent of their incomes replaced.[107] This is the source of the "welfare for the rich" argument against Social Security: the program is not an annuities program, as benefits paid well exceed contributions actually made. Yet it is also not a minimum income support program: even though the replacement formula tilts toward lower income groups, smaller percentages of replacement for middle and upper income groups still cause most of Social Security's transfers to those groups. And the one-third of recipients who depend heavily or solely upon Social Security are in the lower income group, while other income groups have alternative sources of income.[108]

A modest proposal to deal with this would be to alter the replacement to be more inversely proportional to income; more radical proposals are discussed below.

e. Means Testing and Social Security

There are several variations on this theme, but the essential idea is to make Title II a welfare program, providing a minimum income floor for persons age 65 and older. One argument is that that was all Social Security was originally intended to be, and that the current form of the program transfers billions of dollars to persons who have private pensions or other resources which would keep them well above the poverty line.[109] The other argument is that the rationale for non-means based Social Security benefits no longer exists: 1) benefits for spouses and survivors assumed substantial non-participation by women in the economy and dependence on the wage earner; 2) even though benefits were unsupported by contributions, expanding economic growth could be expected to generate sufficient revenues for benefit payments. Arguably, neither assumption is still valid.[110]

Third, it is argued that Social Security at present levels of taxation and expenditure harms the economy. There is some empirical evidence to indicate that the FICA tax decreases private saving and has other negative effects on the economy. Feldstein argues that there is a close to 1:1 tradeoff between increases in Social Security wealth (benefits expected) and decreases in private saving: he concludes that Social Security has reduced private savings by 38 percent, and decreased Gross National Product by 20 percent.[111] Others have put the direct effect on Social Security on private saving much lower, with each $1 increase in expected benefits being associated with a $.25 or $.50 reduction, while still others have concluded that there is not effect at all, or the effect cannot be established based on available data.[112] Meanwhile, Social Security preempts other social spending in the federal budget: unless individual and corporate income taxes are increased, outlays on other federal programs must be decreased by 41 percent by the year 2000 if expenditures on Social Security increase as projected.[113]

There are several criticisms of a wholesale change of Social Security to a welfare program. First, if it were agreed to adopt such a program, it would need considerable lead time to be phased in. Persons who have planned their retirements have done so with the expectation of receiving Social Security benefits. Sufficient notification would be required prior to retirement for savings plans to be altered.[114] In addition, 40 percent of private pension plan members belong to plans which are integrated with Social Security, i.e., they are in defined-benefit plans where the level of pension payment is tied to the level of Social Security benefit received. Large reductions in benefits in a short period of time would spell disaster for these plans.[115]

Aside from phase-in problems, there is the question of whether welfare stigma should be associated with Social Security. As was discussed in the opening section of this chapter, considerable effort was put into separating Social Security from AFDC and "welfare" in the minds of the general public. If Americans came to view Social Security as transfer payments for the elderly poor (rather than mom and dad or grandma and grandpa's monthly check), their attitudes could change considerably, exposing low-income older adults to the type of treatment at present reserved for AFDC recipients.

On a practical basis, a "means test" would require a showing of assets and income by benefit applicants to the Social Security Administration for purposes of establishing eligibility. Currently, the SSA does perform such asset determinations for persons seeking disability benefits before age 65 under Title II or Supplemental Security Income ("SSI") under Title XVI. As is described in the section on SSI in this chapter, being placed at the mercy of the SSA is not without its own problems. If the determinations of the SSA and its Administrative Law Judges ("ALJs") with regard to disability benefits are any guide, means testing will be subject to political and budgetary pressures. Under the Reagan Administration, disability determination procedures by the SSA have come under extreme criticism. Means testing for Title II eligibility would greatly expand the work load of an already overworked agency,[116] even though the SSA has been described as having one of the largest administrative decision-making systems in the world, adjudicating millions of cases every year.[117]

One variation on means testing for Social Security would be to create a common rate of return on contributions for all recipients. Benefit calculation is skewed at present in that it is based on peak years of earnings and that there is a progressive structure in the benefit formula. A common rate of return as a basis for calculating benefits would make Social Security to a larger extent the "insurance" or annuities system it has described itself as being. However, as was discussed earlier, most current retirees' benefits far exceed their actual contributions: unless the rate of return were far in excess of 100 percent of contributions, this approach would reduce benefit levels substantially. Where means testing would come in is that persons over age 65 would be guaranteed the rate of return on their contributions or some minimum level of benefits, if that amount were higher. However, to receive the latter amount where it exceeded the rate of return on contributions, need would have to be established.[118]

Closely allied to this approach would be to increase the correspondence between benefits paid and creditable wages in the beneficiary's earning history: currently, the progressive tilt in the replacement rate breaks down their correspondence.[119] This would still require means testing as described above, because persons with long periods of unemployment or low-paid employment could wind up with wage bases which would entitle them to benefits below the poverty line. This would be a departure from the current system, where persons with more than forty quarters of eligibility (i.e., wages earned beyond a minimum amount during those periods) qualify for minimum benefits even though their total earnings fall below the amount actuarially required to receive that benefit.

A more subtle change with roughly the same consequences would be to alter what are termed the "bend points" in the formula for calculating benefits. The bend points are dollar figures at which greater benefits are paid for additional earnings. The bend points are currently set in a way that permits persons with lower incomes to receive higher rates of replacement in earnings. The proposal would be to reset the bend points so that the amount of additional payments for persons at the middle and upper sections of the earnings scale would be reduced. This would have the effect of decreasing overall Social Security expenditures by decreasing benefit payments to persons above minimum income levels.[120]

f. Transition to Private Pension or Voluntary "Opt-out" Pensions

The concept behind this proposal is one in which taxpayers, like annuitants, would receive a yearly report of their current level of Social Security contributions and estimated monthly earnings on retirement. At the request of taxpayers, these funds could then be transferred to a private pension account or investment portfolio, which the account owner would pay into as in a private pension.

Besides being political anathema, making Social Security "voluntary"[121] has a number of problems. First, private funds would not provide disability or health insurance annuities which would be actuarially fair, due to adverse selection (poor risks opt for insurance, insurers must set rates above a fair level to compensate for unreported risks) and moral hazard problems ("moral hazard" refers to behavior by the insured affecting the insurer's degree of risk: monitoring to insure that such risks are not increased is either impossible or not cost-effective). The only answer to this is to provide compulsory coverage, creating one large group, with no opting out: this is what Social Security currently does.[122] Adverse selection would also prevent actuarially fair annuities for retirement benefits as well.[123]

Second, the effect of "opt out" provisions would be that those for whom Social Security is a bad deal when compared with private investment would leave the program. This would leave a larger relative burden on those remaining in the program.[124] As a practical matter, it would mean transfers of general revenues to what was left of Social Security to make up for the shortfalls between contributions and expenditures.

Third, there would be logistical problems insofar as phasing in such a program is concerned. Benefit payments for current reitrees would need to be maintained while the program would be put into effect. This means that the generation in the labor force while the plan is being phased in would finance two retirement systems: the trust fund for their own retirement and the existent system for persons already retired. Outside of improbably large rates of return on private investment, this means that the current rate of contributions would have to be doubled (taxes plus contributions to private trust funds).[125]

g. Changes in the Cost of Living Adjustment

Two very different types of changes in the Cost of Living Adjustment ("COLA") have been proposed. The first proposal is to reduce annual increases in Social Security benefits to a figure below that of increases in the consumer price index. The most frequent proposal has been "CPI minus 2," or COLAs which would lag two percentage points behind whatever the annual rate of inflation is determined to be. This is a fiscal adequacy proposal, decreasing the amount of money which would be needed to provide for Social Security benefits. It would have negative effects on two groups. First, persons at the lower end of Social Security benefits would suffer substantial erosion in the value of their payments, even though they have a higher replacement rate than other recipients. Each year they would slip farther behind changes in consumer prices, and would eventually fall below the poverty line.[126] Hence, "CPI minus 2" might require periodic increases in the minimum benefit amount, which would at least eat into the cost savings advertised. The other group affected would be persons currently under 32: the value of their future benefits would be decreased through annual discounts below the rate of inflation. They would receive 20 percent less benefits in real present value dollars over the next 75 years.[127]

The other COLA proposal is to create a separate COLA for the elderly. This has received some attention in Congress: Senator Melcher has raised this proposal in the last two sessions of Congress. The basis for this proposal is that the CPI is not reflective of costs of living for persons over age 65. The CPI is based on a survey of urban wage earners, clerical workers, and excludes the elderly.[128] Because of the higher health care costs of the elderly and the high rate of inflation in medical care, it is argued that the CPI underestimates the inflation rate for the elderly. Melcher estimates the inflation rate for the elderly in 1986 was 5.2 percent, while the CPI rose only 1.3 percent.[129]

Boskins and Hurd reached the opposite conclusion. This is because prior to 1983 the CPI calculated interest on home mortgages in a manner which overestimated inflation in housing costs during periods of rising housing prices and interest rates.[130] Since a high percentage of the elderly own their homes, the CPI substantially overindexed the cost of living for the elderly, resulting in a $5-6 billion per year overpayment in benefits to Social Security recipients.[131] Correcting for this, Boskin and Hurd found that differences in cost of living increases for the elderly and nonelderly were small, less than one percent.[132] Relative to the rest of the population, Social Security recipients, receiving COLAs, did better than the rest of the population during the 1970s and 1980s, because price increases were greater than wage increases.[133]

4. Supplemental Security Income

The genesis of SSI was described in the first section of this chapter. SSI functions as a welfare program within Social Security, separate from AFDC. It has two groups of recipients: disabled persons under age 65 who do not have sufficient numbers of quarters of covered income to be eligible for disability insurance under Title II; and persons age 65 and over whose earnings history does not qualify them for old age benefits under Title II. There are approximately 4 million SSI beneficiaries, about half in each group.[134] Recipients must fall below a means test for countable assets (less than $1,800 for an individual, $2,700 for married couples, excluding a home and certain other items).[135]

The basic problem for the elderly in SSI is the benefit amount, which has always been below the poverty line. Currently, the monthly benefit amount for an individual is $358. Increases in the basis benefit amount occur on an ad hoc basis: they are also adjusted annually to keep pace with increases in the CPI.[136] Less than half the states supplement the federal SSI payment.[137] In addition, recipients are not eligible for Medicare, which is tied to Title II eligibility, and must rely instead on Medicaid. Recipients tend to be quite old and generally are women. The cost of bringing this group up to the poverty line would be about $4 billion in additional funds per year.[138]

The major concern on the part of Congress and the Reagan Administration with regard to SSI has been the eligibility of under-65 disabled recipients (and Disability Insurance recipients under Title II). Between the early 1970s and 1980, there was tremendous growth in recipients of both SSI and DI, and Congress instituted stricter regulations to stem this increase.[139] There have been charges of overreaching and questionable conduct by the Reagan Administration, motivated by the desire to keep costs down.[140] The SSA also follows a controversial procedure called "non-acquiescence," in which federal court decisions overruling its determinations are treated as binding only on that case and not precedential in making future determinations.[141]

While this conduct does not directly affect elderly SSI recipients, concerns about overall costs of the program probably impede progress toward bringing all recipients up to the poverty line. In addition, the experience of DI and SSI recipients and applicants under the Reagan Administration may be instructive in considering proposals to have the SSA determine eligibility of all Title II recipients under "means testing" alternatives.

B. PRIVATE PENSIONS

Pension Plans began appearing in the United States in the late nineteenth century, with the first industrial pension plan adopted by the American Express Company in 1875.[142] In the period before the Great Depression, company pension plans were seen as both enlightened corporate action and as a means of avoiding broad government social insurance, which already existed in most Western European nations.[143] Trade unions and fraternal orders also instituted pension plans for their members, although state and municipal employers were the pacesetters, providing pensions for police and fire department workers and for elementary and secondary teachers.[144] The Federal Civil Service Retirement System was not established until 1920.[145]

The number of persons with pension benefits before the Depression was still quite small, and concentrated in large industries and public employment: less than 4 percent of the labor was eligible for pension benefits in 1915, and this had only grown to 15 percent by 1930.[146] The alternatives for persons without pension protection were continued employment past age 65, support by family and children, or the meager old age assistance programs existing in a majority of states by 1933.[147]

Several factors, including Social Security, increased longevity, the postwar economic boom, the rise of labor unions, and tax code changes permitting employers to deduct the full amount of contributions to pension funds, caused tremendous growth in pension coverage and benefit amounts after World War II. By 1975, roughly 34 million employees were covered, and pension plans had assets of $154 billion.[148] By 1986, private pension plan holdings had expanded to $1 trillion, half of all national investment capital: between 1986 and 1990, there will be $450 billion in expenditures for private pension plans.[149] For middle and upper income retriees, replacement rates by Social Security are relatively low. These retirees look to private pensions to either supplement Social Security or to be the major source of retirement income.[150]

Pension plans are of two primary types: defined contribution plans and defined benefit plans. Roughly three-quarters of plan participants are in defined benefit plans, which target a percentage of salary to be replaced by pension payments.[151] The remainder are in defined contribution plans, where there is a contractual agreement as to the amount to be committed to the pension fund by the employer and/or employee.[152] These plans function more like tax-sheltered annuities, as the amount of benefits payable on retirement is determined by the economic performance of the stocks and bonds in which pension contributions are invested. As was discussed above, pension plans can be integrated with Social Security to guarantee an overall benefit amount: as Social Security benefit amounts increase, the amount to be contributed by the pension fund decreases. About 40 percent of defined benefit plans are integrated with Social Security in this manner.[153]

As pension funds grew after World War II, so did problems with these funds. The major problem areas were in vesting, funding, and management. "Vesting" (the point at which employees have sufficient years of service to qualify to receive employer contributions to the pension fund) problems arose because there was no legal requirement that employees vest rights before retirement: in addition, employers often imposed strict vesting requirements which led to forfeiture of pension benefits.[154] Funding problems occurred because employers failed to contribute in amounts sufficient to meet payouts as they became due, a problem which became severe when plans were terminated. Plans werre also damaged by mismanagement, poor investments, and outright theft.[155]

In response, Congress adopted the Employee Retirement Income Security Act ("ERISA") in 1974, which was supplemented by the Multiemployer Pension Plan Amendment Act of 1980 ("MPPAA"). ERISA provided for minimum vesting standards, financing by employers, the establishment of an insurance program to protect against losses due to plan termination, reporting and disclosure by plan trustees, and standards of conduct for benefit plan managers.[156] The MPPAA was enacted in recognition of the fact that multiemployer plans accounted for a substantial portion of the increase in private pension plans and a concern over funding obligations for continuing employers where an employer had withdrawn from a multiemployer plan. The MMPAA established liability for such employers.[157]

There are several narrow questions which will have to be answered through court interpretation of ERISA and the MPPAA or through amendments to those laws. One is the liability of corporate officers and shareholders for pension plan contributions when pension plans are terminated. Section 1145 of ERISA and Section 1381(a) of the MPPAA make "employers" liable for such contributions. The legal question (in doubt, based on conflicting court opinions) is whether corporate officers and shareholders qualify as "employers." Traditional corporate law doctrine is that corporate officers and shareholders are not personally liable for a corporation's debts.[158] The question is whether what is known as "piercing the corporate veil" should be engaged in to reach personal assets to provide for pension contributions.

A second narrow legal question concerns the status of pension fund assets during mergers and takeovers of corporations. Under ERISA, trust fund managers owe a fiduciary duty to prospective and current fund recipients: if they conclude that the status of the fund under new ownership will be either worsened or is in doubt, they must recommend against sale or merger, even though this may conflict with the best interests of shareholders.[159] In addition, pension fund assets may make a takeover attractive. ERISA protects accrued employee benefits (in a defined benefit plan, the benefit beginning at retirement; in a defined contribution plan, the employee's account balance). The law does not protect ancillary benefits, such as medical or disability payments under the pension.[160] On termination of a plan by a new corporate owner, there would be no further accrual defined contributions: in the case of a defined benefits plan, employee benefit levels are frozen at the level supported by prior contributions, which would be below those expected by the employee.[161]

Third, while ERISA provides machinery for suing employers who interfere with pension rights, the process for doing so and the standards set by the courts in interpreting ERISA make this a difficult process. Typically, an employee is terminated on the eve of vesting significant pension and benefit rights, or is terminated when he is only a few years from retirement, losing substantial employer contributions during what would have been peak earning years. The problems in bringing suit under ERISA parallel the problems described in Chapter Seven in bringing suit under the Age Discrimination in Employment Act ("ADEA").

Employees alleging unlawful interference with pension rights must bring suit against their former employer under Section 510 of ERISA. To successfully sue the employer, they must establish three things: 1) the employer engaged in a proscribed activity; 2) the activity was aimed at the employee; and 3) the activity was engaged in either because the employee exercised his or her rights under the pension or ERISA or to interfere with the employee's rights.[162] The courts have interpreted ERISA to mean that the employee must establish that the termination of benefits was the motivating factor behind the conduct of the employer: if the loss of benefits was merely the consequence of behavior engaged in for reasons not violative of ERISA, no Section 510 claim is made out.[163] In other words, it is analagous to age discrimination cases, in which an employer may raise a "reasonable factor other than age" ("RFOA") defense under the ADEA.

A sample case is provided by *Folz v. Marriott Corporation:* Folz was terminated after he reported to his employer that he had multiple sclerosis. He was able to convince the court that the motivating factor behind his termination was his employer's desire to avoid paying his medical costs under the company's pension plan, which promised to be substantial. He was successful in doing so in large part because his employer's proffered reason for termination, poor performance, was clearly pretextual. He had a number of years of good evaluations, receiving only one bad evaluation, the one which occurred after he told his employer of his illness.[164] However, where another employee whose benefits were terminated shortly before retirement either is unable to point to such an obvious motive for termination, or where his or her past employment record is not as pristine as was the case in *Folz,* the employee would have a much more difficult time in establishing that the employer violated the law.

There are also much broader problems facing private pension plans, which are more political and economic in nature. The question is one of whether private pension plans will continue to grow in their coverage of American workers. A secondary question is whether coverage will include post-retirement medical expenses, an important supplement as the percentage of medical bills covered by Medicare declines.

The forces which caused expansion of private pension plan coverage have lost much of their potency. Pension coverage in the United States has always been most extensive among government employees and large industrial enterprises. Government employment, which expanded significantly in the last two decades has been frozen at current levels or contracted in size during the Reagan Presidency. Large industries, such as auto and steel, have declined considerably during this period. The struggle for employees in these industries is maintaining benefit levels provided under earlier agreements. Employment growth has occurred instead in small businesses and in service industries, where pension coverage (and ancillary benefits, such as medical expense coverage) are less common.

A separate development which could affect the extent of pension plan coverage is the proposal to tax fringe benefits, discussed above. Efforts to fund Social Security (especially Medicare) could thus have the effect of reducing pension plan coverage by employers, if they would no longer be able to deduct their contributions.

Two consequences of decreased pension support appear significant. First, since middle-income workers count on pension to make up for lower replacement rates by Social Security, their income status on retirement would decline considerably. In addition to affecting their lifestyles as older consumers, lowered income among previously middle-income wage earners would mean that they would be closer to relying on Medicaid for nursing home reimbursement. Not having pensions, their "spend down" to Medicaid eligibility would occur more quickly, placing greater demands on an already overburdened program. Second, decreased pension plan coverage could increase pressure to expand Medicare benefits. This would occur if health benefits ceased to be a part of pension packages, or if fewer retirees had such pension packages: they would then be solely reliant on Medicare for other than out-of-pocket reimbursement of medical expenses. As is discussed in the next Chapter, America seems to be tolerant of limited or low quality care being provided to Medicare-only low-income patients: it is questionable whether it would tolerate such treatment for the bulk of the elderly.

CONCLUSIONS

Retirement security appears a much more attainable goal today than at any previous time in the history of the United States. The group of the elderly still below the poverty line could be brought above it through a more generous SSI benefit level.

The problem facing elderly Americans in providing for adequate retirement income are primarily problems which occur in the future, in the decades beginning in 2010 and 2020. The solutions to those problems, however, must be implemented in the next few years to provide sufficient lead time for corrections.

In addition to demographic factors, the retirement status of the elderly in the future will also be affected by the economic climate. The phenomenal growth in private pensions and in the levels of benefits provided under Social Security both occurred during the postwar economic boom. Future growth and stability in retirement income will be closely associated with the future course of the economy.

NOTES TO CHAPTER THREE

1. W. Andrew Achenbaum, *Social Security: Visions and Revisions* (New York: Cambridge, 1986), p. 53.
2. Michael J. Boskin, *Too Many Promises: The Uncertain Future of Social Security* (Homewood: Dow-Jones Irwin, 1986), p. 26.
3. Bostkin, pp. 27-28.
4. Boskin, p. 7.
5. Boskin, pp. 102-103.
6. Achenbaum, p. 105.
7. Boskin, p. 47.
8. Boskin, p. 34.
9. Boskin, p. 39.
10. Boskin, pp. 40-41.
11. See, G. John Ikenberry and Theda Skocpol, "Expanding Social Benefits: The Role of Social Security," *Political Science Quarterly* (1987), v. 102, pp. 389-416.
12. Alicia M. Munnell, "The Current Status of Our Social Welfare System," *New England Economic Review* (July-August 1987), pp. 3-4. (Hereinafter, "Munnell 1987").
13. See Munnell 1987, p. 3, and Ikenberry and Skocpol, pp. 414-415.
14. Boskin, p. 28.
15. Ikenberry and Skocpol, p. 412.
16. Ikenberry and Skocpol, pp. 411-412.
17. Ikenberry and Skocpol, p. 413.
18. Munnell 1987, p. 6.
19. Munnell 1987, p. 10.
20. The Omnibus Budget Act of 1981 caused 490,000 families to lose their benefits, most of whom wound up below the poverty level, without medical assistance or food stamps. Munnell 1987, p. 10. See also Geraldine Dallek, "Health Care for America's Poor: Separate and Unequal," *Clearinghouse Review* (1986), v. 20, p. 362.
21. Boskin, p. 8.
22. Munnell 1987, pp. 6, 10.
23. Munnell 1987, p. 3.
24. Ikenberry and Skocpol, p. 390.
25. Munnell 1987, p. 5.
26. Munnell 1987, pp. 5-6.
27. Achenbaum, p. 32.
28. Achenbaum, p. 23.
29. Achenbaum, p. 42.
30. Achenbaum, pp. 38, 210.
31. Achenbaum, pp. 39, 211.
32. Achenbaum, pp. 58, 220.
33. Achenbaum, pp. 211, 143.
34. Achenbaum, p. 22.
35. Munnell 1987, p. 6.
36. Boskin, p. 7.
37. Achenbaum, p. 210.
38. *Congressional Quarterly Weekly Report* (October 10, 1987), p. 2443.
39. Achenbaum, p. 211..
40. Boskin, p. 11.
41. Ikenberry and Skocpol, p. 411.
42. Achenbaum, p. 44. Achenbaum traces the defeat of the proposal to lack of support by the insurance industry, which had found that Social Security sensitized

persons to the need for insurance, the unwillingness of the Eisenhower Administration to be identified with the proposal, and vigorous opposition from organized labor.
43. Achenbaum, p. 62.
44. Achenbaum, p. 62. See also Boskin, p. 98.
45. Achenbaum, p. 91. Achenbaum responds that this is misleading because of a projected surplus in the 1990s, due to scheduled tax increases and only a modest growth in costs in order to take care of current and added retirees. Achenbaum, p. 92.
46. Robert S. Kaplan, *Financial Crises in the Social Security System* (Washington: American Enterprise Institute, 1976); Rita Ricardo Campbell, *Social Security: Promises and Reality* (Stanford: Hoover Institute Press, 1977); *The Crisis in Social Security*, ed. Michael J. Boskin (San Francisco: Institute for Contemporary Studies, 1977); and Peter Ferrara, *Social Security: The Inherent Contradictions* (San Francisco: Cato Institute, 1980).
47. Achenbaum, p. 74.
48. Achenbaum, pp. 67-69, 74-77.
49. Achenbaum, p. 69.
50. Achenbaum, p. 77.
51. Donald E. Chambers, "The Reagan Administration's Welfare Entrenchment Policy: Terminating Social Security Benefits for the Disabled," *2Policy Studies Review* (1985), v. 5, p. 232.
52. Chambers, p. 232.
53. Achenbaum, p. 78. As is discussed above, cuts in AFDC were being made simultaneously with no apparent amount of similar concern for lead time or planning effects for welfare recipients. See Munnell 1987, p. 10.
54. Five members each were appointed by the President, the Speaker, and the Senate Majority Leader, then Howard Baker. Robert Meyers, then Deputy Commissioner of the Social Security Administration, served as Executive Director.
55. Achenbaum, p. 80.
56. Achenbaum, p. 80.
57. Achenbaum, pp. 85-86.
58. See the *New York Times* (July 7, 1982), p. A11; (October 24, 1982), Sec. IV, p. 2; and (November 3, 1982), p. 20. The Democrats gained 26 seats in the House of Representatives, a result not unusual for the party not in the White House in an off-year election, and did not regain control of the Senate.
59. Achenbaum, p. 83.
60. Achenbaum, p. 84.
61. Achenbaum, pp. 86-87. The NCSSR required a fifteen-day extension of time to reach these recommendations.
62. Achenbaum, p. 87.
63. Achenbaum, p. 87.
64. Achenbaum, p. 103.
65. Achenbaum, pp. 87-88.
66. *Congressional Record* (March 9, 1983), p. H954.
67. Boskin, p. 10.
68. See Achenbaum, pp. 91-92.
69. As NCSSR member Alexander Trowbridge commented when the Commission had to ask for an extension of time to complete its recommendations, "... you almost have to be up to the precipice before you get a decision." *New York Times* (December 20, 1982), Sec. B, p. 17.
70. Boskin, pp. 11, 2.
71. Boskin, pp. 11, 13.
72. Achenbaum, p. 115.

73. Alicia Munnell, "Paying for the Medicare Program," *Journal of Health Politics, Policy, and Law* (1985), v. 10, p. 502. (Hereinafter, "Munnell 1985")

74. Munnell 1985, p. 500.

75. Munnell 1985, p. 500.

76. Munnell 1985, pp. 497, 500.

77. See Boskin, p. 2. Boskin adds other factors into the equation besides demographics (the number of baby boomers retiring, increased life expectancy). The fund crisis predicted is also the result of projected decreases in the percentage of the elderly working and in the rate of private saving. The 1983 Amendments provided some incentives for working beyond age 65, and Boskin's argument is that increased fund accumulations would decrease consumption and, probably, private saving.

78. Achenbaum, p. 124.

79. Achenbaum, p. 125.

80. Achenbaum, pp. 124-125.

81. Boskin, pp. 14-15.

82. Boskin, pp. 35-36.

83. Boskin, pp. 35-36. But see note 77 above.

84. See Achenbaum, pp. 239-240, n. 52, describing Boskin's "Personal Security Accounts" proposal.

85. Boskin, p. 7.

86. Boskin, pp. 9, 38.

87. See Achenbaum, pp. 93-96.

88. Achenbaum, pp. 88-89, 143-144.

89. *Congressional Quarterly Weekly Report* (July 25, 1987), p. 1656.

90. Munnell 1985, p. 505.

91. Boskin, pp. 98-99.

92. Achenbaum, p. 144.

93. Boskin, p. 99.

94. Munnell 1985, p. 504.

95. Munnell 1985, pp. 503-504.

96. See note 62 and accompanying text.

97. Achenbaum, p. 87

98. Boskin, pp. 107-108.

99. Munnell 1985, p. 505.

100. Boskin, pp. 57-58.

101. Achenbaum, p. 119.

102. Achenbaum, p. 118.

103. Boskin, p. 60.

104. Achenbaum, p. 119.

105. Achenbaum, p. 120.

106. Boskin, p. 114.

107. Boskin, pp. 31-33.

108. Boskin, p. 9.

109. Boskin, pp. 7, 9.

110. Boskin, p. 111.

111. Martin Feldstein, "Social Security, Induced Retirement, and Aggregate Capital Accumulation," *Journal of Political Economy* (September-October, 1974), v. 82, pp. 905-926.

112. Boskin, pp. 76-80.

113. Boskin, p. 4.

114. Boskin, p. 38.

115. Boskin, p. 103.

116. Donna Price Cofer, "The Question of Independence Continues: Administrative

Law Judges Within the Social Security Administration," *Judicature* (1986), v. 69, pp. 230-231.

117. Chambers, p. 230.

118. Boskin, p. 112.

119. Boskin, p. 112.

120. Boskin, p. 112.

121. It would be "voluntary" in the sense that the taxpayer would be permitted to remove funds from and cease paying into the Social Security trust funds. The government would require proof of alternative investment in other retirement schemes.

122. Boskin, pp. 72-73.

123. Boskin, p. 101.

124. Boskin, p. 100.

125. Boskin, p. 100.

126. Boskin, p. 110.

127. Boskin, p. 110.

128. *Congressional Quarterly Weekly Report* (August 22, 1987), pp. 1948-1949.

129. *Congressional Quarterly Weekly Report* (August 22, 1987), pp. 1948-1949.

130. Michael J. Boskin and Michael D. Hurd, "Indexing Social Security Benefits: A Separate Price Index for the Elderly?" *Public Finance Quarterly* (October, 1985), v. 13, pp. 440-441. Before 1983, expenditures on half the interest over the lifetime of a home mortgage were taken to have occurred in the year of purchase. The CPI now uses a rental equivalency concept, i.e., the annual expenditure on housing is the amount the house would rent for.

131. Boskin, pp. 108-109.

132. Boskin and Hurd, pp. 442-443.

133. Boskin, p. 109.

134. Munnell 1987, p. 11.

135. Munnell 1987, p. 9.

136. Munnell 1987, p. 8.

137. Munnell 1987, pp. 6-7.

138. Munnell 1987, p. 11.

139. Chambers, p. 230.

140. Chambers, pp. 231-232. See also Cofer, pp. 228-229. The Association of Administrative Law Judges charged in a suit against Secretary Heckler that maximum benefit allowance rates given to ALJs by the Department of Health and Human Services. Intra-agency reviews of ALJs exceeding these levels were conducted.

141. Ann Ruben, "Social Security Administration in Crisis: Non-Acquiescence and Social Insecurity," *Brooklyn Law Review* (1986), v. 52, pp. 101-102.

142. Thomas J. Grady, "Liability for Unpaid Pension Contributions: Are Corporate Officers or Shareholders 'Employers' Under ERISA?" *Labor Lawyer* (1984), v. 4, pp. 1-2.

143. Ikenberry and Skocpol, pp. 398-399.

144. Achenbaum, p. 15.

145. Achenbaum, p. 15.

146. Achenbaum, p. 15.

147. In 1933, at the depth of the Great Depression, only 21 states, Alaska, and Hawaii had such programs. The nationwide average monthly benefit was $19.25. Achenbaum, pp. 16, 201.

148. Grady, p. 2.

149. Randy L. Gegelman, "The ERISA Trustee: Saying 'No' To a Tender Offer," *Washington University Law Quarterly* (1986), v. 64, p. 953, n. 2.

150. Boskin, pp. 9, 33.

151. Boskin, pp. 102-103.

152. Boskin, pp. 102-103.
153. Boskin, pp. 102-103.
154. Grady, pp. 2-3.
155. Grady, pp. 2-3.
156. Grady, pp. 2-3.
157. Grady, pp. 14-15.
158. Grady, pp. 4-20.
159. Gegelman, pp. 955-963.
160. Gegelman, pp. 963-964.
161. Gegelman, p. 964.
162. William C. Martucci and John L. Utz, "Unlawful Interference with Protected Rights Under ERISA," *"Labor Lawyer* (1986), v. 2, p. 257.
163. Martucci and Utz, p. 257.
164. Martucci and Utz, p. 255. The case is reported at 594 F. Supp. 1007 (W.D. Mo. 1984).

4 Health Care and the Elderly

Health care costs in the United States have been rising rapidly over the past few decades. Only 4.4 percent of the gross national product ("GNP") in 1950, health care costs were 10 percent of the GNP in 1984.[1] Health care expenditures increased from $69 billion in 1970 to $230 billion in 1980,[2] and to $387.4 billion in 1984.[3] While there are various causes for this phenomenal growth in health care spending, government financing of health care services, particularly those for the elderly and the poor, has been a major factor.[4] The two major federal medical programs, Medicare and Medicaid, serve over 50 million Americans.[5] The elderly are major consumers of health care through these programs: 38 percent of hospital revenues come from Medicare reimbursement.[6] The fiscal year 1987 budget authorization for Medicare was $92.8 billion.[7] Increases in the numbers of the elderly, and of "the oldest old," those seventy-five and older, should cause increases in health care outlays, absent major changes in health care financing.

The adoption in 1983 of the Prospective Payment System ("PPS") for Medicare's reimbursement of hospitals was a response to the increased cost of government health care for the elderly.[8] Congress has also established a Physician Payment Review Commission to make recommendations for a fee schedule for the repayment of doctors under Medicare. The manner in which health care providers are reimbursed by the government has major implications for the quantity and quality of services provided to the elderly. Efforts to control government medical care expenditures can be broadly characterized as supply controls and demand controls: supply controls emphasize regulation and health resources planning (e.g., Certificates of Need for expansion in the number of hospital beds), while demand controls attempt to reduce utilization of health care services.[9] PPS uses Diagnosis Related

Groups ("DRGs") to regulate the supply of hospital services by forcing hospitals to decrease utilization.[10]

This Chapter examines the recent history of health care for the elderly, analyzes the Prospective Payment System, and then discusses other approaches to health care cost containment. The focus of this Chapter is on government health care programs for the elderly. This is in part because Medicare and other programs pay a major portion of the medical bills of the elderly; it is also because private health insurers tend to follow the lead of the federal government in attempting to control their own costs.[11]

A. MEDICARE AND COST CONTROL, 1965-1983

After years of resistance by the organized medical community, Congress passed the Medicare proposal in 1965. Medicaid, passed shortly thereafter, was aimed at the health care problems of the poor. In a sense, Medicare is to Medicaid as OASI is to Aid to Families With dependent Children ("AFDC"). Medicare is funded principally through a portion of the Social Security tax, placed in a trust fund, and is limited to the elderly and disabled. On the other hand, Medicaid is run more like a general assistance program: it is a general-revenue financed, means-tested welfare benefit.[12] Medicare was intended to guarantee health care access to the elderly, while Medicaid was to guarantee health care to the poor.[13] However, much of Medicaid's spending goes to the elderly. Two-thirds of Medicaid spending in 1984 went to institutionalized care (mainly nursing homes) for the elderly and the mentally retarded.[14] And for the elderly poor on Medicare, Medicaid has a "buy-in" arrangement with Medicare which provides that Medicaid will absorb the large majority of cost increases (e.g., costs which would otherwise be co-payments made by the health care consumer).[15]

Medicare serves the elderly through two separate programs, hospital insurance ("HI") and supplemental insurance ("SMI"). HI pays for inpatient hospital care, home health care, and skilled nursing facility ("SNF") care, while SMI pays for physical outpatient services. HI is funded through the Social Security payroll tax, while SMI is paid through insurance premiums paid by the elderly, as well as general revenues.[16] As is discussed in later chapters, Medicare's payment for skilled nursing facilities is quite limited, and the Reagan Administration has resisted growth in spending for home health care.

Medicare and Medicaid have had a tremendous impact on the health status of the elderly and poor. One measure of this is that the mortality rates for diseases that afflict the poor disproportionally—diabetes, heart disease, stroke, and pneumonia—have decreased over 30 percent since the inception of these programs.[17] Medicaid and Medicare have never been universal in their coverage:[18] Medicaid recipients must pass means tests and

Medicare eligibility is a derivative of Social Security eligibility under Title II and Title XVI. Medicare covers 95 percent of the non-institutionalized elderly and Medicaid covers 15 percent of the elderly, considerably higher than the percentage of the elderly receiving employer-related private health insurance.[19]

The extent of coverage provided by Medicare is also a concern. One governmental response to the increased cost of Medicare has been to increase deductibles and cost-sharing under the program. In 1984, the average Medicare enrollee had mean out-of-pocket expenses of $1,055.00, $505.00 of which was in non-Medicare related expenses.[20] Moreover, this average masks the higher cost-sharing ($897.00 per person) for the SMI enrollees who used Medicare sufficiently to incur cost-sharing for persons over and above the Medicare Part B SMI deductible.[21] As a consequence of higher medical costs and higher cost-sharing and deductibles under Medicare, the percentage of income spent out-of-pocket by the elderly has begun to creep back to where it was in pre-Medicare days. Although the percentage of the medical bill paid for directly by the elderly is less than 36 percent now, as opposed to 70 percent before 1965, the percentage of elderly household income spent on medical care increased from 8 percent in 1962 to 14 percent in 1980, and 15 percent in 1984.[22] And the average medical care expenses for the elderly vary from 21 percent of income for those with family income under $5,000.00 to 2 percent of income for those with family incomes of $30,000.00 or more.[23]

A key to the huge increase in health care costs for the elderly following the adoption of Medicare and Medicaid is the role of the medical community in the design of that system. After resisting government involvement as "socialized medicine," Congress made physicians and hospitals the principal architects of the benefit packages and payment methodologies for Medicare and Medicaid.[24] The Medicare statute stated as a central policy non-interference with the practice of medicine in health care institutions.[25]

The result has been a clash between the egalitarian goals of these programs (equal access to medical care) and the maintenance of a health care delivery system still libertarian in nature as regards pricing of services.[26] Medicare reimbursed hospitals initially on a simple retrospective payment for services provided basis, and still reimburses physicians on the basis of "customary, prevailing, and reasonable" rates of payment ("CPR"). Although prospective payment has been intended as a major reform of this system, it can be seen as a new fee-for-service system, libertarian in principle, with health care providers choosing whom they will serve and what they will do for them.[27]

Prior to the institution of the Prospective Payment System for hospitals, there had been several attempts to control escalating health care costs. These were universally resisted by health care providers as unwarranted governmental intrusions; proposals were either rejected outright or came out watered down and largely ineffective. In 1972, the federal government passed Professional Standards Review Organization ("PSRO") legislation to control the use of services: the same legislation enacted provisions limiting increases in professional fees and placing cost limits on hospital expenses subject to reimbursement.[28] These were replaced in November, 1984 by peer review organizations ("PROs"), operating as part of the prospective payment system.[29] The idea behind PSROs (and PROs) was to involve health care professionals in utilization review, a "self-regulation" approach.

The Carter Administration attempted to contain medical care costs generally, in an effort to reduce the high rates of inflation which plagued the late 1970s. The cost containment plan was to limit costs for all hospital patients, as well as to limit capital expenditures for hospitals.[30] The hospital industry lobbied vigorously to defeat this proposal, promising "self-restraint" in the form of voluntary control of health care cost increases: the inability of the industry to fulfill this promise set the stage for the cost containment measures of the Reagan Administration.[31] As Sapolsky has noted, there is some irony in the success of the Reagan Administration in passing cost control measures, as conservatives resisted and weakened such proposals prior to 1980.[32]

Reagan Administration efforts to control governmental health care costs began with the Omnibus Budget Reconciliation Act of 1981 ("OBRA 1981), enacted immediately after the Economic Recovery Act of 1981. OBRA 1981 introduced block grants for categorical social and health programs and sharply reduced funding for regulatory programs (health planning and certificate of need programs, PSROs for Medicare and Medicaid), as well as reducing federal funding for Medicaid.[33] 1981 can be described as the year that the federal government changed course as far as access to health care was concerned: after 15 years of commitment to increased access, even amid growing concerns about costs, OBRA 1981 marked the shrinking of federal programs and efforts designed to provide health care to the poor and elderly. OBRA 1981 terminated federal programmatic responsibility for nearly all U.S. Public Health Service categorical programs, placed funding for these programs into block grants to be administered by the states: funding for these block grants was reduced by 25 percent in 1981 and has been reduced subsequently.[34] The tightening of criteria for Medicaid and other public programs financing health care for the poor, along with loss of private health insurance due to unemployment during the recession of 1981-1982 and increased poverty during the same period has led observers to conclude that the health status of mothers and infants and persons with chronic diseases has been significantly worsened since 1980.[35]

In 1982, Congress passed the Tax Equity and Fiscal Responsibility Act of 1982 ("TEFRA"). This Act placed limits on the costs that Medicare would pay for each patient case, and required the Department of Health and Human Services to develop a prospective payment system by December,

1982.[36] Such a system was adopted as part of the Social Security Amendments of 1983.

B. THE MEDICARE TRUST FUND CRISIS

Before examining prospective payment and other solutions, some attention should be given to the problem to which they were addressed, the impending crisis in the Medicare Trust Funds. Prospective payment was enacted at a time when it was projected that the Trust Funds were about to go bankrupt, resulting in a reliance on general revenues which would have doomed the program.[37] Despite the cost control measures which have been put into place, several analysts still project a Medicare Trust Fund Crisis, possibly as early as 1992 or 1994.[38]

Between 1974 and 1977, Medicare and Medicaid outlays doubled.[39] Three factors were seen as causes for increases in health care costs: 1) payment methodologies which reimbursed providers on the basis of charges incurred, encouraging overutilization of services and attitudes about medical care which were not cost-conscious; 2) increases in costly medical technology; and 3) health insurance, including government programs, with low or no co-insurance, which also encouraged indiscriminate and wasteful health care services.[40] Put a different way, cost increases in government medical programs are due to three differently stated factors: 1) expansions in the number of persons served by the programs; 2) expansions in the volume of services provided per program enrollee; and 3) increases in the prices of services rendered. One study found that nearly all of the growth rate increases in total physician expenditures between 1976 and 1982 were due to increases in the volume of services rendered, while 40 percent of the increases in Medicare payments for physicians' services between 1980 and 1982 was due to this factor.[41] Of the 21 percent annual increase in SMI benefits between 1978 and 1982, about 21 percent was due to expansions in Medicare enrollment, while the remainder was due to increased prices and service utilization.[42]

The hospital insurance ("HI") and supplemental insurance ("SMI") funds are each projected to experience imbalances, although the two are growing at different rates. To this date, prospective payment only deals directly with HI, although some form of prospective payment for physicians' services may be instituted.

In 1982, the total income of the HI fund was $25.6 billion, while its expenditures were $36.1 billion: this reduced the trust fund from $18.8 billion to $8.2 billion.[43] For its 1983 Annual Report, the HI Trust Fund Board made projections of income and disbursements under four sets of assumptions, one optimistic, two intermediate, and one pessimistic: under the optimistic projection, the fund would be exhausted by 1996, while under the intermediate projections the date was 1990, and the pessimistic set of assumptions had bankruptcy taking place by 1988.[44] SMI, which is funded through general revenues and co-insurance payments has grown to the point where it is now the third largest domestic program in the federal budget, exceeded only by Social Security and by HI.[45] In fiscal 1985, general revenue contributions to make up for the difference between premium payments and outlays were in excess of $17.9 billion.[46] Moreover, the percentage of the budget spent on SMI was projected to increase from 3.7 to 5.7 percent between 1982 and 1988, as SMI reimbursements increased at a rate of 17 percent per year.[47]

The Reagan Administration responded by cutting Medicare outlays by 5 percent between January 1981 and July 1983 compared to what would have been spent under the previous law.[48] The Deficit Reduction Act of 1984 was also projected to further reduce outlays by another 2 percent between 1984 and 1987 through higher deductions for HI and SMI, as well as higher SMI premiums and co-insurance.[49] The Social Security Act amendments of 1983, by enhancing revenues and decreasing some benefits, have eased this situation somewhat. Prospective payment was instituted in 1983 as a way to reduce the fund imbalance in HI, keeping the fund from having to borrow from the OASI portion of Social Security.

Despite the Reagan Administration's cost controls, the HI fund is still projected to be completely exhausted during the next decade. This leads to a longer-range problem. The Social Security trust fund as a whole is projected to run at a surplus until 2020: the surplus built up between the current date and that time will then be drawn upon to pay for projected OASI and disability insurance fund imbalances in the years between 2020 and 2060.[50] However, if those reserves are depleted to cover HI deficits after 1994, no surplus will ever be developed.

SMI's situation is slightly different. It must either increase insurance premiums or compete with other domestic programs for remaining portions of federal general revenue. A third option is merging HI and SMI into a single program.[51] The risk of increasing premiums is that more of the elderly will be excluded from the program. Greater reliance on general revenue would mean that the SMI portion of Medicare would become a welfare program for the elderly, which could possibly weaken its support in Congress. Combining SMI with HI would simply add to the pressures on the HI trust fund, as well as on the Social Security fund generally.

Medicare recipients currently have 60 percent of their total noninstitutional care bills paid by Medicare, 17.4 percent through other governmental health programs (such as Veterans Administration benefits), and 22.1 percent paid out of pocket (for direct care or for "medigap" insurance premiums).[52] Reductions in benefits under Medicare would hit hardest two different but overlapping groups, those who have no insurance other than Medicare, and those with very high medical costs. Persons reliant on Medicare are already paying over 40 percent of their health costs out-of-pocket.[53] These tend to be the "near poor," persons with incomes below 125 percent of the government poverty line, who were ineligible for Medicaid because they possessed some liquid assets.[54] Persons making heavy use of Medicare exceed care maximums and wind up paying the excess out-of-pocket. 75 percent of all Medicare reimbursements in 1978 went to 11 percent of the enrollees: that proportion of the program population pays 36 percent of all Medicare-related individual costs.[55] For these groups, further limitations on reimbursement under Medicare would have a great impact on health care consumption, as they would be forced to make up for more medical care costs through direct payment. Yet to avoid inroads on the Social Security trust fund or greater general revenue deficits, some cuts in benefits (or increases in co-insurance) appear likely.

C. PROSPECTIVE PAYMENT

In 1983, Congress adopted a prospective payment system for Medicare beneficiaries in acute care hospitals. This system was implemented between 1984 and 1986. PPS reimburses hospitals based on the Diagnosis Related Group ("DRG") category in which a patient is classified. DRGs are based on the International Classification of Diseases: PPS does not apply to pediatric, psychiatric, long-term care, or rehabilitation hospitals.[56]

DRGs are a patient classification system for relating a hospital's "case mix" (i.e., the types of patients a hospital treats) to the costs incurred by the hospital: they were developed in the 1960s at Yale University as a means of monitoring the quality of health care and hospital utilization of services.[57] DRGs were first applied on a large scale in the late 1970s by the New Jersey Department of Health, which used them as the basis for a prospective payment system under which hospitals were reimbursed a fixed amount for each patient treated.[58] Although DRGs have undergone four complete revisions since their original development,[59] one concern raised about them is that they are based on an early 1980s "snapshot" of medical practice and disease categories, enshrining that particular status quo.[60]

The basic concept of the DRG system is that all human diseases can be classified according to organ system, length of stay, resource utilization, morbidity, and sex: such categories theoretically reflect costs incurred by hospitals in treating patients falling under the system.[61] There are 470 categories under the system.[62] Payment to hospitals for inpatient care is based on four criteria: the patient's principal diagnosis or surgical procedure, whether there is an important secondary diagnosis, the patient's age, and whether or not the patient was alive upon discharge.[63] The DRG system was formed by physician panels dividing all principal diagnosis into 23 mutually exclusive Major Diagnostic Categories, each related to a major organ system, such as respiratory system or circulatory system, further dividing categories into medical and surgical classifications, and then further partitioning according to age of patient and discharge status: additional categories are provided for patient types whose resource utilization is significantly different (burn patients, newborns transferred to an acute care facility, substance abuse patients, myocardial infarction patients, newborns who die).[64]

The agency involved in making reimbursements under the PPS-DRG system is the Health Care Financing Administration ("HCFA") of the Department of Health and Human Services ("HHS"). Under PPS, HCFA was to initially adjust reimbursement to regional variations in costs, as well as each hospital's own historical costs in 1982: ultimately, such adjustments are to be phased out, creating a reimbursement amount based on national average costs per case.[65] The legislation creating PPS also provided for additional amounts to be paid for "outliers," cases that have an extremely long length of stay or extraordinarily high costs compared to most discharges within that particular DRG.[66] However, the amount of additional payment is only a percentage of the actual excess cost and is provided only where the cost of care exceeds a predetermined amount or length of stay exceeds the mean length of stay for a DRG category by a predetermined amount.[67] As a result, the DRG payment level is effectively a statement about the ideal amount of care to be provided, with deviations above this amount being seen as financially inappropriate.[68]

D. EFFECTS OF PPS ON COSTS: PRELIMINARY FIGURES

The purpose of PPS is to reduce federal expenditures on Medicare. PPS, through the use of DRGs, accomplishes this through creating disincentives for hospitals to provide care in excess of the DRG amount: whereas Medicare was initially created with incentives to increase the amount of health care provided to the elderly, PPS creates an incentive to do less.[69] Although DRGs also eliminate the previous tendency to provide unnecessary and inappropriate services, the concern for eliminating waste was generated by cost-saving purposes, but those of increasing the quality of care or reducing risks to patients.[70] Under PPS, the federal government makes no direct decisions about the provision of care to the elderly: rather, it shifts those decisions to hospitals. Two types of savings can occur through the DRG system: savings in federal expenditures, which can be shifted by hospitals to non-Medicare patients; or real aggregate savings, in which the total actual cost of providing services decreases.[71] To a considerable extent, the federal government is only interested in the first type of savings, which represents federal budgetary savings. The second type of savings can generate profits for hospitals, if they can provide services for less costs than the DRG amount. The federal government would be concerned about this second type of savings under two circumstances: 1) if Medicare patients' care were jeopardized through cutting corners; and 2) if it meant that the DRG price was set too high, meaning that the government had "left money on the table." In practice, the first has been a matter of great concern, while the second has not: hospitals have complained about the inadequacy of the DRG rates and the reluctance of HCFA to adjust them.[72]

To generate either type of savings described above, PPS-DRG must force hospitals to alter their operations to achieve cost reductions. Hospitals can accomplish this in at least four ways: 1) elimination of excessive or unnecessary services (the most benign approach); 2) cuts in labor costs; 3) reductions in length of stay or amount of resources used per patient within a given DRG category; and 4) adjust the "patient mix," i.e., attempt to screen out patients who would be likely to exceed DRG reimbursement amounts. There is evidence that hospitals have attempted to do all four, with some success: the latter three methods, of course, can have very negative effects on the quality of care, and are discussed below, as criticism of PPS-DRGs.

What cost savings have been achieved through PPS? After the system was implemented, hospital expenditures which had been increasing at an annual rate of over 61 percent, fell to an increase of 5.4 percent in 1984.[73] Medical payments rose only 9 percent in the fiscal year ending June 1985, compared to an average annual increase of 19 percent in each of the three preceding fiscal years.[74] To some extent, hospitals anticipated PPS, and this may have affected these results: for example, although hospital admissions declined 4 percent in 1984, they were already levelling off in 1982 and 1983.[75] And, although hospitals have complained about DRGs (as is discussed later, hospitals whose service population includes a disproportionate number of the elderly and non-elderly poor have been hit the hardest), hospitals overall showed profits in 1984 increasing 27.4 percent over 1983.[76] That is the result of the other side of PPS: while hospitals must absorb expenses exceeding scheduled payment rates, they can retain savings where costs are below those rates.[77]

The savings described are preliminary in nature.[78] Some critics think that DRGs will only create temporary savings, as hospitals will adjust to them: what is needed is control on hospital admission rates.[79] Others note that when New Jersey first instituted DRGs, there were substantial savings during its first two years of operation; however, in the third year, per capita expenditures increased nearly 15 percent.[80]

How can hospitals adjust to PPS in such a way as to maximize reimbursement (i.e., "beating the system"[81])? A principal technique is called "DRG creep," under which patient problems are redefined to fit into higher DRG categories to obtain greater payment amounts.[82] This is not necessarily fraudulent, as there is enough ambiguity in the definition of primary patient conditions to permit such behavior.[83] There is some empirical evidence that hospitals are engaging in this activity: there has been a marked increase in some of the costlier DRGs (e.g., major hip and joint procedures)[84] and the case mix index (a national measure of the severity of patient illnesses) has been rising much more rapidly than expected.[85]

Another "beating the system" technique is the use of multiple admissions for the same patients. A patient is admitted under the DRG category, treated, released, then readmitted under a new principal diagnosis and treated, and so on, permitting multiple DRG reimbursements. This is more easily controllable through retrospective chart review: HCFA should be able to identify cases that should have been treated in one hospitalization, rather than multiple admissions occurring in rapid sequence.[86] This approach may also jeopardize patient health, as patients may be discharged without having received adequate care for the multiple conditions affecting them on their initial admission.[87]

A third approach is called "unbundling," under which hospitals react to PPS's current limitation to acute care, inpatient facilities. Treatment which would formerly have been provided on an inpatient basis (and hence part of costs subject to the DRG ceiling) are instead performed on an outpatient basis. This permits the hospital to receive its DRG payment plus full reimbursement for the outpatient service.[88] This approach not only means the government saves no money on Medicare, but non-Medicare patients treated on the same basis actually can see a cost increase.[89] A related technique is to shift Medicare patients to DRG exempt wards, such as psychiatric wards.[90]

The above methods of circumvention do not mean that DRGs will not reduce expenditures, although they may impede cost savings: HCFA review and refinement of DRGs can probably alleviate some of these abuses.[91] The more significant concern is the effect of PPS-DRGs on the quality of care dispensed, especially as regards the elderly poor, who generally do not have health care resources other than Medicare and charity care.

E. PPS AND THE QUALITY OF CARE

PPS affects Medicare payments both directly and indirectly in ways which could have an adverse effect on the quality of care. The criticisms of PPS most frequently mentioned—restricted access, compromised quality of care, and impeding the development and use of new biomedical technologies— are direct effects: in addition, hospital administrative decisions can affect care indirectly, through changes in hospital employment, cessation of unprofitable services, and cost-shifting. In addition, PPS may also contribute to a trend in hospital ownership by for-profit corporations, which may result in adverse effects on the factors noted above (access to care, quality of care, appropriate use of technology).[93]

1. Reduced Employment

Labor costs are the single largest budget item for hospitals, constituting over one-half of operating costs: therefore, they were a predictable target for DRG-related cost cutting and hospital employment in general medical and surgical hospitals declined for the first time in 1984.[94] These cutbacks were largely in patient care occupations, especially nursing.[95] Simultaneously, there has been an increase in administrative and marketing jobs in hospitals.[96] This could be a reaction to PPS, as hospitals attempt some of the circumvention strategies above, which increase administrative and paperwork requirements. Marketing costs may reflect the efforts of hospitals to attract non-Medicare patients. One other response to PPS has been to attempt to shift as many patients as possible to home health care agencies operated by hospitals, which also increases hospital administrative costs.[97]

2. Reduced Length of Hospital Stay

Perhaps the chief criticism of PPS has been that it has created an incentive for hospitals to engage in the premature discharge of Medicare beneficiaries from hospitals,[98] releasing them "sicker and quicker." In 1985, hospitals began discharging Medicare patients involuntarily with the explanation that the number of covered days had "run out": although there was an appeal process, few patients were aware of it.[99] The General Accounting Office's study of the issue concluded that patients were being discharged in a poorer state of health than before DRGs were implemented, often without adequate prior notice of discharge.[100]

Early release is a direct result of DRG incentives. While there has been a general trend toward decreased length of hospital stay which antedates PPS—in large part due to private health insurer ceilings on hospital reimbursement—Medicare length of stay reductions have far exceeded those for the general population. The average length of a hospital stay declined by 2 percent in 1983 and 5.1 percent in 1984, but about 20 percent for Medicare patients, from 9.6 to 7.4 days.[101]

Decreased length of stay can have particularly negative effects for the frail elderly and for the elderly poor, who are often the same people. This is because the poor tend to defer seeking health care, so they enter the hospital in worse condition than other patients: they also tend to have poorer nutrition and to be overweight, causing increased time and expense in medical treatment.[102] DRGs also create serious problems for the frail and the poor in post-release care. Persons who are rushed through hospitalization and discharged prematurely place a greater strain on families and home health care agencies, who may not be equipped to provide the level of care needed.[103] One study found that where heavy care would need to be provided over an extended period, one-third of family caregivers would withdraw some support.[104] Early release often also means hasty release, with inadequate discharge planning, further complicating post-release care.[105] The poor and the frail elderly also suffer where there is no support group available to them in the form of family or friends: they either cannot afford nursing home care, or discover that nursing homes will not accept them because of their care needs.[106]

Congress and HHS reacted to publicity about early release through the development of a notice to be given to patients upon admission to hospitals explaining the patient's rights to appeal decisions about release, as well as suspending the Medicare beneficiary's financial liability for continued care during the appeal period.[107]

Early release also creates a conflict-of-interest problem for patients' physicians. While physicians determine 60-80 percent of hospital expenditures, hospitals can exert pressures on resident and non-resident physicians to perform their services in a manner which is cost-effective for the hospital.[108] It is also the case that senior physicians often have profit-sharing arrangements with hospitals which would encourage them to provide care maximizing hospital returns under DRGs.[109] Hence, rather than acting as the Medicare patient's advocate in arguing that all medically necessary services be provided by the hospital, the physician may be in a position in which he or she makes cost-effective decisions about services provided which are related to the patient's Medicare and insurance status.[110] In addition, physicians themselves may be subject to prospective payment reimbursement in the future,[111] discussed later in this Chapter.

3. Changes in Patient Mix

The charge is made that PPS influences how hospitals view some types of Medicare patients. Under PPS, it is argued, the tendency is to attempt to avoid admitting those patients requiring heavy or unreimbursed care and those who have no private health insurance in addition to Medicare. Both groups create risks of loss to hospitals under PPS. Although DRGs include adjustments and different categories for complications and coexistent disease conditions, there are no adjustments per se for severity of illness.[112] And, as explained above, the poor and the frail elderly will be more likely to have severe illnesses. Hospitals also prefer patients with private insurance coverage which does not rely on DRG-type reimbursement.[113]

Hospitals have identified these diseases which are profitable for them under the DRG system: they want a "patient mix" which increases admissions of patients with those diseases, while avoiding persons whose diseases would probably cause the hospital to lose money under DRGs.[114] A leading management consulting firm has gone so far as to create what it labels "a survival guide for the hospital industry" which advises hospitals as to "winners" and "losers" in terms of how to identify patients as to the contribution margin between the DRG reimbursement amount and the actual cost of care, which DRGs are most and least profitable, and which physician should be encouraged to use hospital resources.[115]

Persons who are Medicare/Medicaid dual eligibles are also undesirable patients. Again, they tend to be sicker than other patient groups, increasing treatment costs. They also tend to be more difficult to place in nursing homes on their release because of low Medicare reimbursement rates.[116] Therefore, the tendency is to shunt these persons to city and public hospitals, a problem described later in this section.

4. Effects on Medical Technology

Under PPS, HCFA was to provide separate payments under Medicare for capital expenses.[117] This was thought to favor the use of capital-intensive techniques and to encourage hospitals to experiment with equipment leasing and innovative accounting procedures so that hospitals could qualify for reimbursement for capital outlays.[118] Congress had intended to incorporate capital costs in DRG rates after PPS had been in place for a few years but in fact has only imposed limits on reimbursement of hospitals' capital costs over the next few years.[119]

However, there are several reasons why DRGs may discourage purchase of new technologies. First, new technologies initially raise costs, as they are used in addition to, rather than instead of, old technologies and persons must be trained to use new technologies. At the same time hospitals would be forced to use present dollars to buy equipment whose cost may not be reflected in DRGs for several years (and may not be reflected at all if the equipment is supposed to save money).[120] The tendency would be reluctance to employ new techniques until hospitals could determine their cost-effectiveness, yet cost-effectiveness studies require that a technique be in use for study to take place.[121]

Second, Congress has strictly limited money available for the purchase of new equipment, because it has attributed the increase in medical expenditures in part to the costs of high technology in hospital care.[122] Finally, the time lag between equipment purchase and DRG payments adjustments or recalibrations may discourage purchases of new technology. The cost basis for DRGs is 1983 data, the year of PPS's adoption: recalibration therefore adjusts the amount of payments for one DRG relative to other DRGs in 1983 costs, reflecting the differences in health care costs under different types of medical conditions. To the extent that 1983 is an imperfect proxy for the current cost of health care, the cost basis for future payments will be understated. Hospitals are unlikely to purchase new equipment where they will not receive payment for the cost of equipment or its use for several years after its acquisition, and then receive only a discounted amount of that cost.[123]

5. Omission of Services

Closely related to the "patient mix" problem described above is the simple closing down of services which are determined to cost more than DRG revenues provide. This determination may be affected by the number of persons potentially using a service and whether such services are available elsewhere: but if all hospitals (or hospitals in a given area) find that certain services are simply cost-inefficient under DRGs, a widespread unavailability will have serious adverse consequences for the quality of care.[124] DRGs in particular provide incentives to reduce or omit certain costly diagnostic procedures: while diagnostic procedures can be redundant in some cases, they are critical in others.[125] Hence, PSS-DRGs may compromise the quality of care by restricting diagnostic procedures to only those which can be "costed out," even though their omission could result in a failure to diagnose a serious illness in a patient, or a failure to treat an illness effectively.[125] The related approach is to shut down "loser services" where the costs of such services can be shifted to public hospitals or other providers: while the hospital shutting down the services saves funds, there is no net national savings in medical care unless fewer services are offered in the aggregate.[127]

6. Cost-Shifting and Patient-Shifting

As alluded to above, another effect of PPS is to cause private hospitals to attempt to displace costs subject to DRG reimbursement. As indicated earlier, they can achieve this in one respect by billing Medicare for out patient services not subject to DRGs. This only has a negative effect on care if the patient's treatment would have been improved had he or she received these an an inpatient, rather than having had them delayed until after he or she had been discharged. The other two methods have negative consequences for both Medicare patients and others. One method of displacing costs is "cost-shifting," over charging non-Medicare patients to make up for losses incurred under DRGs. This technique has been used in the past by hospitals to compensate for charity care. Private insurers, who have borne the brunt of cost-shifting, have cracked down on this by negotiating the rates they will pay for services, their own form of PPS-DRGs.[128] Hence, the real "victim" of cost-shifting is the hospital patient who either is uninsured or incurs costs in excess of the amount their insurers will pay.

"Patient-shifting" refers to the efforts of private hospitals to avoid high risk Medicare patients altogether, causing them to be shifted to public or city hospitals. This is akin to "dumping," under which private-pay hospitals transfer uninsured persons who have been admitted on an emergency basis to public hospitals once they have been stabilized. Of course, there is no assurance that public hospitals can provide for such "displaced" patients, as they are also subject to PPS: losses will be absorbed by their funding agency, i.e., states, counties, and municipalities.[129]

Patient-shifting has two consequences. First, as with dumping, a separate and unequal system of health care is highlighted, one in which the poor are treated in overcrowded, financially stressed public institutions, while others go to private hospitals.[130] Patient-shifting for Medicare patients is ironic, since the purpose of the program was to provide access to hospitals and health care to the elderly. The second consequence is that some hospitals od a great deal better under PPS than do others. PPS encourages hospitals to attract patients who will make relatively less use of the hospital's resources than other patients within the same DRG: in one study, some institutions were found to have received payments that were as much as 59 percent too high, while others received 25 percent too little in relation to the actual costs incurred in patient treatment.[131] An Office of Technology Assessment study found wide variation and uneven distribution in the use of hospital services for patients within the same DRG category.[132] This is because DRGs do not account sufficiently for severity of illness. As discussed earlier, the "outlier" provision does not fully compensate hospitals treating persons whose costs exceed DRG limits. And, as is discussed in the next Section, HHS-HCFAA has resisted additional compensation to public hospitals under "disproportionate share" legislation.

7. Overall Comments

The criticisms discussed above can be distilled into two general comments about PPS. First, PPS makes the choice of who receives what care a matter of health care provider preference, which will be shaped by the economic "carrots and sticks" of DRG reimbursement, and is unrelated to and probably in conflict with the goal of equal access to care.[133] Second, PPS-DRG can be thought of as a system in which decisions about the macroallocation of health resources at a societal level are forced into microallocation decisions by health care providers about the care provided (or not provided) to individual patients.[134] As commented earlier, PPS is a system under which HHS, makes no direct decisions to reduce the amount of health care services to the elderly by private providers are given economic incentives to do so.

F. ADJUSTMENTS AND RESPONSES TO PROBLEMS UNDER PPS

PPS legislation in the form of the Social Security Act Amendments of 1983 provided for some built-in devices to attempt to correct the problems and abuses described above. One such device, outliers, has already been described. The track record of these devices is spotty at best: the conclusion of one author is that their effectiveness is a function of the degree to which

Congress is willing to be an advocate for the elderly as regards their health problems.[135] This section examines three devices within the PPS system designed to provide adjustments to meet problems in the system: 1) disproportionate care legislation: 2) the Prospective Payment Assessment Commission ("PROPAC"); and 3) Peer Review Organizations ("Pros"). Finally, a fourth element, Hill-Burton uncompensated care, is briefly discussed. Although Hill-Burton antedates PPS by several decades, it was meant to serve as a method of providing services free of charge where no other form of reimbursement was available.

1. Disproportionate Share Legislation

As alluded to earlier, studies have concluded that the average Medicare costs per case in hospitals serving a disproportionate number of low-income persons are higher than costs of other hospitals because low-income persons are often more severely ill and take longer to place in nursing homes than average patients.[136] As a result, Section 601(e) of the Social Security Amendments of 1983 required HHS to provide exceptions and adjustments to the PPS reimbursement rate for "public or other hospitals that serve a significantly disproportionate number" of low-income or Medicare patients.

HHS has resisted "disproportionate share" legislation. After the 1983 amendments were enacted, then HHS Secretary Margaret Hechler announced on January 3, 1984 that she would not implement this provision because department data dis not indicate that an adjustment was warranted. Congress responded by including a section in the Deficit Reduction Act of 1984 which required the Secretary to develop and publish a definition of "significantly disproportionate number" and to compile a list of hospitals meeting the definition by December 31, 1984: HHS did not meet this deadline.[137] After a federal district court ordered by the Secretary to do so, the HCFA issued interim rules solely to comply with the judge's order: the HCFA rescinded these regulations after Justice Rhenquist, sitting as Circuit Judge, stayed the court's order.[138]

In December, 1985, HHS published a definition of disproportionate hospitals under which an eligible hospital is one which serves 39.55 percent low-income patients and 91.01 percent Medicare patients. Only 108 hospitals nationwide fit this definition: large public hospitals that one would expect Congress intended to assist with the disproportionate share provisions were not included.[139] In response, Congress included in the Consolidated Budget Reconciliation Act of 1985 ("COBRA '85") its own definition, which was more generous than that of HHS, including urban public hospitals.[140] Further, in the Omnibus Budget Reconciliation Act of 1986 ("OBRA '86"), Congress extended disproportionate assistance to hospitals serving the rural poor.[141]

The lesson of disproportionate share legislation is that HHS views PPS as a cost-cutting measure: it views the needs of hospitals serving underserved groups narrowly and has attempted to restrict the allocation of Medicare resources to these hospitals.[142]

2. ProPAC

Section 1395(c) of the Social Security Amendments of 1983 required the Director of the Congressional Office of Technology Assessment to appoint a Prospective Payment Assessment Commission ("ProPAC"), to be composed of experts in the provision and financing of healthcare.[143] ProPAC has two responsibilities under the law: 1) to recommend to the Secretary of HHS how to update DRGs; and 2) to recommend necessary changes in DRGs, including new DRGs, or modifications in currently existing DRGs.[144] In addition, Congress required HHS to update DRGs annually, adjusting DRG amounts to reflect inflation, hospital productivity, and new technology, as well as to readjust DRGs to reflect changes in resource consumption by hospitals. The Secretary was required to consider the recommendations of ProPAC in its annual adjustment of DRG rates.

Given that ProPAC's recommendations are not binding on HHS, the Secretary has not adjusted any of its recommendations and has always developed lower rates than would have been the case had Formulas suggested by ProPAC been followed.[146] Congress, however, has relied on ProPAC's analysis and has legislatively supplanted HHS rules on updating hospital payment rates to establish more generous payment rates.[147]

The ProPAC experience again underscores the Reagan Administration's cost-cutting view of PPS. ProPAC has not operated as intended: that it has any significance at all stems only from Congressional disagreements with HHS as to rate-setting and rate-adjustment. This is also an area where HHS has less authority within the executive branch than does the Office of Management and Budget ("OMB"). This was illustrated in 1986, when the new Secretary of HHS, Otis Bowen, himself a physician, took the position that if the hospital payment rates were not updated at least 1.5 percent, quality of care would be jeopardized: OMB, which had proposed an updated rate of only 0.5 percent evenutally prevailed.[148]

3. PROs

As was mentioned earlier, Peer Review Organizations ("PROs") replaces PSROs in 1984: PROs are to conduct utilization reviews of hospital services provided under Medicare.[149] HHS designates a PRO for each state: PROs, which are largely made up of health care providers, review the necessity, appropriateness, quality, and cost-effectiveness of care provided to Medicare beneficiaries, and can deny Medicare payment if it determines that a procedure was unnecessary.[150]

Initially, HHS delayed entering into contracts with PROs and many PROs were slow getting started and their performance was so deficient that HHS terminated their participation in the program.[151] The chief complaint about the program in its first two years was that HHS in its contracts with PROs required them to focus excessively on cost-containment goals to the detriment of quality of care goals, with concentration chiefly on reducing unnecessary hospital admissions.[152] PROs were criticized by Congress because they were constrained by their contractual objectives from determining whether hospitals were providing high quality services under PPS, particularly as regarded early release of patients.[153] Some of the early PRO contracts were seen by critics as containing quotas for reductions in Medicare procedures (e.g., the Kentucky PRO agreed to reduce the number of fatal heart attacks by 20 percent).[154] HHS viewed these numbers as reasonable goals, not quotas, although they appeared to emphasize concern with overutilization, rather than underutilization of care produced by DRGs.[155]

As a result of these problems, HHS and Congress altered PROs' utilization review responsibilities in 1986, HHS changed procedures and objectives of quality of care reviews substantially, while in COBRA '85 Congress gave PROs the authority to deny payment for substandard care (although HCFA was to define substandard care) and imposed additional responsibilities on PROs to review outpatient and other surgery procedures.[156] OBRA '86 required PROs to spend more of their time and resources reviewing quality of hospital services, to review "early readmission" cases and to determine if previous inpatient services and post-release services met professional standards (presumably, a reaction to the early release problem).[157]

If PROs were meant to be a counterwieght to HCFA motives to reduce costs, they have been ineffective. This is because, under the law, HHS runs the program, controlling the monitoring process through its contracts, which set the agenda for utilization reviews: since HHS-HCFA is more interested in cost containment than in monitoring the quality of care, the contracts reflect this.[158] The effect of PROs, then, is one of enforcing DRGs, not one of providing a counterincentive to hospitals which are induced to alter care under the cost-cutting incentives of DRGs.[159]

4. Hill-Burton Care

The Hospital Survey and Construction Act, better known as Hill-Burton, was passed in 1946 to assist construction and modernization of hospitals after World War II.[160] In return for government grants and loans, Hill-Burton facilities were to provide a "reasonable volume of free or reduced cost care" to "individuals unable to pay," and to make such services "available to all" persons residing within the facility's service population area.[161] There is a 20-year limitation from the opening date of the portion of the hospital modernized or constructed.[162]

Hill-Burton requirements would appear to be a method for requiring that hospitals which would otherwise "dump" patients or attempt to screen them out provide free or low-cost care. In practice, Hill-Burton has been relatively limited in its impact. Most hospitals which received funds either have passed the 20-year limitation already or will do so in the next few years.[163]

Hospitals which were obligated to provide free or reduced cost care often did not do so during the 1950s and 1960s because there was no monitoring of their compliance: although the 1946 Act required states to designate an agency to enforce its provisions, none did until the early 1970s.[164] Although HHS (then the Department of Health, Education, and Welfare) issued administrative standards and procedures in 1972, uncompensated care did not increase, because state agencies failed to establish eligibility criteria or procedural guidelines and failed to monitor hospital compliance.[165] Under the Reagan Administration, the General Accounting Office has cited the HHS Office of Health Facilities as poorly enforcing uncompensated care compliance: Hill-Burton facilities submit triennial compliance reports which are accepted as true by HHS after only cursory review.[166] Audits by state attorney generals, legal services offices, and others have revealed undisputed noncompliance, nonprovision of free care to be a substantial number of providers, and the fraudulent crediting of ineligible accounts or bad debts.[167] Litigation to force HHS to enforce compliance has failed: a federal court of appeals has rules that the duty of HHS to monitor and enforce compliance was deemed discretionary unless HHS enforcement amounted to "wholesale neglect."[168]

The result is that Hill-Burton is not likely to provide much assistance to the indigent in obtaining health care. Although community service regulations require that all persons residing in the service area of a Hill-Burton hospital be provided emergency care regardless of ability to pay, hospitals routinely exclude indigent patients to their detriment by stating that, in their opinion, the situation was not an emergency. Although the HHS Office of Civil Rights is responsible for monitoring such violations, it has failed to disseminate a uniform definition of emergency.[169] Hence, dumping, even under emergency conditions, continues to take place. HHS regulations adopted in 1986 further streamlines hospital compliance requirements.[170]

G. OTHER APPROACHES TO MEDICARE COST CONTROL

In terms of health care cost controls, PPS is not the only possible option. However, HHS appears to frown on state cost control approaches which are at variance with PPS.[171] Additional steps can be taken to deal with the health care costs of the elderly. These are: 1) extending PPS to physicians; 2) Health Maintenance Organizations ("HMOs") and Preferred Provider Organizations ("PPOs"); and 3) a variety of state cost controls.

1. Physician Prospective Payment Systems

When Congress created PPS for hospitals under Medicare, it also required the Secretary of HHS to submit a report on the advisability and feasibility of paying for physician services to hospital inpatients based on a DRG similar to the one used in hospital reimbursement.[172] HHS-HCFA funded studies by the Center for Health Economics Research ("CHER"). CHER examined the experimental use of physician DRGs in New Jersey and North Carolina. While CHER declined to state any conclusions, it did reach three major findings: 1) there is greater variation for treatment costs in medical as opposed to surgical DRGs; 2) a DRG-based physician payment system could unfairly redistribute Medicare funds from physicians with more complex and less costly practices; and 3) most physicians would be unable to engage in cost-shifting, due to the relatively small number of patients they treat within each DRG category.[173]

Medicare at present reimburses physicians based on the "customary, prevailing, and reasonable" ("CPR") rate of payment for particular specialties, which is opposed by payers (large insurance companies and employers) because of disparities in rates of payment and because it provides no incentives to encourage efficient use of services. The Congressionally-appointed Physician Payment Review Commission has tentatively proposed a nationwide fee schedule.[174]

PPS for physicians would pose several problems. First, as CHER implies, there would be a built-in bias toward physicians in large, multispecialty group practice, such as Health Maintenance Organizations. Such doctors would be better able to spread the risks inherent in DRG rates, based on averages of high-and-low-cost cases, over large numbers of heterogeneous patients than physicians in solo or small group practices.[175] This would operate to the disadvantage of specialists or solo practitioners seeing a higher proportion of patients with complex, hard-to-treat problems; it might also encourage medical staff to eliminate such specialists, as they would have a negative effect on the ratio between costs incurred and reimbursement received.[176]

Second, under such a system, physician freedom of choice about who they treated under Medicare and their association with hospitals might have to be substantially limited. At present, physicians can decide to accept or reject Medicare cases: under a DRG system, this would encourage doctors to reject assignment for complicated cases and to accept assignment for simple ones, i.e., treatment would be based on a profit-maximization basis. A PPS reimbursement system would probably force Congress to require that doctors who treat Medicare beneficiaries to accept all Medicare claims to avoid such behavior.[177] In addition, HCFA would be unlikely to reimburse attending physicians directly: the government would be funding fee-splitting arrangements in which the attending physician would be responsible for reimbursing consulting or assisting physicians. Also, from the perspective of administrative efficiency, it would make more sense of HCFA to reimburse a hospital with which a physician was associated: the hospital could contract with the physician for reimbursement rates.[178] This could substantially alter the nature of medical practice but would be necessary for the efficient administration of such a system.

Third, there would be a problem in the equity of reimbursement. especially for medical as opposed to surgical practice. The CHER study determined that while relatively few surgical expenses are discretionary, the only constant for most medical DRGs is the presence of the attending physician, whose charges are a function of length of stay of the patient. In CHER's study of total charges by New Jersey doctors for treating patients 70 years and older for pneumonia, charges for two-thirds of patients ranged between $72 and $1,136: the DRG payment of $604 thus substantially underpaid or overpaid most physicians treating such patients.[179]

Finally, a physician PPS-DRG program would intensify the conflict of interest problem noted earlier. The incentive for physicians would be to provide minimally adequate services to a patient: provision of services above this amount would reduce the profitability of treatment and would not result in any additional return on investment by the physician.

2. HMOs and PPOs

Health Maintenance Organizations and Preferred Provider Organizations can be thought of as both possible alternatives to and supplements to PPS. Critics of PPS-DRG who doubt its long-term effectiveness without some control on hospital admission rates and other adjustment strategies by hospitals see HMOs and state and local government cost-control plans as having a more enduring effect on costs.[180] HMOs would also be a method for extending DRGs beyond Medicare: private insurers might utilize DRG or DRG-like rates simply to prevent cost-shifting by hospitals, and HMOs would provide a mechanism to prevent this from occurring.

Health Maintenance Organizations function as contracts between the health care provider and enrollees or subscribers. HMOs are reimbursed using a capitation fee, a fixed periodic fee per enrollee that is not dependent upon the enrollee's use of services.[181] Federal and state governments have encouraged HMO expansion, largely because HMOs expend fewer funds than traditional insurance plans. HHS has authorized HCFA to enter into capitation contracts with HMOs for Medicare beneficiaries in which HMOs would receive an amount equal to 95 percent of what HCFA estimates would be the average per capita cost for a Medicare recipient receiving care under a fee-for-service arrangement.[182]

HMOs create some of the same problems for care of the elderly noted for DRGs. The incentive for the HMO is to provide care at or below the capitation rate. This has positive effects on health care if this is accomplished through preventive medical care and out patient care, thereby reducing the incidence of hospitalization. Negative effects occur where HMOs reduce costs through reduced numbers of staff, creating long delays for enrollees in receiving services. This can result in beneficiaries seeking "out-of-plan" care. This occurred in the pilot HMO-Medicare demonstration in South Florida, but this did not deter HHS from going nationwide with the program.[183]

A different problem is posed by proprietary HMOs, about one-fourth of all U.S. HMOs. Proprietary HMOs are a response to cutbacks by the Reagan Administration in loans to HMOs after 1982. Such HMOs avoid federal requirements and can limit both the groups with which they contract and the scope of coverage in ways not possible for federally-qualified HMOs.[184] Of course, such HMOs will avoid older, lower-income, less healthy persons as adverse financial risks. As was mentioned earlier, one criticism of PPS for Medicare is that it encourages proprietary hospitals and medical care systems. Health care providers will avoid limited reimbursement and federal regulation under Medicare and focus on populations not covered by Medicare. This means that HMOs with Medicare enrollees will be serving higher-risk patients and will compensate through either rising rates (which would be limited by HCFA) or reducing or restricting services. Public hospitals seeing the bulk of low-income Medicare beneficiaries will be faced with the same prospects.

Preferred Provider Organizations ("PPOs") are consortiums of hospitals and physicians who have agreed to provide services to enrollees for a discount. Panel providers obtain a semi-guaranteed volume of patients in return for discounts: most PPOs are for-profit entities.[185] Unlike HMOs, PPOs are fee-for-service, not capitation-based. PPOs are attractive to hospitals in urban, over-bedded areas.

PPOs have negative consequences for the elderly poor in two respects. First, providers are willing to provide care at a discount so long as reimbursement at that rate is guaranteed. If DRG ceilings were below the discounted amount for care, this would not be true. And if Medicare enrollees had no other form of insurance, the health care provider would go unreimbursed. Hence, for-profit PPOs have an incentive to avoid Medicare patients, especially heavy care or low income ones. Second, PPOs are under fiscal pressure to avoid providing charity care or care to the uninsured. Since the provider is already discounting services to the rest of its patients, it cannot afford to provide care which may be totally uncompensated.[186] PPO hospitals (and physicians) would have substantial reasons for avoiding the elderly poor, or dumping them on public facilities.

3. State Cost Controls

Many states have enacted their own cost containment measures, although the impetus for these measures was the Medicaid program, not Medicare (although, as described below, states can obtain a waiver from PPS and set rates for Medicare). Medicaid is administered by state public aid agencies and is funded by the states, with federal matching grants. The Reagan Administration has cut back sharply on Medicaid, although over half the states have adopted programs providing care for the medically needy.[187] These programs largely deal with acute care institutions: they affect the elderly poor and other poor persons alike. The primary effect of Medicaid on the elderly is in its reimbursement of nursing homes, discussed in Chapter Five. So while the state approaches discussed below affect the elderly to some extent, they can also be thought of as alternative approaches to PPS in dealing with health care cost problems.

The weakest form of cost control is rate regulation: this requires hospitals to file publicly their rates and budgets. Although facilities remain free to set their own charges, disclosure of a hospital's rates can exert some pressure over costs.[188] A somewhat stronger approach is budget review, in which a hospital submits its proposed budget to a state authority, which then uses a formula or a negotiation process to review the reasonableness of the hospital's proposal.[189] In some states, the state authority can only recommend a more appropriate budget ("voluntary review"): in others, budget review places mandatory limits on the hospital's budget.[190]

The strongest form of state regulation is rate setting, a public utility approach in which a state authority prospectively establishes hospital rates through formulas, a bidding process, or negotiation.[191] The chief problem with this approach is that the rates set for state reimbursement (for Medicare, Medicaid and the medically needy) may conflict with federal Medicare DRG rates. Under Section 1886(c) of the Social Security Act, states may obtain a waiver to exempt themselves from Medicare PPS-DRG. However, under the regulation proposed by HHS, obtaining waivers are discouraged through requirements that the state show its estimated payments will not exceed those under federal DRGs and that states provide a larger amount of complicated data to support the state's application.[192]

CONCLUSIONS

Some things are unlikely to change. The demand for health care services by the elderly will continue to increase; so will the costs of providing such care. PPS attempts to control costs by limiting reimbursement to predetermined national averages. The questions raised by PPS are whether the savings it produces are net savings or merely transfer costs elsewhere and whether savings achieved are at the expense of decreases in the quality of care for the elderly. Other factors that seem unlikely to change are increases in the amount of the Social Security tax devoted to the HI program and in the amount of the insurance policy premiums for SMI. Solutions may be possible in the manner in which health care for the elderly is funded as well as in controlling the rate of payment for services. In any event, as the amount expended on HI and SMI continue to grow, the pressure on the Medicare trust fund and the federal budget will continue to grow as well.

NOTES TO CHAPTER FOUR

1. Eileen Applebaum and Cherlyn Skromme Granrose, "Hospital Employment Under Revised Medicare Payment Schedules," *Monthly Labor Review* (August 1986), p. 38.

2. W. Andrew Achenbaum, *Social Security: Visions and Revisions* (New York: Cambridge University Press, 1986), p. 172.

3. Wendy K. Mariner, "Prospective Payment for Hospital Services: Social Responsibility and the Limits of Legal Standards," *Cumberland Law Review* (1987), v. 17, pp. 379-380.

4. Edgar Davidson Charles and William Willard Higdon, "Medicare: the Prospective Payment System," *Cumberland Law Review* (1987), v. 17, p. 417. Charles and Higdon list as other causes rising national expectations about the value of health care services, rapid development and dissemination of medical technology, third-party reimbursement, and the lack of competition in the health care system.

5. Eleanor D. Kinney, "Making Hard Choices Under the Medicare Prospective Payment System: One Administrative Model for Allocating Resources Under a Government Health Insurance Program," *Indiana Law Review* (1986), v. 19, p. 1160.

6. Applebaum and Granrose, p. 38.

7. *Congressional Quarterly Weekly Report* (October 10, 1987), p. 2443.

8. Mariner, p. 379.

9. Jane Perkins, "The Effects of Health Care Cost Containment on the Poor: An Overview," *Clearinghouse Review* (December 1985), v. 19, pp. 832-833.

10. Perkins, pp. 833-834.

11. See Mariner, pp. 384-385. See also Steven Culler and David Ehrenfried, "On the Feasibility and Usefulness of Physician DRGs," *Inquiry* (1986), v. 23, pp. 40-55.

12. Timothy M. Smeeding and Lavonne Straub, "Health Care Financing Among the Elderly: Who Really Pays the Bills?" *Journal of Health Politics, Policy, and Law* (1987), v. 12, p. 38. Medicaid also receives state funding.

13. Mariner, p. 386.

14. Donald N. Muse, "States Not Protected from Medicaid Growth," *State Government News* (February 1986), p. 12.

15. Smeeding and Straub, p. 46.

16. Charles and Higdon, p. 481.

17. Kinney, p. 1160.

18. Kinney, p. 1160.

19. Smeeding and Straub, p. 37.

20. Smeeding and Straub, p. 36.

21. Smeeding and Straub, pp. 36-37.

22. Smeeding and Straub, p. 36.

23. Smeeding and Straub, p. 36.

24. Kinney, pp. 1160-1161.

25. 42 U.S.C. Section 1395 (a). See Kinney, pp. 1160-1161.

26. Mariner, pp. 411-412.
27. Mariner, p. 412. As is discussed later in this chapter, doctors and hospitals can still choose which Medicare patients they wish to treat, a decision complicated by the DRG system's cap on reimbursement.
28. Charles and Higdon, p. 419.
29. Perkins, p. 833.
30. Charles and Higdon, p. 419.
31. Harvey M. Sapolsky, "Prospective Payment in Perspective," *Journal of Health Politics, Policy, and Law* (1986), v. 11, p. 634. See also Linda E. Demikovich, "Who Can Do A Better Job of Controlling Hospital Costs?" *National Journal* (February 10, 1979), pp. 219-223.
32. Sapolsky, p. 633.
33. Kinney, p. 1168.
34. Kinney, p. 1168, n. 75.
35. Kinney, p. 1169.
36. Kinney, p. 1170.
37. Mariner, p. 380.
38. Smeeding and Straub, p. 35; Perkins, p. 831..
39. Achenbaum, p. 170.
40. Kinney, pp. 1165-1166.
41. Culler and Ehrenfried, p. 42.
42. Alicia Munnell, "Paying for the Medicare Program," *Journal of Health Politics, Policy, and Law* (1985), v. 10, p. 496.
43. Charles and Higdon, p. 418.
44. Charles and Higdon, pp. 418-419.
45. Culler and Ehrenfried, p. 40.
46. Munnell, pp. 495-496.
47. Munnell, pp. 496-497.
48. Smeeding and Straub, p. 46.
49. Smeeding and Straub, p. 46.
50. Munnell, p. 497.
51. Munnell, p. 497.
52. Smeeding and Straub, pp. 41-42.
53. Smeeding and Straub, p. 48.
54. Smeeding and Straub, pp. 44-45.
55. Achenbaum, p. 173.
56. Mariner, p. 380, n. 9.
57. Charles and Higdon, p. 420.
58. Charles and Higdon, p. 420.
59. Charles and Higdon, p. 420.
60. Mariner, p. 393.
61. Kinney, p. 1176.
62. There are 467 classes, plus three categories compensating for errors (surgical procedures unrelated to principal patient diagnosis, medical record coding errors preventing DRG assignment). See Charles and Higdon, p. 423.
63. Applebaum and Granrose, p. 37.
64. Charles and Higdon, pp. 421-423.
65. Mariner, p. 381, n. 9.
66. Charles and Higdon, p. 427.
67. Mariner, p. 381, n. 9.
68. Mariner, p. 381, n. 9.
69. Mariner, pp. 380-381.
70. Mariner, p. 385.

71. Mariner, p. 385.
72. See Statement of Jack Owen, Executive Vice President of the American Hospital Association, cited by Kinney, pp. 1183-1184, which among other comments states that "the primary motivating factor in the development of each component of the rate calculation is budget reduction" and that "HCFA is not truly interested in the adequacy of the rates promulgated."
73. Perkins, p. 833.
74. Applebaum and Granrose, p. 38.
75. Applebaum and Granrose, p. 38.
76. Kinney, p. 1171.
77. Applebaum and Granrose, p. 37.
78. There is a problem in lag time of reporting of data collected by hospitals which debaters will confront. As is illustrated above, 1986 articles will generally cite 1984 figures..
79. Munnell, pp. 493-494.
80. Culler and Ehrenfried, p. 43.
81. Achenbaum, p. 40.
82. Mariner, p. 388.
83. Mariner, p. 388, n. 20.
84. Perkins, p. 834.
85. Applebaum and Granrose, pp. 40-41. This funding is somewhat at odds with the one prediction about hospital reaction to PPS, that they would alter patient mix to exclude "heavy care" patients. A response is that "heavy care" but uninsured patients are shunted to public hospitals, while the "heavy care" patients in private hospitals either are insured (and hence can cover amounts in excess of DRG limits) or are patients whose care needs have been exaggerated, i.e., been subjected to "DRG creep."
86. Mariner, p. 388.
87. Mariner, p. 389.
88. Mariner, p. 389.
89. Mariner, p. 389.
90. Perkins, p. 834.
91. Mariner, p. 391.
92. Mariner, p. 382.
93. Mariner, p. 382, n. 10. About 14 percent of U.S. hospitals are owned by for-profit corporations, which are investor-owned or are corporate chains. This is a considerably lower proportion than is the case with long-term care facilities.
94. Applebaum and Granrose, p. 38.
95. Applebaum and Granrose, p. 44.
96. Applebaum and Granrose, p. 45.
97. Robert Newcomer, Juanita Wood, and Andrea Sankar, "Medicare Prospective Payment: Anticipated Effects on Hospitals, Other Community Agencies, and Families," *Journal of Health Politics, Policy, and Law* (1985), v. 10, p. 279.
98. Kinney, p. 1193.
99. Kinney, p. 1193.
100. See Perkins, p. 834, n. 32 and accompanying text.
101. Applebaum and Granrose, p. 38.
102. Mariner, p. 403.
103. Perkins, p. 384.
104. Newcomer, et al., p. 279.
105. Perkins, p. 834.
106. Mariner, p. 403. This problem is discussed further in Chapter Five.
107. Kinney, p. 1194. HHS worked with consumer groups to develop the notice:

appeals take place immediately. The change in financial liability was instituted through the Omnibus Budget Reconciliation Act of 1986.

108. Mariner, p. 392.
109. Mariner, pp. 396-397.
110. Mariner notes an example in which the Seattle Artificial Kidney Center's lay committee selected patients for dialysis on the basis of age, sex, marital status, income, net worth, educational background and occupation, prefering Scout leaders and Sunday school teachers. As one set of commentators noted, "(t)he Pacific Northwest is no place for Henry David Thoreau with bad kidneys." See Mariner, p. 398, n. 46.
111. Mariner, p. 392.
112. Mariner, p. 402.
113. Applebaum and Granrose, p. 41.
114. Applebaum and Granrose, p. 41.
115. Applebaum and Granrose, p. 42.
116. Perkins, p. 834.
117. Applebaum and Granrose, p. 41.
118. Applebaum and Granrose, p. 41.
119. Kinney, p. 1176, n. 115.
120. Mariner, pp. 389-390.
121. Mariner, p. 390.
122. Mariner, p. 394.
123. Mariner, pp. 394-395.
124. Mariner, p. 394.
125. Mariner, p. 393.
126. Mariner, p. 393.
127. Mariner, p. 389.
128. Mariner, p. 404.
129. Mariner, p. 404.
130. See Geraldine Dallek, "Health Care for America's Poor: Separate and Unequal," *Clearinghouse Review* (1986), v. 20, pp. 361-371.
131. See Applebaum and Granrose, p. 41.
132. Cited in Mariner, p. 402, n. 60.
133. Mariner, p. 410.
134. Mariner, pp. 413-414.
135. Kinney, p. 1195.
136. Perkins, pp. 833-834.
137. Perkins, p. 834.
138. Kinney, pp. 1187-1188.
139. Kinney, p. 1188.
140. Kinney, p. 1189.
141. Kinney, p. 1189.
142. Kinney, p. 1189.
143. Charles and Higdon, pp. 428-429.
144. Kinney, p. 1178.
145. Kinney, p. 1177.
146. Kinney, p. 1183.
147. Kinney, p. 1183.
148. Kinney, p. 1185.
149. Perkins, p. 833.
150. Perkins, p. 833.
151. Kinney, p. 1190.

152. Kinney, p. 1190. The quality objectives in the first PRO contracts were: 1) reduce unnecessary hospital admissions resulting from substandard care; 2) assure provision of medical services which, if not performed, are likely to cause complications; 3) reduce "avoidable deaths;" 4) reduce unnecessary surgery; and 5) reduce postoperative and other complications.
153. Kinney, pp. 1190-1191.
154. Perkins, p. 833.
155. Perkins, p. 833.
156. Kinney, p. 1192.
157. Kinney, p. 1192.
158. Kinney, p. 1196.
159. Mariner, p. 398.
160. Michael A. Dowell, "Hill-Burton: The Unfulfilled Promise," *Journal of Health Politics, Policy, and Law* (1987), v. 12, p. 155.
161. Dowell, pp. 155-156. The "available to all" provision had more to do with racial segregation in hospitals than with access limitations produced by poverty.
162. Dowell, p. 161.
163. Dowell, p. 162. 2,500 hospitals had Hill-Burton obligations in 1985, but that figure was to drop to 1,000 by 1990 and to 400 by 1995.
164. Dowell, p. 156.
165. Dowell, pp. 156-157.
166. Dowell, p. 162.
167. Dowell, p. 163.
168. *Gillis v. Hechler,* 759 F.2d 565 (6th Cir. 1985). See also *Davis v. Ball,* 640 F.2d 30 (7th Cir. 1980), 753 F.2d 1410 (7th Cir. 1985).
169. Dowell, pp. 166-167.
170. Dowell, pp. 167-168.
171. Perkins, p. 837.
172. Culler and Ehrenfried, p. 40.
173. Culler and Ehrenfried, p. 41.
174. Associated Press, "Medicare Fee Schedule Sought," *Chicago Tribune* (April 5, 1988), Sec. One, p. 8.
175. Culler and Ehrenfried, p. 41.
176. Culler and Ehrenfried, p. 43.
177. Culler and Ehrenfried, p. 48.
178. Culler and Ehrenfried, pp. 43-44.
179. Culler and Ehrenfried, p. 45-46.
180. Munnell, p. 494.
181. Perkins, p. 843.
182. Perkins, p. 843.
183. Perkins, p. 843.
184. Perkins, p. 844.
185. Perkins, p. 844.
186. Perkins, p. 844.
187. Kinney, p. 1160, n. 29.
188. Perkins, p. 835.
189. Perkins, pp. 835-836.
190. Perkins, p. 836.
191. Perkins, p. 836.
192. Perkins, p. 836.

5 Nursing Homes and Long-Term Custodial Care

As life expectancy among persons over age 65 continues to increase, so will the numbers of the elderly who will need long-term custodial care. In 1985, 5.2 million persons over age 65 were mildly or severely disabled and in need of assitance to perform activities of daily living.[1] Approximately 1.3 million persons over age 65 lived in nursing homes in 1980.[2] Nursing home expenditures rose from $480 million in 1960 to $10.1 billion in 1975, $28.8 billion in 1983, and $35.2 billion in 1985.[3] Increasing at a rate of almost 20 percent per year during that period, nursing home costs are growing faster than any other component of health care costs.[4] Nursing home care can cost $1,500-$3,000 per month.[5] However, care is often provided by unskilled or low-skilled employees, and abuse and neglect of residents is all too common.[6] A factor which is of great importance in understanding nursing home issues and answers is that most nursing homes are for-profit entities, operated as corporations.[7] About 80 percent of nursing home beds are in for-profit facilities.[8]

This chapter examines problems in the provision of long-term care to persons over 65, problems of access, ability, and availability of care, as well as the quality of the care provided. The last part of the chapter discusses solutions, including methods of reimbursement and types of regulation.

A. PROBLEMS

1. Accessibility and Heavy Care, Low Income Elderly Persons

At the outset, a few facts about nursing home care may help provide a clearer picture of the problem. Nursing homes are divided into Skilled Nursing Facilities ("SNFs") and Intermediate Care Facilities ("CIFs"). A

1983 study by the Institute of Medicine of the National Academy of Sciences ("IOM") found that there were 13,326 nursing homes, of which 5,759 were ICF, only 5,064 were ICF and SNF, and 2,504 were SNF only.[9] State licensing requirements differ for each, requiring different staffing. SNFs are for persons with greater care needs, although the reality is that 90 percent of direct patient care in nursing homes is delivered by nurse's aides.[10] The American Association of Retired Persons opposes the distinction between standards and conditions of participation for SNFs and ICFs in Medicaid and Medicare, proposing that they be replaced by a single consolidated standard based on SNF requirements.[11] Almost one-third of nursing home admissions, many within a few days, one-half leave within three months, nearly two-thirds leave within six months. The primary reasons for "leaving" nursing homes are deaths and transfers back to the hospital, although about one-fourth of admissions return to their homes and another 3 percent go to retirement homes.[12]

As is discussed more extensively later in this chapter, Medicare and private insurance pay less than 3 percent of the total nursing home bill.[13] Medicaid accounts for nearly half of nursing home costs, while the rest is paid out-of-pocket by residents and their families.[14]

Because most nursing homes are profit-making enterprises which must be concerned about return on equity to investors, persons who require significant amounts of care or who are unable to provide more than minimal reimbursement to the nursing home for services are unattractive residents. As was discussed in Chapter Four, one of the effects of PPS is to cause earlier releases of elderly patients from acute care hospitals. Nursing homes absorb a relatively small proportion of early-discharged patients who continue to require heavy care. They instead select private paying patients with limited nursing-care requirements. Such selectivity is possible, as is discussed later in this section, because nursing home bed occupancy is already high in most communities.[15]

Because SNF beds are unlikely to be available to them, heavy care patients are likely to be retained in hospital-based nursing beds.[16] Some might also receive Medicare or Medicaid reimbursement for home health care, although government regulations make this problematic.[17] This is an inappropriate use of hospital beds: what is needed is nursing, not acute care treatment. Heavy care patients are shuffled from one part of the hospital to another, the result of PPS, yet they are unlikely to be transferred to SNFs, due to nursing home economic motivations and the current level of Medicare-Medicaid reimbursement.

Low income elderly persons may find most nursing homes simply inaccessible to them. Medicaid reimbursement rates have lagged behind privat pay rates. If there is continued expansion of long-term care insurance, which seems likely, nursing home care rates will reflect the payment rates of those policies.[18]

Because nursing home costs are very responsive to rate changes under cost-based reimbursement systems, increased Medicaid reimbursement rates result in increases in costs (reflecting increased staff and amenities) and no net increase in accessibility.[19] Medicaid-reimbursed patients, less desirable than private pay patients to nursing homes because government reimbursement levels, are adversely affected by increasing private demand and shortages in nursing home beds. Hence, Medicaid reimbursement rates must increase just to maintain existing levels of access.[20] The result is nursing home discrimination against Medicaid recipients in favor of private-pay patients, which is estimated to be practiced by up to 80 percent of nursing homes voluntarily participating in Medicare and/or Medicaid programs.[21]

Such institutions can discriminate against the low income elderly by signing limited-bed provider agreements with Medicaid, restricting the number of beds available to Medicaid-only prospective residents. they may also claim to have no beds available when inquiries are made for Medicaid recipients, placing the person's name instead on a waiting list. Nursing homes may also engage in such subterfuge as asking for "voluntary" contributions to a building fund or requiring that residents agree to pay for care out of their own or their families' private funds for a specified period of time before Medicaid payments will be accepted on the resident's behalf. Nursing homes may also limit Medicaid-pay residents to a certain wing, or, perhaps most importantly, limit the use of Medicaid funds to pay for the expenses of formerly private-pay patients who have exhausted their resources. This means that Medicaid-only nursing home candidates are unlikely to be admitted directly from the community.[22]

2. Nursing Home Demand and Construction

Unlike the hospital industry, which has been characterized by excess capacity, the nursing home industry has failed to keep up with the growth in the demand for beds.[23] Occupancy rates in nursing homes nationally are about 90 percent, with many facilities having waiting lists.[24] This in part reflects the resource base of proprietary nursing homes, which is limited to reimbursement for services from private-pay patients, plus reimbursement from Medicaid, and must pay not only costs of doing business but compensate investors as well.[25] Unlike hospitals, there is no Hill-Burton program to fund the construction of nursing homes, nor is the government likely to repeat the problems of over-supply created by that program.[26]

From another perspective, an undersupply of beds is desirable for the nursing home industry. In the case of for-profit institutions, tight supply and rising demand permits increases in rates which can be charged. This not only increases revenues, it permits nursing homes to market selectively, restricting admissions to private-pay and light care residents.[27] The ceiling becomes what private-pay patients are able to pay. And statistics about rates of construction and relative shares of public and private payment are consistent with the application of this viewpoint. Between 1981 and 1984, the number of nursing home beds grew at a rate of only about 2 percent per year. During the same period, the Medicaid nursing home population declined slightly, Medicaid spendings as a share of all nursing home spending fell from 46 percent in 1982 to 44 percent in 1984, and private expenditures increased from 46 percent to 49 percent of the total.[28]

At their current rate of growth, nursing homes would be able to meet less than half of the projected demand by the end of the century.[29] This would mean that there would be very few admissions of low income elderly persons to nursing homes: Medicaid would be used, as mentioned above, as a supplement for long-term nursing home residents who had been private-pay patients on admission. Therefore, unlike hospitals, which have allocated too many resources and overbuilt supply, for-profit nursing homes have underallocated resources.[30] Of course, this assumes that nursing homes have some commitment to providing access to all prospective nursing home residents, a commitment which they demonstrably do not have.

In addition, current forms of capital reimbursement under state Medicaid reimbursement formulas may actually discourage investment in nursing homes. As a result, these systems discourage maintenance and rehabilitation in homes in which the Medicaid-reimbursed elderly are residents and encourage nursing homes to operate outside of the Medicaid system.[31]

Restrictions on reimbursement of nursing homes' capital expenses stem from efforts to deal with "trafficking," in which nursing homes were resold on a frequent basis. Traditional cost-based capital reimbursement paid owners at rates that reflected the full costs they incurred in purchasing nursing home buildings and equipment. While this encouraged investment (and thus increased numbers of beds and therefore access to Medicaid patients) and the construction and maintenance of high-quality nursing homes, it also encouraged abuses. Since the base cost of a nursing home was equal to the owner's construction cost or purchase price, the only way the value of the home could be increased for reimbursement purposes was through resale at a higher rate. Each resale created a new base cost to be reimbursed by the government, and encouraged further resales to generate profits, new buyers being assured of government reimbursement. Besides funding owner profits through Medicaid revenues, this approach also provided few incentives for efficiency in investment and financing by owners, as interest rates were fully reimbursed. In addition, excessive renovation and maintenance expenses were encouraged, since they added to the resale value of the home.[32]

If the traditional method of reimbursement encouraged abuse, its replacements have discouraged investment and maintenance. One technique was to set as the base rate for capital reimbursement the original cost of the facility, not the recent purchase price. While eliminating incentives for trafficking, this approach also removes the ability to generate profits on capital investments and hence discourages such investments. It also reduces the incentives of owners to maintain and renovate their facilities, since profitability is not tied to the purchase price of the home.[33] Another method, the "flat rate" approach to reimbursement, pays nursing homes on a rate based on the category to which the home belongs (e.g., its location, number of beds, SNF and ICF), regardless of actual costs incurred. this holds down capital costs but, in the process, discourages investment and creates disincentives for maintenance and renovation. Since the rate sets a cap on reimbursement, it encourages higher-cost programs to avoid Medicaid altogether, since their costs above the cap would not be reimbursed by Medicaid but would be reimbursed by private-pay patients.[34] Holahan and Coen suggest as an alternative the payment of nursing home owners on a "fair rental" basis, the state "renting" the facility on behalf of Medicaid patients and reimbursing owners on the basis of a current appraised value to be set by the state. While this would be more expensive, it would encourage long-term ownership. This would have a positive impact on quality of care, as this would be reflected in the appraisal value, and would avoid opting out of providing nursing home space for Medicaid patients.[35]

3. Quality of Care

Quality of nursing home care is tied to two factors: 1) skill levels and training of nursing home staff; and 2) regulations and their enforcement by state agencies. The first factor is affected by the resources available to the nursing home and the profit motives of proprietary institutions, while the second is affected by the degree of state and federal commitment to regulation.

One of the most serious problems in nursing home care is related to staffing patterns. Only 5 percent of nursing home employees are Registered Nurses ("R.N.s") and another 6 percent are Licensed Practical Nurses ("L.P.N.s"). On an average, the ratio of nurses to residents is 3 R.N.s and 4 L.P.N.s per 100 patients. Since care must be provided on a 24-hour, 7-day per week basis, while the average full-time nursing employee works 33 hours per week, this translates into 1.5 licensed nursing personnel actually on duty per 100 patients at any time. Hence, the balance of care is provided by nurse's aides, who are not required to have formal training or education, and are usually unskilled, untrained, and poorly paid.[36] One recommendation that has been made is to require that in every certified facility a registered nurse who has received gerontology and geriatric nurse training be responsible for seeing that accurate assessments of residents be made and updated.[37]

Abuse and neglect are associated with the low quality of care provided by nurse's aides. In Arkansas, which has more nursing home residents than any other state except Florida, aides start at minimum wage, and usually are making only $3.55 per hour after two years.[38] Nursing home residents have been physically and sexually abused, as well as underfed, dehydrated, and permitted to become hypothermic.[39] Residents who "act out" are restrained by aides by being tied to beds, developing bed sores which can become infected. Alternatively, they may be unsupervised and wander away from the grounds and be harmed.[40]

There is some question as to whether infusions of funds to nursing homes through increased reimbursement would necessarily correct this problem. The IOM concluded that, while substantially more study was needed, there was no evidence showing a straightforward link between level of reimbursement, nursing home costs, and the quality of care: nursing homes were found to provide wildly different quality of services at any level of reimbursement.[41] Moreover, according to the IOM, in most instances improvements in the quality of services were possible without significant additional costs to Medicaid or other payors.[42] This may reflect a problem in supervision and management rather than just a problem in rates of reimbursement of nursing homes and consequent rates of pay for staff.[43]

Regulation is influenced by both federal and state commitment to enforcement of standards. Nursing homes must meet federal conditions of participation to receive reimbursement from either Medicare or Medicaid, and 75 percent of nursing homes fall into this category.[44] Other nursing homes must still meet state licensing regulations, which are similar to federal regulations but often more specific.[45] There have been criticisms of state enforcement of these standards. Surveyors inspecting nursing homes tend to focus on facility characteristics, reviewing documents with nursing home supervisors rather than soliciting views of residents and observing care received. The Health Care Financing Administration ("HCFA") has been criticized for cutting funds, forcing states to curtail their survey and enforcement efforts. HCFA has also been criticized for erratic behavior in pursuing deficient nursing homes, undermining the credibility of state investigations.[47] In its fiscal 1987 budget, the Reagan Administration called for a reduction of federal:state matching for state inspections from $1:$.75 to $1:$.50. And, despite 1981 Congressional authorization to ban admissions to nursing homes with serious deficiencies, no bans occurred because HCFA failed to prommulgate regulations.[48] Congress has recently amended the Medicaid nursing home law in an attempt to improve the quality of care through participation requirements, survey and certification procedures, and enforcement remedies for SNFs and ICFs.[49] As is discussed later, Congress is attempting to set higher standards for the quality of nursing home care: it remains to be seen whether these will be carried out.

B. SOLUTIONS

1. Paying for Care

Forms of reimbursement, and the conditions under which government reimbursement will be provided have a major effect on the accessibility of nursing home care to the elderly. This section discusses Medicare and Medicaid reimbursement for nursing home care, private long-term care insurance, and suggestions for modifications in reimbursement systems, including the implementation of PPS for nursing home care.

Medicare provides coverage only for SNFs and only for short-term post-acute care that requires daily skilled nursing or related rehabilitative services.[50] The benefit was designed to reduce hospital stays by substituting care in nursing homes when medically appropriate and is limited to 100 days, although the average length of Medicare-covered stays is only 30 days. There are only 275,000 Medicare SNF admissions per year, in contrast to more than 1 million general nursing home admissions.[51] Hence, Medicare at present is of considerably less significance in nursing home reimbursement policy than is Medicaid.[52]

Medicaid covers both SNF and ICF-provided care. Institutionalized individuals are eligible for Medicaid as categorically needy at state option: once the state agrees to provide coverage for them, its program must conform to federal statutory and regulatory requirements.[53] Individuals may be eligible for Medicaid assistance prior to institutionalization; more typically, they are institutionalized and then spend down all of their resources to the poverty-level resource standard for their state's Medicaid program before they are eligible for assistance.[54] About 68 percent of all Medicaid spent on persons over age 65 went to nursing homes in 1984.[55] This was 43 percent of Medicaid's total budget: it has in effect become the nursing home insurance plan of the middle class as well as low income elderly persons.[56]

Medicaid nursing home reimbursement has followed flat-rate and facility-specific approaches. Under the former, the state pays a fixed amount per day of care to all nursing homes, the rates set prospectively. Facility-specific reimbursement involves payment of each nursing home by the state of a rate based on that facility's costs. In contrast, Medicare reimburses SNFs on a retrospective, facility-specific basis, with an overall ceiling on routine operating costs per patient day.[57] State and federal budget constraints have limited upward adjustments in these rates. Since 1981, Medicaid nursing home spending has increased by just 7.7 percent.[58] States have attempted to contain costs, as nursing home reimbursement begins to virtually preempt alternative uses of Medicaid funds.

Private long-term care insurance can best be described as embryonic at this point. In early 1985, an estimated 50,000 to 75,000 persons were covered by long-term care ("LTC") insurance policies nationwide, offered by 12 to 16 companies. By 1986, about 40 companies had entered the market, including such major carriers as Aetna, Mutual of Omaha, and Prudential.[59]

One of the reasons the growth of LTC insurance plans has been slow is the mistaken belief on the part of the elderly that Medicare will pay for their nursing home costs. A 1983 survey by the American Association of Retired Persons ("AARP") of its members found that 79 percent thought they could rely on Medicare to pay for nursing home care.[60] If insurance companies can overcome consumer ignorance there seems to be a market for such insurance: improved economic status is anticipated for a significant portion of the elderly population. In addition, the AARP survey found that 40 percent of respondents worried that they would not have enough money to pay for nursing home or home health services if needed, and 47 percent said they were interested in learning more about LTC insurance.[61]

At best, private life insurance would provide a supplement to Medicaid and Medicare coverage. This is because the economics of offering such insurance virtually exclude the poor and near poor, who also tend to be the greatest users of institutional long-term care.[62] A 1985 study performed for HHS found that, using 5 percent of cash income per person and $3,000 or more in assets as a cutoff for affordability, only 21 percent of persons aged 67 to 69 could afford LTC insurance; using 10 percent of income and $3,000, the study found that 47 percent could afford the insurance.[63] Therefore, only the elderly who are middle income and above are likely to ever have LTC insurance.

Even if all LTC insurance did was supplement government assistance, it might increase access of nursing home care to the low income elderly. This is because middle income persons currently spending down to Medicaid eligibility would instead be able to rely on LTC insurance, making more Medicaid funds available. Conversely, it might be the result that LTC insurance would actually hurt low income persons unable to afford such insurance. This is because nursing homes would be presented with a greater market pool of non-Medicaid residents to drwa from if middle income elderly had LTC insurance as well as their liquid assets. It is also conceivable that the availability of third party payment might cause further inflation in nursing home charges, as has been true of hospital costs, making care less accessible to Medicaid-only elderly persons.

PPS has been discussed as a new technique for Medicaid reimbursement of nursing homes. The 1985 Consolidated Budget Reconciliation Act enacted a limited prospective payment option for the payment of SNFs: facilities serving fewer than 1,500 Medicare SNF patient days per year could choose to be reimbursed prospectively on a basis separate from the current rate-setting formula for Medicare SNF payments.[64]

Three approaches could be taken in developing a PPS system for nursing home care. One would be to focus on activities of daily living ("ADLs"), focusing on the physical, mental, and social disorders of patients to form groups which could be expected to use a similar mix of resources.[65] Another would be to use what are called resource utilization groups ("RUGs"), in which groups are identified according to resource consumption.[66] RUGs are developed on the basis of 5 broad types of categories. Patients can be classified as being in one of the following groups: special care, rehabilitation, clinical complex, severe behavioral problems, or reduced physical functioning. After a first grouping, a second stage would divide these clinical groups into 16 patient categories as distinguished by the level of physical functioning (as defined by the ADL index).[67] A final approach is nursing resource use, in which prospective payments would be based on time devoted to direct patient care. Patients are groups according to need for specialized care, then subgrouped according to presence or absence of a catheter/ostomy.[68] All three systems make heavy use of the ADL system, which in fact is a loose description of a resident's condition, made on a subjective basis.

Unlike the PPS-DRG system for hospitals discussed in Chapter Four, the purpose of PPS for nursing homes would not be primarily that of cost-containment. This is because the supply and demand situation of nursing homes is the reverse of that for hospitals. PPS in a nursing home context would credit institutions for providing heavier care, where indicated, to less healthy residents. The purposes of the prospective payment for nursing home services would be those of improving access to care, ensuring quality, expanding capacity, and inducing the more appropriate use of resources.[69] In other words, PPS classification would be useful in improving quality and responsiveness of nursing home services to patient needs. Case mix reimbursement systems, as opposed to flat-rate and facility-specific reimbursement, might make it possible to include heavy care, low income patients who would otherwise have been avoided.[70]

2. Assuring Quality of Care

Assuring the quality of care in nursing homes is primarily the task of a combination of federal and state regulation. As was alluded to above, current approaches to regulation have come under criticism. This part of this section looks at different types of governmental regulation and then addresses briefly tort litigation as a means of dealing with nursing home abuse and neglect.

OBRA '87 substantially amended and added to Medicaid nursing home law. These changes occurred in the areas of requirements for nursing homes participating in Medicaid, survey and certification procedures, and enforcement remedies.[71] Participation requirements included nurse staffing requirements (one R.N. on duty eight hours per day, seven days per week, plus one L.P.N. on duty at all times), procedures for accommodation of individual rights of residents, administrative requirements, and preadmission screening for mentally ill and mentally retarded persons.[72]

Survey and certification changes, effective October 1, 1990, provide for unannounced standard surveys of all participating nursing homes, with extended surveys to be required of nursing facilities found to have provided substandard care: federal matching payments for state costs would be at a rate of 90 percent in fiscal 1991, declining to 75 percent in fiscal 1994 and thereafter.[73] Federal enforcement procedures expand remedies available to HHS and the states. Where facilities are not in compliance with participation requirements and jeopardize the health and safety of residents, the state or the Secretary is required to take immediate corrective action or terminate the facility's participation in Medicaid: where residents are not jeopardized by noncompliance, intermediate remedies can be imposed instead (these include denial of payment for new admissions, civil fines, temporary management by a receiver, or, in emergencies, authority to close the facility and/or transfer residents).[74]

These are significant changes, most of which are yet to be implemented. Nevertheless, they fail to deal with some key problems. First, they rely on state agencies for enforcement. State agencies do not have a good track record in this area, often having been co-opted by state nursing home lobbies.[75] A second problem is that of providing credible sanctions. Sanctions which involve home closure and transfer of residents are not seen as credible threats. In addition to it being unlikely that state agencies will carry out these measures, closure would aggravate demand problems and transfer could place residents in even less hospitable surroundings.[76] Third, the new regulations perpetrate the separation of nursing home inspection and enforcement agencies from state attorney general's offices, which have generally been tougher and more innovative in dealing with nursing homes.[77]

It has also been suggested that regulation by the government could take on new forms altogether. One approach which has been used in some states is the appointment of a state ombudsman as an advocate for nursing home residents.[78] This would differ from current state regulatory approaches, where agencies view themselves either as "counselors" to nursing homes, encouraging improvements, or as law enforcement agents, engaging in confrontations with nursing home operators.[79] While the latter is more effective than the former in achieving change, the agency is still primarily representing the interests of the state, and only indirectly represents the interests of nursing home residents when it acts as parens patriae for them. An ombudsman would instead act directly on their behalf.

A second approach to to extreme problems in compliance is the appointment of receivers to manage nursing homes. This avoids the problems of several different alternatives. As mentioned earlier, closure ie neither credible nor desirable, given bed shortages. Another state procedure, forced sale of nursing homes not in compliance permits a well-compensated exit for nursing home operators who are in violation of the law.[80] Appointment of a receiver would avoid both of these problems, as well as threats by owners to withdraw from Medicaid certification.[81]

Tort litigation against nursing home operators, primarily for abuse and neglect of residents, has been successful in some circumstances, but must overcome some significant obstacles. A formidable barrier is fear of retaliation on the part of elderly residents, who must remain residents during the course of proceedings. They may also fear the unknown if litigation forces them to move to a different setting. There are also proof problems: the physical frailty of residents may make plausible claims by the nursing home that injuries occurred without fault, and residents can be less than credible witnesses because of failing memories. A final barrier is damages which may be sought. Residents cannot claim lost income, many states have statutory limits on pain-and-suffering awards permitted to surviving spouses or children, and states also limit punitive damages in actions brought by survivors and in wrongful death actions.[82]

Despite these limitations, tort actions against nursing homes have been successful.[83] Tort actions provide a private remedy to victims and the relatives of victims; they may also stir otherwise complacent regulatory agencies into action. These suits may also have more clout if brought as class actions against the nursing home operators, rather than restricting them solely to the trauma suffered by an individual resident. A modification of the current procedure would be to permit suits against nursing home operators (for money damages or injunctive relief) by ombudsmen or the equivalent of the public guardians on behalf of residents. Suits for injunctive relief could also be brought against negligent state agencies; for punitive damages to be awarded, state immunity laws would need to be modified.

CONCLUSION

Nursing home care has become a big business. At the same time, problems have been created in the access of heavy care and low income elderly to needed custodial care, and in the quality of services rendered. Solutions dealing with these problems must take into account the profit motivation of most nursing homes, the weakness of state agencies and the lack of support by the NCFA of state enforcement efforts. America faces a situation of dual care for adults in need of custodial care services. Moderately impaired, middle and upper income persons will reside in nursing homes meeting high quality standards, as such institutions cater to the resources and service requests of these persons. Meanwhile, heavy care patients and those with little income will either congregate in Medicaid-only nursing homes or will simply not receive formal care at all, receiving instead substitute nursing services from friends and relatives, or doing without necessary care altogether.

NOTES TO CHAPTER FIVE

1. Charles P. Sabatine, "An Advocate's Primer on Long-Term Care Insurance," *Clearinghouse Review* (1986), p. 351.

2. U.S. House of Representatives, Select Committee on Aging, Subcommittee on Health and Long-Term Care, *The Attempted Dismantling of the Medicare Home Health Care Benefit*, 99th Congress (Report, 1986), p. 11. (Hereinafter, "House Committee Report, 1986")

3. John Holahan and Joel Cohen, "Nursing Home Reimbursement: Implications for Cost Containment, Access, and Quality," *Milbank Quarterly* (1987), v. 65, no. 1, p. 112; and Michael D. Rosko, Robert W. Broyles, and William E. Aaronson, "Prospective Payment Based on Care Mix: Will it Work in Nursing Homes?" *Journal of Health Politics, Policy, and Law* (Winter 1987), v. 12, p. 683. (Hereinafter, "Rosko, et al.")

4. Holahan and Cohen, p. 112.

5. Eugenie Denise Mitchell, "Spousal Impoverishment: Medicaid Burdens on the At-Home Spouse of a Nursing Home Resident," *Clearinghouse Review* (1986), p. 358.

6. Sandy McMath, "The Nursing Home Maltreatment Case," *Trial* (September 1985), v. 21, pp. 52-53.

7. Rosko, et al., p. 685.

8. Rep. Mario Biagg, U.S. House of Representatives, Select Committee on Aging, Subcommittee on Human Services, *Quality of Life in Nursing Homes*, 99th Congress (Hearings, 1986), p. 4. (Hereinafter, "House Hearings, 1986")

9. House Hearings, 1986, p. 34. Statement of Barry Gurland.

10. House Hearings, 1986, p. 70. Statement of Tom Spicuzza.

11. House Hearings, 1986, p. 54. Statement of Lou Krieger.

12. William G. Weissert, "Hard Choices: Targeting Long-Term Care to the 'At Risk' Aged," *Journal of Health Politics, Policy, and Law* (Fall 1986), v. 11, p. 468.

13. Sabatine, p. 353.

14. Robert E. Schlenker, "Case Mix Reimbursment for Nursing Homes," *Journal of Health Politics, Policy, and Law* (Fall 1986), v. 11, pp. 445-446.

15. Robert Newcomer, Juanita Wood, and Andrea Sankar, "Medicare Prospective Payment: Anticipated Effects on Hospitals, Other Community Agencies, and Families," *Journal of Health Politics, Policy, and Law* (Summer 1985) v. 10, pp. 277-278. (Hereinafter, "Newcomer, et al.")

16. Newcomer, et al., p. 278. See also, Charles Brecher and James Knickman, "A Reconsideration of Long-Term Care Policy," *Journal of Health Politics, Policy, and Law* (Summer 1985), v. 10, p. 249.

17. Brecher and Knickman, p. 249. Home health care reimbursement problems are discussed in Chapter Six.

18. Sabatine, p. 355.

19. Holahan and Cohen, p. 129.

20. Holahan and Cohen, p. 129.

21. Toby Edelman, "Discrimination by Nursing Homes Against Medicaid Recipients: Improving Access to Institutional Long-Term Care for Poor People," *Clearinghouse Review* (1986), v. 20, p. 339.

22. Edelman, p. 340.

23. Rosko, et al., p. 686.

24. House Hearings, 1986, p. 4. Statement of Rep. Mario Biaggi.

25. Rosko, et al., pp. 685-686.

26. Rosko, et al., p. 686.

27. Rosko, et al., p. 688.
28. Holahan and Cohen, p. 113.
29. Holahan, p. 113.
30. Rosko, et al., p. 686.
31. Holahan and Cohen, pp. 131, 135-137.
32. Holahan and Cohen, pp. 131, 133.
33. Holahan and Cohen, p. 134.
34. Holahan and Cohen, pp. 134-135.
35. Holahan and Cohen, pp. 145-146.
36. House Hearings, 1986, p. 70. Statement of Tom Spicuzza.
37. House Hearings, 1986, p. 35. Statement of Barry Gurland.
38. McMath, p. 52.
39. McMath, p. 52.
40. McMath, p. 52. See also, Patricia Newmore, "Protecting Nursing Home Residents," *Trial* (December 1985), v. 21, p. 56.
41. House Hearings, 1986, p. 29. Statement of Bruce C. Vladeck.
42. House Hearings, 1986, p. 29. Statement of Bruce C. Vladeck.
43. House Hearings, 1986, p. 17. Statement of Teresa Tuliericio.
44. Newmore, p. 56.
45. Newmore, p. 56.
46. House Hearings, 1986, p. 28. Statement of Bruce C. Vladeck.
47. Timothy S. Jost, "Enforcement of Quality Nursing Home Care in the Legal System," *Law, Medicine and Health Care* (September 1985), p. 168.
48. House Hearings, 1986, p. 4. Statement of Rep. Mario Biaggi.
49. Roger Schwartz and Jane Perkins, "The Omnibus Budget Reconciliation Act of 1987: Legislative Changes in Medicaid," *Clearinghouse Review* (April 1988), v. 21, pp. 1301-1302.
50. Schlenker, p. 445.
51. Korbin Liu, Joshua Wiener, George Schieber, and Pamela Doty, "The Feasibility of Using Case Mix and Prospective Payment for Medicare Skilled Nursing Facilities," *Inquiry* (Winter 1986), v. 23, pp. 365-366. (Hereinafter, "Liu, et al.")
52. Schlenker, p. 445.
53. Mitchell, p. 358.
54. Mitchell, p. 358.
55. Sabatine, p. 353.
56. Meg Delaney, "Who Will Pay for Retiree Care?" *Personnel Journal* (March 1987), pp. 85-86.
57. Schlenker, p. 446.
58. Holahan and Cohen, p. 113.
59. Sabatine, p. 353. Prudential was test marketing a policy for members of AARP.
60. Delaney, p. 86.
61. Sabatine, p. 353.
62. Sabatine, p. 353.
63. Sabatine, p. 353.
64. Liu, et al., pp. 365, 369.
65. Rosko, et al., p. 688.
66. Rosko, et al., pp. 690-691.
67. Rosko, et al., p. 690.
68. Rosko, et al., pp. 691-692.
69. Rosko, et al., p. 688.
70. Schlenker, pp. 452-454.

71. National Health Law Program, "The Omnibus Budget Reconciliation Act of 1987: Legislation Changes in Medicaid, Medicare, and Related Programs," *Health Advocate* (February 1988), p. 10.

72. National Health Law Program, pp. 10-12.

73. National Health Law Program, pp. 12-13.

74. National Health Law Program, pp. 13-14.

75. Jost, p. 170.

76. Jost, p. 170.

77. Jost, p. 170. See also, Diane Horvath and Patricia Newmore, "Nursing Home Abuses as Unfair Trade Practices," *Clearinghouse Review* (November 1986), v. 20, pp. 801-810, for a discussion of innovative approaches by state attorney generals' offices.

78. House Hearings, 1986, pp. 39, 66-67. Statements of Joe Michaels and Nicholas Rango.

79. Jost, pp. 162-163.

80. Jost, p. 170, where a consumer advocate is cited referring to a facility that had been responsible for a patient's death, it received a $500 fine and then brought its owner $1.5 million at a forced sale. Unless adequately policed, such sales can transfer the property to another substandard owner, or to the same owner under a different guise.

81. Horvath and Newmore, p. 807.

82. Newmore, p. 56.

83. Newmore, p. 59. See also, McMath, pp. 52-53.

6 Specialized Services for the Elderly

This chapter discusses a number of programs which do not fit precisely in any of the three previous chapters. However, they have an impact on the retirement status, well-being, and health care of the elderly. The most controversial of these, reimbursement for home health care, can be thought of as either an adjunct or an alternative to either acute-care hospitalization or custodial care. Others, such as drug prepayment and mental health screening, are proposals for services, ways of treating the elderly which could improve upon their quality of life.

A. HOME HEALTH CARE

"Home health care" refers to government reimbursement of professional services providing certain types of medical care in the elderly person's residence. It does not refer to "informal caregivers," i.e., assistance in activities of daily living by relatives or friends. Informal caregivers provide 60-80 percent of the care provided at home.[1] Home health care services are becoming of greater importance because of the increased pressures placed on these caregivers by PPS. As was mentioned in Chapter Four, the tendency of PPS-DRGs to cause elderly patients to be released "quicker and sicker" has placed greater care demands on families caring for them.[2] Where nursing home care is unavailable or unaffordable, home health care services would provide improved quality of care to the elderly, as well as avoiding possible deterioration of the care-giving relationship within families.[3]

The idea of providing home health care as a benefit to provide an alternative to nursing home placement dates from before the passage of Medicare legislation.[4] Between 1974 and 1981, both the Senate and House Committees on Aging issued reports criticizing the Department of Health.

Education, and Welfare and, later, the Department of Health and Human Services ("HHS") for making it impractical for Medicare recipients to receive reimbursement for home health care.[5]

In the Omnibus Budget and Reconciliation Act ("OBRA") of 1981, Congress authorized waivers for providing home and community based care. These waivers, which have been reauthorized by OBRA 1987, were intended to produce deinstitutionalization of the elderly and to reduce the costs of care.[6] In 1980, Congress had improved access to home care for Medicare patients by reducing many restrictions on such care, and it also made it easier for private, for-profit agencies to enter the market by eliminating state licensure requirements for proprietary agencies seeking to participate in Medicare programs.[7] This led to a rapid increase in the number of home health care agencies. Between 1977 and 1982 there was an annual increase of 8.5 percent in the number of Medicare-certified home health agencies; between 1980 and 1982, Medicare-certified proprietary agencies increased 241 percent.[8] The inclusion of home care as a benefit by many private health insurance carriers has also influenced this growth.[9]

The remainder of this section discusses a number of issues created by the growth of home health care. These are: 1) effect of the use of home health care on the cost and quality of care for the elderly; 2) the role of for-profit agencies in home health care; and 3) the apparent opposition of the Office of Management and Budget ("OMB"), the Department of Health and Human Services ("HHS") and the Health Care Financing Administration ("HCFA") to expanded funding of home health care.

1. Home Health Care, Costs and Quality

A primary motivation behind encouraging home health care is the desire to reduce the tremendous costs of caring for the elderly. Nursing home care, as described in Chapter Five, is enormously expensive. Home health care advocates also urge that many persons institutionalized in nursing homes could stay in their own homes or apartments if home care were available. General Accounting Office reports have estimated that 25-40 percent of nursing home residents fall into this category.[10] In addition, home health care can function as an alternative to inpatient, acute-care hospital provision of services.

Whether home health care actually saves money over nursing home institutionalization is tied to current home health care regulations, which are discussed in the final part of this chapter. HCFA has sought to avoid the states shunting persons from community care of the aged to home health care. The states would do so because they could thus transfer elderly persons from a state-funded budget to Medicaid, which is jointly funded by the federal government and the states, and Medicare, which is federally funded. As a result, federal waivers for home health care are limited to those persons

who but for the waivered services would be at high risk of institutionalization, limiting federally reimbursed home health care to those with high care
needs.[11]

Therefore, home and community based care, although advanced as a
substitute, is often instead a complement to nursing home care. This typically
raises overall health uses and costs by the small number of persons who
are eligible for home health care reimbursement by HCFA.[12] The result
is that community based services will provide care for the following types
of patients: 1) persons with relatively light care needs, whose expenses are
reimbursed by the states; 2) persons with very heavy care needs who would
otherwise be (and frequently just were) in nursing homes, and whose expenses
are paid for by the federal government; and 3) persons whose home health
care is paid for by private health insurance or out-of-pocket. There is a
perverse incentive for families, physicians, and the states to place the elderly
in hospitals or nursing homes where their care needs may tax community
resources, but are not sufficiently high to qualify for federal reimbursement
of home health care. This is because the "but for" requirement in the law
is interpreted by HCFA to disqualify for federal reimbursement all but extreme
cases.[13]

Meanwhile, private employers and private health insurance carriers have
apparently embraced home health care as an alternative to inpatient, acute-
care hospitalization for cost reasons.[14] Home health care plans for persons
being treated for orthopedic disorders, cancer, and cardiovascular conditions
made up 70 percent of home health care patients in one study, while another
study showed home health treatment costs of $25-75 per day compared
with $350-400 per day hospital costs.[15] These programs apply to persons
under 65 as well as the elderly. It is also the case that states have paid
for home health care: New York's Long Term Home Health Care Program
has shown the cost of services for patients in such programs to be
approximately 50 percent of the cost of corresponding institutional care.[16]

Hence, what may be beginning to emerge is a home health care system
with the following contours: 1) state-funded community care services, subject
to state budgetary constraints; 2) home health care services with hospitals,
paid for through private health insurance, largely provided to persons under
age 65 under employer-connected insurance; and 3) federally reimbursed
home health care for noninstitutionalized, heavy care elderly persons.
Although there will be cost savings by private insurers, federal regulations
have the effect of minimizing the savings of home health care under Medicare-
based programs.

The other response to current regulations is to simply avoid formal
providers of care. If the elderly person has a spouse or other relatives, he
or she received unskilled care from them. As was noted above, this
characterizes the bulk of home health care. This would appear to be the
response of choice of the elderly without insurance to provide for home

health care, who do not meet federal "but for" standards and hence cannot receive Medicare reimbursement, and who resist institutionalization or cannot afford it.[17]

As a result, any system which provided greater access to home health care would intitially show a significant increase in such costs, as it dealt with pent-up demand. There could be cost savings as compared with hospitalization, if it could be demonstrated that persons foregoing services which could be provided at home eventually have hospitalization costs which would have been avoided or reduced had such services been available. This is analgous to the preventive medicine argument made by HMO advocates. However, there would be no net savings as opposed to nursing home costs, unless it could be established that such persons would have had their entry into long-term care institutions delayed by the presence of home health care services. This leads to a discussion of the quality of care effects of home health care system availability.

Quality of care in the context of home health services has two related but distinct meanings: medical status and, of equal importance, mental outlook or emotional status. Particularly with reference to the comparison between hospitalization and home health care, what is claimed is that home health care can achieve the same levels of outcomes, but for considerably lower costs. The primary focus is on cost savings: quality of care is addressed secondarily, and on the basis that since the same results can be achieved, there is no justification for the expense associated with hospitalization. As was discussed in Chapter Four, home health care has been used by hospitals as a means of beating DRG reimbursement limitations: Medicare is billed for both inpatient services and the additional outpatient care.[18] Provision of outpatient care by hospitals also can be profitable because inpatient care provided by Registered Nurses can be replaced by home health services provided by less expensive Licensed Practical Nurses, or nurse's aides.[19]

Community care studies have found that community care's only real improvement is in patient contentment, and even that is raised only by a small amount. Community based care does little for physical and mental functioning, mortality, or institutionalization. In fact, such care is as likely to be associated with an accelerated decline in physical functioning as with an increase.[20] Home health care has significant support as an alternative to nursing home residence, based on public opinion polls.[21] However, such perceived desirability may reflect attitudes of the adult children of the elderly as well as the elderly, and have more to do with perceptions of the preferability of home health care than its reality.

2. Proprietary Home Health Care Agencies

As was noted above, legislative changes in 1980 and 1981 resulted an influx of proprietary, for-profit home health care agencies into the provision of services for the elderly. Much of the pressure on Congress to relax HCFA restrictions on home health care reimbursement comes from the National Association for Home Health Care, which functions as an industry lobbyist.[22]

For-profit agencies present several advantages over nonprofit agencies or the use of state employees in providing home health services. First, proprietary agencies have superior cash flow situations compared with nonprofit groups. This permits them to set up and expand operations more quickly.[23] Second, for-profit agencies as opposed to state employees are not unionized and are not subject to civil service controls, thus reducing personnel costs.[24] A more fundamental argument is that for-profit agencies are more reflective of market forces than are nonprofit groups or state agencies.[25] This is an argument that the government receives the advantages of economic decision-making by agencies operating under contract, as opposed to nonprofit groups and state agencies, which may make diseconomic choices which are underwritten by others.

There are also disadvantages to reliance on for-profit agencies in providing home health care services. The flip side of the comments above about costs is that proprietary agencies, drawing on the experience of similar operations in nursing homes, will attempt to provide services for the lowest cost possible and will attempt to water down regulatory standards and their enforcement.[26] And as the flip side to the economic decision-making argument, proprietary home health care agencies are accused of engaging in "creaming." "Creaming" involves the selection of affluent areas, higher-paying clients, and easier-to-serve clients.[27] This is analogous to the comments made about proprietary nursing homes in Chapter Five. Hill, et al. note that in a study in two states, proprietary home health costs were higher than of nonprofit visiting Nurse Associations, due to higher management and clerical costs per patient. Yet proprietary groups have lower costs per hour of service delivered because they take advantage of Medicare-Medicaid financing systems by delivering more hours per visit and more visits per case than nonprofit agencies, as profit motivations provide no incentive to restrict care where it is reimbursed.[28]

Hill, et al.'s study of proprietary vendors in Illinois led them to conclude that where there is competition, for-profit agencies provide services at about the same price as nonprofit groups. State oversight and the setting of standards for training of home health care workers, qualifications of supervisors, their ratio to workers, and their performance of on-site visitations to clients' homes were utilized to maintain quality of care.[29]

One other factor that is of importance is the increased number of heavy care elderly adults released from hospitals because of DRG influences who have sought home health care. The General Accounting Office reported a 37 percent increase in the number of patients sent to home care after the DRG system went into effect.[30] The "creaming" motives of for-profit agencies suggest that they would avoid such prospective clients. These elderly persons at present are cared for by hospitals as part of outpatient care.[31] However, if Medicare decided to reduce reimbursement for such services, there persons might be forced into nursing homes, where proprietary homes would avoid them, or into public hospitals for brief periods of time.

3. Current Government Regulations and Limitations on Home Health Care

The controversy over home health care under Medicaid involves conflicting signals between Congress, which supports home health care strongly, and the OMB and MCFA-HHS, which has dragged its feet at the implementation of reimbursement legislation because of its cost implications. In 1981, Section 2176 of the Omnibus Budget Reconciliation Act amended the Social Security Act to authorize the Secretary of HHS to waive most or all statutory provisions of Medicaid law which discouraged or restricted coverage of home and community long-term care.[32] Despite this action, as of 1986, Medicare was spending less than 3 percent of its budget for home health care.[33] This amounted to about $2 billion and was up from 1 percent of Medicare expenditures in 1971. Medicaid provided an additional $600 million, about half of it in New York. About 1.2 million persons took advantage of the benefit.[34]

Part of the explanation for the limited implementation of waivers is that the initial legislation included permissive language, allowing discretion by HHS.[35] HHS has pointed to the fact that (after the 1981 legislation) expenditures for home health care doubled from $1 billion, the number of certified home health agencies increased from 3,000 to 6,000, and the average agency per-visit cost increased. It has contended that these facts are evidence that the home health benefit is out of control.[36] In response, in OBRA 1987 Congress changed the language authorizing home health care waivers to mandatory language: Section 4102 of the Act states that meet Congressional standards.[37] Although HHS (and OMB) see home health care as growing precipitously, health care advocates view HHS as having delayed or refused waivers to limit cost increases.[38]

Another problem in the 1981 legislation was created by the Congressional Budget Act of 1974, which restricts Congressional committees from introducing legislation that would raise expenditures. Since the Congressional Budget Office had estimated that broadened coverage would add to utilization and spending, Congress had to come up with language to comply with the 1974 Act.[39] It did so by requiring that services offered under waiver programs must result in aggregate Medicaid expenditures no higher than what they would have been without the waiver. This is accomplished through cost containment and through the requirement that those served by the waiver authority must be persons who "but for the waivered services" would be at high risk of institutionalization.[40] NCFA used this requirement to thwart reimbursement requests. It has interpreted the legislation to mean not only that each community care slot must produce an empty nursing home bed (even though there is excess demand for such beds) but that states show that the total cost of a patient's consumption of all goods and services (including food stamps and Supplemental Security Income) does not exceed what would have been spent on the patient in a nursing home.[41]

The 1987 legislation provided that home care be provided to persons age 65 and over who would otherwise "be likely" to require institutional care.[42] It remains to be seen whether this language change will produce any change in the number of waivers actually approved. HCFA has interpreted other provisions in the home health care legislation narrowly, restricting the approval of waivers.[43]

Given Congressional support of home health care and OMB-HHS concerns about health care costs, future conflict over this issue appears likely. And given other budgetary constraints, Congress is unlikely to broaden home health care coverage beyond Medicare recipients with significant care needs.[44] While private insurance coverage of home health care can be expected to grow, this will not help most of the persons who must look to Medicaid for health care assistance.

B. REIMBURSEMENT FOR OUTPATIENT PRESCRIPTION DRUG USE

This is an idea which has been tried on an experimental basis, with good results: have Medicare pay for prescription drugs used by the elderly while not hospitalized. While Medicare reimburses hospitals for drugs during hospitalization, it does not cover outpatient prescription drug use.[45]

There are several arguments for providing such a service to the elderly. First, large numbers of the elderly suffer from one or more chronic conditions[46], and are under programs of medication on a regular basis. One-third of all prescriptions are written for persons over age 65.[47] And such medications are both expensive and rising in cost. Between 1981 and 1986, the price of prescription drugs increased 79 percent, while the Consumer Price Index went up only 28 percent: in 1986, they went up a record 8 times the CPI rate.[48] Although there have been some attempts to regulate drug costs under Medicare and to impose limits on drug payments under Medicaid, these have been unsuccessful.[49] For the elderly with high drug costs, outpatient reimbursement would provide a significant economic benefit.

Second, outpatient reimbursement of prescription drug use would provide a significant health benefit to the elderly. Some elderly persons, faced by rising costs for rent, energy, food, and other essentials cut corners by reducing usage of medications where possible. This seems to be true in particular of persons with high blood pressure, who take medication intermittently, when symptoms flare up. The result is that chronic conditions are not effectively controlled, leading to medical complications and avoidable hospitalizations. There is also the view that programs of medication, if followed, are a desirable alternative to other medical options, which usually involve surgery. One example of this is use of drugs such as Tagamet to control stomach ulcers, as opposed to ulcer surgery.[50]

The state of New Jersey conducted a program of Pharmaceutical Assistance for the Aged. It was limited to those elderly persons with incomes of less than $9,000 for individuals, $12,000 for couples.[51] Program participants were required to make a $2 copayment per prescription.[52] Lingle, et al. studied the records of program participants between 1975 and 1979, comparing them with persons of comparable age and income who were hospitalized across the state line in eastern Pennsylvania.[53] The study found a significant difference in inpatient hospital reimbursements, which were $238.50 less for patients in New Jersey than in Pennsylvania.[54] Because HFCA would not release data on length of stay or dates of admission, the study was unsure whether the cost reductions were due to reduced length of stay or reduced numbers of hospital admissions.[55] Inpatient utilization of hospital services did not differ between samples, nor were the numbers of hospital admissions between the samples significantly different.[56]

HHS and HCFA have opposed reimbursement of outpatient drug use, on program cost grounds. While there are administrative costs of such a program, the argument is that these are made up through decreased hospitalization costs.[57] PPS masks such a savings, as it reimburses on the DRG estimate of patient costs, not on actual hospital expenditures. The HCFA fear is that reimbursement of drug use would become enormously expensive. A Congressional proposal was made in 1987 to have Medicare help pay for the drug costs of just those elderly with drug costs above $500 per year.[58] Roughly 20 percent of Medicare recipients have such expenses; the proposal would have required them to make a 20 percent copayment. The proposal was estimated by HHS to have a price tag of $5.8 billion, although the Congressional Budget office estimated its cost at $850 million.[59] HCFA-HHS' concern is that availability of assistance would lead to overprescribing.

The economics of this issue are both a matter of short-term versus long-term savings and of different accounts being affected. The argument that can be made for reimbursement of outpatient prescription drug use is that its positive health effects will result in a net decline in medical care expenditures for the elderly. This is because some hospitalizations may be avoided, or patients may be hospitalized for less serious conditions. These are long-term savings, and really are savings in the sense of reductions in the rate of increase: Medicare expenditures are likely to keep growing as the number of elderly continues to increase, to prescription drug based "savings" will cut into this increase.

On the other hand, reimbursement of outpatient prescription drug use would definitely create increased Medicare outlays. HCFA would have to pay for drug purchases, as well as for administrative expenses. Even if decreased medical costs eventually show up in the form of adjusted DRGs, interim Medicare expenditures would be increased.

An intermediate approach to drug expenses would be to treat them as an addition to Part B SMI expenses. This would require an increase in the SMI premium. Expenses not covered through premiums would have to be made up through general revenues, like other SMI expenses. The increased premium would be an additional burden on the elderly, but would provide funding which would cover the expenses of the elderly with very high outpatient drug costs. It would also avoid adding another expense to the Medicare trust fund.

Another intermediate approach has to do with the prescribing of generic name over brand name drugs. The biomedical equivalent of brand name drugs cost a fraction of their price, so this could have a major effect on the drug outlays of the elderly.[60] In 1984, Congress passed legislation which permitted the prescribing of biomedical equivalents. As of 1985, generics comprised approximately 20 percent of the prescription market and 35 percent of all prescriptions written.[61]

The argument is made that the rate of substitution could be even greater. The drug industry, through the Pharmaceutical Manufacturing Association, has lobbied hard against generics. As a result, state laws often make it cumbersome for doctors to allow substitution. Where forms must be filled out to permit substitution, doctors lean toward brand name drugs.[62] Drug companies have used direct mail contracts with pharmacists and advertising with physicians (detailmen, convention displays, medical magazine inserts) to encourage use of brand name drugs.[63] And pharmacists have an incentive to dispense brand name drugs, because they receive higher percentage markups on them than generic name drugs.[64]

The brand name vs. generic name drug battle has been going on for a number of years. Greater use of generics would increase the palatability of government underwriting of outpatient prescription drugs. The Congressional Budget Office has estimated that incentives to use generics would cut spending 10 percent under the Congressional proposal discussed earlier.[65]

C. MENTAL HEALTH CARE AND THE ELDERLY

This section discusses the provision of mental health care services to the noninstitutionalized elderly, or, more properly, the absence of utilization of such services by persons over 65. While part of the explanation for this can be found in deficiencies in reimbursement policies covering outpatient mental health treatment of older persons[66], the problem is more complex than that.

Only 4-5 percent of community mental health center patients are over 65, while psychiatrists in private practice spend only 2 percent of their time with elderly patients.[67] These are surprisingly low figures considering the increased prevalence of organiz mental disorders and the risk of depression associated with age.[68]

Several explanations can be offered for under-utilization of mental health care services. A primary explanation is ageist behavior on the parts of general practitioners treating the elderly. Since the elderly are much more likely to use a general practitioner than a mental health professional even where treatment of a mental health symptom is desired[69], the attitudes of the general practitioners are of critical importance. Ageist beliefs include views that decline and deterioration in functioning are natural and that mental disorders among the elderly are not "true" illnesses, meriting institutionalization rather than treatment.[70] This ties in with a belief that the elderly are not good candidates for therapy, especially psychotherapy because of arteriosclerosis or senility.[71]

The elderly are also responsible for underutilization of mental health services. The attitudes of the elderly toward mental illness, combined with a fear of institutionalization, can lead to underreporting of mental health problems, including depression.[72] A survey of 88 elderly senior center participants revealed that 63 percent would not reveal symptoms of depression to any health professional, preferring instead to keep this information to themselves or to reveal it to a family member or friend.[73]

Finally, the shortage of trained geriatric mental health specialists and the limited ability of general practitioners to identify mental health problems reduces the utility of the medical community to deal with mental problems of the elderly.[74] For example, elderly patients may exhibit somatoform disorders, presenting physicians with complaints that do not seem to have a physical basis. Somatization often reflects an underlying depressive disorder, but the tendency of general practitioners would be to attempt to treat the complaint described by the elderly person.[75] A study of 140 elderly patients waiting in physicians' offices revealed failure to diagnose mental disorders, false diagnosis of other patients as depressed, and a failure to refer these patients to mental health professionals.[76]

Dealing with the problem requires two sets of solutions. First, as mentioned above, reimbursement under Medicare and Medicaid is inadequate and should be improved upon. Second, even if funds were available, the following needs to be done so that the elderly know to avail themselves of mental health services and medical professionals know how to deal with them. This involves increased geriatric training in the mental health profession, changed public attitudes toward mental health in the elderly (distinguishing between aging and mental disorders), and education of general practitioners to correctly diagnose (and refer) mental health problems of the elderly.[77]

D. TRANSPORTATION PROBLEMS OF THE ELDERLY

What will be said here about the transportation problems of the elderly to a certain extent parallels the comments about housing needs of the elderly in Chapter Seven. There are really two different transportation problems: 1) problems of the middle income elderly, generally those who live in suburban and rural areas, and own automobiles; and 2) problems of the low income and physically handicapped elderly, generally those who live in urban areas.

1. Personal Mobility and the Suburban and Rural Elderly

As is discussed in Chapter Seven, over 70 percent of the elderly own their own homes. In addition, a growing proportion of persons over age 65 live in suburban areas.[78] This coincides with the growth in the numbers of the elderly who are over 75 to present transportation problems for these elderly: although most own cars, they may be reluctant to use them, and no public transportation alternative is available.

As is discussed in the next part of this section, there are reasons for the elderly and the disabled to avoid public transportation even when it is available. The decline in public transit ridership and services over the years has been associated with the growth in the use of private automobiles, which in turn was associated with greater residential dispersion and distance from traditional central areas of the city.[79] The result is that persons age 65 and older are more dependent on private vehicle transportation than the under 65 population. Without private cars, social costs will be higher and the elderly's quality of life will be reduced.[80] For the suburban elderly, the automobile is the lifeline to both needed services (trips to the doctor's office, the grocery store, the pharmacist, etc.) and to continued membership in the community (to social events, to the homes of friends, to church, etc.).

The problem for these elderly comes in the form of declining abilities to operate motor vehicles after age 65. According to the National Institute on Aging, "motor vehicle accidents are the most common cause of accidental death among persons in the 65 to 74 age group."[81] The ability of an elderly person to drive "may be impaired by such age-related changes as increased sensitivity to glare, poor adaptation to dark, diminished coordination, and slower reaction time."[82] This is controversial to the extent that it implies age-based changes in the ability of the elderly to exercise a basic privilege in American society, that of being able to operate a car. A study sponsored by the American Automobile Association ("AAA") Foundation for Traffic Safety concluded that older drivers show a wide range of capabilities, with limitations more directly associated with physical mobility than with chronological age.[83]

Statistics concerning the traffic accident and fatality potential of the elderly are mixed. Per capita involvement of older persons in fatal accidents is greater than the per capita involvement of those of middle age, but less than for the population 65 and older continues to grow, so does the share of involvement in fatal accidents by the elderly, but the rate of increase is not as fast as their increase in the population share.[85] Barakat and Mulinazzi conclude that there is "convincing evidence" that "the skills necessary for safe driving begin to deteriorate around age 55, perhaps dramatically so after age 75."[86] The AAA study found that at about age 75 older drivers tend to recognize a deterioration of some skills important to safe driving may be justifiable.[87] According to the Highway Users Federation, older drivers suffer from reduced vision, alertness, range of motion and risk evaluation and decision-making skills. However, they compensate by being more risk-averse and more law-abiding, self-imposing driving limitations under hazardous circumstances.[88]

Several types of solutions are available. First, the paratransit alternatives described in the next part of this section could be imported from urban to suburban areas. Given the low density of population and long distances between elderly residences and destinations, this could be extremely expensive.

A second alternative is what the elderly do informally: rely on friends and children to transport them. This is generally becoming a less viable option as a result of smaller family sizes and increases in geographic distances between parents and their children. A growing phenomenon is that persons age 75-80 have children who are age 55 and above and thus subject to their own mobility limitations. A formalized version of this alternative is to make transportation services part of home health care, and this is provided for under existing legislation.[89]

A more elaborate approach would be the implementation of technical solutions. These are of two principal types. First, traffic and highway systems could be redesigned in more "user-friendly" fashion. Second, cars could be redesigned to be made easier to drive for physically limited people.[90] According to the National Highway Safety Advisory Committee there are no programs at the federal or state level that are concerned exclusively or even primarily with helping older people maintain independent mobility.[91] Traffic and highway system redesign would be very expensive, as those systems are designed primarily for work-trip community and business transportation uses by younger drivers. Car redesign might be more viable, paralleling work done for physically handicapped drivers. Of course, passive restraints such as airbags and automatic seat belts would be valuable as "crash attenuators" for the elderly, who are more significantly affected by frontal collisions than are younger drivers and passengers.[92]

2. Transportation Access for the Urban Handicapped and Low Income Elderly

This group of the elderly presents a very different set of transportation problems. Few, if any, can afford to operate an automobile, making them highly dependent on public transportation.[93] And, although public transportation is more available in urban areas, significant barriers to its use by these elderly exist. These "transportation disadvantaged" are served mostly by taxis, school buses, personal transportation, and special services sytems.[94]

Urban public transportation (buses and rail rapid-transit systems) are designed to be responsive to the needs of work-trip commuters. A first problem is design feature, i.e., having to step up into buses and use stairways or escalators to subways and elevated trains. These features not only create problems for the physically impaired but also demand that passengers move quickly, a problem for many of the elderly as well as the handicapped.[95]

A second barrier to the use of public transportation by the elderly is route flexibility. The elderly, especially those with mobility problems, require close to door-to-door service. In addition to problems created by walking distances, waiting for service also limits the usefulness of public transportation to the elderly. Inconvenient scheduling and fear of crime make the elderly less inclined to use public transportation.[96]

The major alternative to public transportation systems in serving the transportation disadvantaged is the development of paratransit services. These can be publicly run or publicly compensated, as in "Dial-a-Ride" services. They can also be privately managed, as is the case with "Senior Citizens Buses" provided by churches, community groups, and senior citizen centers. This alternative generally amounts to transportation of the elderly and the physically impaired by school buses and vans.

Paratransit services correct some of the problems described for public transportation but create others. The cost to the low income elderly is minimal, since the public services are subsidized and private services are free. They also provide door-to-door access. The quality of paratransit service, however, is inferior to that of traditional public transit. In addition, many paratransit services provide little advantage over public transit in assisting elderly and handicapped passengers when transferring to and from vehicles.[97] The cost of publicly-funded paratransit services is a concern to municipalities. There are also problems of duplication of effort among governmental programs, franchise conflicts, labor requirements problems, and users' restrictions concerns.[98] Although such systems provide door-to-door access, limited numbers of vehicles available means users must wait long periods of time to be picked up, requiring pre-planning on their part. The result is that the elderly in urban areas, like their counterparts in suburbia, rely on relatives and neighbors, as well as limiting the number of their trips.[99]

Possibilities for solutions are more limited for this group of the elderly. A hidden dimension of the problem is that the Reagan Administration has placed a lower priority on urban mass transit than had previous administrations. As has been the case with heating assistance, discussed in Chapter Seven, mass transit's political appeal has declined as Congress and the public have become less concerned about energy costs. Public transportation systems, operating at deficits anyway, are less capable of adapting to the special needs of the elderly and the physically impaired. The elderly may be helped by the activities of militant handicapped rights groups, which have sued municipalities to provide wheelchair lifts and who generally regard dial-a-ride programs as an insult.

NOTES TO CHAPTER SIX

1. Meg Delaney, "Who Will Pay for Retirement Care? *Personnel Journal* (March 1987), p. 86.
2. Robert Newcomer, Juanita Wood, and Andrea Sankar, "Medicare Prospective Payment: Anticipated Effect on Hospitals, Other Community Agencies, and Families," *Journal of Health Politics, Policy, and Law* (1985), v. 10, p. 279. (Hereinafter, "Newcomer, et al.")
3. Newcomer, et al., p. 279.
4. U.S. House of Representatives, Select Committee on Aging, Subcommittee on Health and Long-Term Care, *The Attempted Dismantling of the Medicare Home Health Care Benefit*, 99th Congress (Report, 1986), p. 3. (Hereinafter, "House Committee Report, 1986")
5. House Committee Report, 1986, pp. 4-5.
6. Roger Schwartz and Jane Perkins, "The Omnibus Budget Reconciliation Act of 1987: Legislative Changes in Medicaid," *Clearinghouse Review* (April 1988), v. 21, p. 1302.
7. Newcomer, et al., p. 278.
8. Newcomer, et al., p. 278.
9. Newcomer, et al., p. 278.
10. House Committee Report, 1986, p. 6.
11. William G. Weissert, "Hard Choices: Targeting Long-Term Care to the 'At Risk' Aged," *Journal of Health Politics, Policy, and Law* (Fall 1986), v. 11, p. 465.
12. Weissert, pp. 476, 479.
13. See the examples provided in the House Committee Report, 1986 at p. 61, e.g., a 65 year old diabetic with several circulatory problems and gangrene of the toe who was denied daily wound care as not medically necessary (three times per week was deemed appropriate) and who was subsequently rehospitalized for amputation of her lower leg.
14. House Committee Report, 1986, pp. 26-27.
15. House Committee Report, 1986, p. 69.
16. House Committee Report, 1986, p. 69.
17. House Committee Report, 1986, pp. 58-59, reporting results of a survey of home health care agencies conducted by the National Association for Home Care.
18. See, Chapter Four, n. 88 and accompanying test.
19. Newcomer, et al., pl. 276.
20. Weissert, p. 476.

21. See, House Committee Report, 1986, pp. 82-85, citing a 1985 study conducted for the National Association for Home Care.

22. However, Congressional support long antedates the entry of for-profit groups into the field. See notes 4 and 5 and accompanying text, above. The American Association of Retired Persons also supports home health care. See, House Committee Report, 1986, pp. 5-6.

23. Bette S. Hill, C. Jean Blaser and Pamela W. Balmer, "Profits Vs. Nonprofit Contracts for Home Health Care," *Policy Studies Review* (February 1986), v. 5, p. 589. (Hereinafter, "Hill, et al.")

24. Hill, et al., p. 589.

25. Hill, et al., p. 589.

26. Hill, et al., p. 589.

27. Hill, et al., p. 590.

28. Hill, et al., p. 590. Presumably, if a PPS-type Formula were applied, the results would be reversed.

29. Hill, et al., p. 596.

30. House Committee Report, 1986, p. 58.

31. Newcomer, et al., pp. 276-277. Hospital based home health agencies accounted for 15 percent of home health agencies certified by Medicare prior to PPS, a number expected to grow.

32. Weisert, p. 463.

33. Relaney, p. 86.

34. House Committee Report, 1986, pp. 15, 38.

35. Schwartz and Perkins, p. 1302.

36. House Committee Report, 1986, p. 37.

37. Schwartz and Perkins, p. 1302.

38. Schwartz and Perkins, p. 1302.

39. Weissert, p. 465.

40. Weissert, p. 465.

41. Weissert, p. 476.

42. Schwartz and Perkins, p. 1302.

43. See, House Committee Report, 1986, pp. 39-47, for a summary of HCFA regulations restricting the home health care benefit.

44. Weissert, p. 477.

45. Earle W. Lingle, Jr., Kenneth W. Kirk, and William R. Kelly, "The Impact of Outpatient Drug Benefits on the Use and Costs of Health Care Services for the Elderly," *Inquiry* (Fall 1987), v. 24, p. 203. (Hereinafter, "Lingle, et al.")

46. Delaney, p. 85. See also, House Committee Report, 1986, p. 14. The most frequently occuring conditions in 1981 were arthritis (46 percent), hypertension (38 percent), hearing impairments and heart conditions (28 percent each), sinusitis (18 percent), visual impairments and orthopedic impairments (14 percent each), arteriosclerosis (10 percent), and diabetes (8 percent).

47. Julie Kosterlitz, "Prescribing Pain," *National Journal* (July 18, 1987), p. 1846.

48. Kosterlitz, p. 1846.

49. Kosterlitz, pp. 1846, 1848. Between 1977 and 1983, there was a limited program of drug payment ceilings, which was suspended and has not been replaced.

50. KJosterlitz, p. 1845.

51. Lingle, et al., p. 204.

52. Lingle, et al., p. 204.

53. Lingle, et al., p. 204.

54. Lingle, et al., pp. 209-210.

55. Lingle, et al., p. 210.

56. Lingle, et al., p. 210.

57. Lingle, et al., p. 204.
58. Kosterlitz, p. 1848.
59. Kosterlitz, p. 1848.
60. U.S. House of Representatives, Select Committee on Aging, Subcommittee on Housing and Consumer Interests, *High Drug Costs and Older Americans: A Prescription for the Future*, 99th Congress (Hearings, 1986), p. 73. (Hereinafter, "Hearings, 1986")
61. Kosterlitz, p. 1847.
62. Kosterlitz, p. 1847. See also, Hearings, 1986, p. 47.
63. See, Kosterlitz, p. 1847. See also, *Forbes* (June 18, 1986), p. 50 (campaign by drug manufacturers to discourage them from prescribing generic drugs: one compnay, Sandoz Pharmaceuticals, was censured by the Food and Drug Administration for "flagrant, repeated and willful" violations of drug marketing regulations).
64. Kosterlitz, p. 1847.
65. Kosterlitz, p. 1848.
66. Howard M. Waxman, "Community Mental Health Care for the Elderly—A Look at the Obstacles," *Public Health Reports* (May-June 1986), v. 101, p. 294.
67. Waxman, p. 294.
68. Waxman, p. 294.
69. Waxman, pp. 295-296.
70. Waxman, p. 295. See also, C.M. Gaitz, "Barriers to the Delivery of Psychiatric Services to the Elderly," *Gerontologist* (June 1974), v. 14, pp. 210-214.
71. Waxman, p. 295. See also, E. Mumford and H.J. Schlesinger, "Economic Discrimination Against Elderly Psychiatric Patients Under Medicare," *Hospital Community Psychiatry* (June 1985), v. 36, pp. 587-589.
72. Waxman, p. 295.
73. Waxman, p. 295. Of the persons surveyed, 29 percent showed mild to moderate symptoms of depression and 17 percent were cognitive impaired, according to rating scales completed by the participants. Yet only 3 percent had seen a psychiatrist or psychologist in the previous year.
74. Waxman, pp. 296-297.
75. Waxman, p. 297.
76. Waxman, p. 296. Of the 140, 32 displayed some evidence of mental disorder, 18 with depression, 8 with an organic impairment, and 6 with both. Of these, 21 were diagnosed as depressed. However, the group with the lowest scores on tests was just as likely to be diagnosed as depressed. None of the persons had seen a mental health professional in the past year, and only one was seeing his doctor for a complaint even remotely resembling a mental health problem (difficulty in sleeping).
77. Waxman, pp. 298-299.
78. M.H. Hoeflich, "Housing the Elderly in a Changing America: Innovation Through Private Sector Initiative," *University of Illinois Law Review* (1985), v. 1985, pp. 3-4.
79. Sami Jamil Barakat and Thomas E. Mulinazzi, "Elderly Drivers: Problems and Needs for Research," *Transportation Quarterly* (April 1987), v. 41, p. 194.
80. Highway Users Federation and Automotive Safety Foundation, *Workshop on Highway Mobility and Safety of Older Drivers and Pedestrians* (Washington: Highway Users Federation, 1985), cited by Barakat and Mulinazzi, p. 194.
81. Cited by Barakat and Mulinazzi, p. 202.
82. Barakat and Mulinazzi, p. 202.
83. AAA Foundation for Traffic Safety, *Needs and Problems of Older Drivers* (Falls Church: AAA, 1985), cited by Barakat and Mulinazzi, p. 202.

84. Barakat and Mulinazzi, p. 197. This data reflects the fact that the age group most prone to accidents and fatalities consists of persons, especially males, under 25.

85. Barakat and Mulinazzi, p. 197.

87. Cited by Barakat and Mulinazzi, p. 202.

88. Cited by Barakat and Mulinazzi, p. 197.

89. See, Weissert, pp. 463-464. Transportation is included in the array of services which can be provided under Medicaid.

90. Barakat and Mulinazzi, p. 201.

91. Barakat and Mulinazzi, p. 201.

92. Barakat and Mulinazzi, p. 204. The elderly are more prone to bone breakage (e.g., hipbones), which has serious consequences for future mobility.

93. Joe King, Jr., "Adequacy of Transportation in Minority Communities for Handicapped, Low Income and Elderly Groups," *Transportation Quarterly* (April 1987), v. 41, pp. 247-248.

94. King, p. 247.

95. King, p. 249.

96. King, pp. 249, 253.

97. King, 248.

98. King, p. 249.

99. King, pp. 253-254.

7 Special Issues

This chapter considers three major concerns or issues affecting the elderly. In most cases they cut across all three of the resolutions for debate, although they may be of greater relevance for a particular topic. Some of these issues may be distinct affirmative cases on one of the topics, e.g., age discrimination on the retirement security topic. All of the areas discussed below are affected by the systems of health care, transfer payments, and custodial care discussed in Chapters Three through Five and, in turn, affect the quality of services for the elderly provided by those systems.

A. ELDER ABUSE

Elder abuse is a problem which has begun to receive national attention in the past few years. A basic document in the literature on Elder Abuse is the 1981 report of the House Select Committees on Aging.[1] Two other basic documents relied on by authors are a law review article by Katheryn Katz in the Journal of Family Law[2] and a study by Block and Sinnott in 1979.[3]

1. Dimensions and Causes of the Problem

Several studies have been conducted on elder abuse; however, conclusions and generalizations from such data must be guarded against, because of differing methodologies and criteria used, varying state definitions of abuse, and the probability of underreporting.[4]

As was the case in the 1970s with child abuse and spousal abuse, estimates of the extent of the problem are problematic. The 1981 House Select Committee estimated that there are one million cases of elder abuse per year, but it also comments that only one in six such cases is reported.[5] State adult protective services prepare annual reports listing numbers of reported and confirmed cases. As was (and is) the case with child abuse and spousal abuse, there seems little doubt that there is an extensive problem, its precise dimensions being difficult to ascertain. The issue of underreporting is linked closely to solutions to the problem, and the consequences of those solutions, and is discussed later in this section.

"Elder Abuse" refers to several different kinds of maltreatment, and state law definitions vary. Four types of abuse and neglect are generally included under this heading: 1) physical abuse of the elderly; 2) emotional abuse; 3) neglect (failure to provide adequate food, shelter, medical care, and other necessities); and 4) financial exploitation. A Florida Department of Health and Rehabilitative Services study in 1985 reported on 22,485 allegations of adult abuse, neglect, or exploitation, of which 56 percent were confirmed. Of the reports, 52 percent involved neglect, 18 percent physical abuse, 15 percent emotional abuse, and 6 percent financial exploitation.[6]

While elder abuse occurs within nursing homes and other long-term care facilities, it also occurs in private residences, the abuse being inflicted by a relative or other care taker. The Florida study cited above found that 43 percent of the reported cases of abuse took place in private homes.[7] This presents different issues for solutions. A principal benefit to be claimed for improved nursing home care is decreased maltreatment (neglect as well as physical and emotional abuse) of the residents. However, dealing with abuse by relatives raises the issue of possible institutionalization of the victim, which may be resisted by the victim and which would expose the victim to the problems of nursing home care described earlier.

Three primary causes can be identified for elder abuse. With regard to nursing home abuse, the problem can in large part be traced to the problems of nursing homes discussed earlier, particularly the tendency of proprietary nursing home operations to cut corners on labor costs, resulting in the hiring of low paid and poorly trained attendants, hiring them in numbers minimally sufficient to meet state regulations and skimping on professional supervisors to oversee them.

For both nursing homes and private residential abuse a second, and in some ways more troubling, cause has to do with the care needs of the elderly victim. A consistent finding is that victims tend to be disproportionately over seventy-five or women.[8] Elder abuse seems to be correlated to the amount of care needed and the degree of emotional, physical, and financial stress of caring for the dependent elderly.[9] While the stresses of caring for the "heavy care" elderly adult can create problems for nursing homes, nursing homes also tend to avoid such patients because of cost efficiency reasons as was discussed previously. However, such stresses are less easily avoided by relatives. And, as life expectancy increases, more and more middle-aged adult children will be asked to assume responsibility for their parents, just as those children are nearing retirement age themselves.[10] Hence, elder abuse can be expected to expand significantly as baby boomers start retiring in the 21st century, a factor possibly aggravated by the smaller family size of retirees available to care for them.[11] The problems discussed previously of limited nursing home capacity, preference for private-pay patients, and Medicaid reimbursements may in turn aggravate the problem by increasing care stress within nursing homes catering to low-income, Medicaid-reimbursed patients. In addition, the increasing number of low and moderate income elderly who will be unable to locate nursing home care when they or their relatives attempt to place them in a nursing home will increase emotional, physical, and financial stresses on the relatives who will then be asked to take care of them. Such relatives, usually with children, are likely to be of low or moderate income themselves and may not be equipped to care for the elderly, especially those of advanced years who are no longer able to care for their basic needs.

A final cause of elder abuse has to do with stereotypes about persons over age 65. This is discussed further in this section under the heading of SOLUTIONS, with regard to the effects of adult protective services ("APS") and involuntary provision of such services. "Ageism" is the product of social beliefs about the mental and physical capabilities of the elderly. There is an implicit assumption that infirmities associated with aging are "natural,"[12] as well as a presumption of incompetence on the part of the elderly.[13] This results in a dehumanizing process with regard to the view of the elderly adopted by their caretakers (nursing home staff and relatives) and government social and protective service agencies mandated to act on behalf of the elderly: they are viewed as infantile in thought and behavior.[14] Maltreatment of the elderly—whether physical abuse, emotional abuse, neglect, or (to a lesser extent) financial exploitation—proceeds from a beginning rationalization that the elderly are mentally incompetent, less human than their caretakers, and that the caretaker is justified in his or her actions. Some authors note the similarity in attitudes toward the institutionalized or dependent elderly and other members of the "therapeutic state," persons who are too mentally incompetent to ask for services voluntarily: the mentally ill, the mentally retarded, juvenile and defective delinquents, drug abusers, alcoholics, sex offenders, and other wards of public guardians, all of whom are seen as socially deviant.[15]

2. Dealing with Elder Abuse

Most, but not all, states deal with elder abuse through a combination of mandatory reporting laws and adult protective services. Most of this legislation has been enacted within the past ten years and there have been few court cases dealing with the issues created by such laws. States which have not enacted reporting laws for elder abuse or adult protective services rely on more traditional guardianship laws.[16] Elder abuse has not been dealt with through legislation by the federal government. The states, in their traditional role of providing social services, have been the exclusive agencies dealing with the problem. The remainder of this section examines the current status of mandatory reporting laws and adult protective services, as well as public guardianship operations. The following section considers criticisms of these systems, as well as suggestions for reform. One fact to be borne in mind is that mandatory reporting statutes and statutes creating adult protective services were both modeled on child abuse legislation, which in most states had been passed into law somewhat earlier than elder abuse legislation.[17] This modeling is itself the subject of criticism, which is discussed in the next section. The point to be made is that legislators appear to have applied most of the same assumptions made about children and child abuse to the elderly and elder abuse in the laws passed.

39 states require the reporting of in-home adult or elder abuse.[18] Reporting laws specify professionals required to report elder abuse: in most state laws, reporting is mandatory.[19] Generally, medical professionals are required to report, but some states require a few other professionals to report suspected cases of elder abuse: accountants, social workers, law enforcement officials, coroners, and attorneys.[20] Failure to report by a statutorily designated person is punishable by fines and imprisonment.[21]

Adults who are physically or emotionally abused or neglected include others besides the elderly. Some state's laws are not age-specific and include abuse of the mentally and physically disabled, of whatever age.[22] Even in these states, the elderly are lumped in with persons considered (like children) incapable of asking for assistance, with the state acting in parens patriae for the elderly.[23] Elder abuse laws are distinct from domestic violence laws, which appear to make different assumptions about the victim, even though the same or related state agencies may be involved in dealing with abuse.[24]

The standard for deciding when a statutorily-defined professional must report in most states is a fairly minimal one, that of having a reasonable cause to believe an incident of abuse or neglect has taken place.[25] States do not have central registries for maintaining reports of abuse.[26] In most states, the reporting person is immune from civil suit.[27] However, confidentiality of communications, principally between victims and medical personnel, is not provided and is admissible at administrative hearings.[28]

Incidents of abuse or neglect are to be followed by an initial investigation by the state's adult protective services or social service agency: based on this report, a recommendation of protective services for the victim or a referral to a law enforcement agency can be made.[29] "Protective services" can be a euphemism for institutionalization: most states stipulate that the services to be provided include home care and are to be the least restrictive of freedom available and that institutionalization will occur only when there is no alternative.[30] Thorny issues are presented by two situations: 1) where there is an administrative hearing, confidentiality of the investigative report and the information needs of the protective service agency conflict with the privacy rights and defense needs of the caretaker accused of victimization; 2) where the victim refuses assistance, the state's role in protecting the elderly conflicts with the individual's right of independence and self-determination.[31]

States with mandatory reporting laws for elder abuse generally also have adult protective service agencies. Although one would seem to go hand-in-hand with the other, this has not always been the case: adult protective services have been created as specialized agencies separate from other state social service agencies to deal with elder abuse. In fact, one issue concerning elder abuse has been the need to separate protective services from broader state services to avoid conflicts of interest between the state and the elderly victim. The protective services agency should act as the surrogate for the victim who cannot (and in some cases, will not) ask for assistance, while the social services agency is to be a provider of care, therapy, or rehabilitation.[32] In the 1978 Mary Northern case in Tennessee, a conflict arose because the Department of Human Services was to make decisions both as to whether services should be requested involuntarily for the "victim" (the protective services role) and as to whether those services should be made available (the social services role).[33]

Administrative hearings are held by adult protective services agencies to determine the proper course of action to be taken with regard to the elderly person. There are wide variations among states as to notice of hearing, representation by a lawyer at the hearing, presence of the elderly victim at the hearing (especially where the victim is considered incompetent and has resisted care), and the standard of evidence (a mere preponderance, clear and convincing, etc.) to be met at the hearing.[34] There are two different scenarios for such hearings. The first is an adversarial setting, where a caretaker is accused of abuse or neglect, with the protective services agency acting as the elderly accuser's surrogate. In the second setting, as in the Mary Northern case, the surrogate is being resisted by the elderly person, who is either the "victim" of his or her own neglect, or who (for a variety of reasons) does not wish to be removed from a setting in which he or she has been abused or neglected. The first situation creates due process concerns as regards the person accused of victimizing the elderly person, while the second creates concerns as to privacy rights of the elderly person. A third situation is a variation on either of the first two situations: an emergency situation requires immediate action by the agency. In this situation, intervention by the state is compulsory, generally on a showing that there is a substantial, immediate risk of death.[35] While it is generally the case that it is the state agency which is seeking to act on an emergency basis, in at least one case advocates for homeless elderly persons successfully argued that the state was required to provide emergency services over a resistance to extend such services by the state.[36]

The area of operation by adult protective services which has generated the most controversy is involuntary protective services. 15 states permit protective services agencies to provide services on such a basis as an alternative to civil commitment or public guardianship proceedings.[37] Hearings to determine whether protective services should be provided on an involuntary basis were criticized by the 1978 Presidential Commission on Mental Health as providing fewer procedural due process protections than comparable guardianship and involuntary commitment laws. Where an abused adult refuses protective services, the state begins incompetency proceedings, at which due process protections are limited.[38] A study of state agency proceedings concluded that the proceedings themselves contributed to infantilization of the elderly, as well as implying the failure of preexisting criminal and civil laws.[39] Of course, the agency may start proceedings before involuntary services are provided: the legal status of the person as a result of such a proceeding is no different than that of a child.[40]

States without involuntary protective service statutes rely on traditional public guardianship and civil commitment proceedings. In practice, courts tend to blur the distinction between the two, treating them as if they were the same entity. The controlling U.S. Supreme Court case in the area as regards procedural due process is *Mathews v. Eldridge*, which held that a recipient of disability benefits under the Social Security Act was not entitled to a hearing prior to his termination, Justice Powell reasoning that the disabled have alternative sources of assistance and that medical assessments are "sharply focused and easily documented."[41] Courts interpret *Mathews* to tolerate state laws covering guardianship and civil commitment which are inclusive in scope and provide truncated due process protections.[42]

3. Criticism and Recommendations for Change

This section examines criticisms of mandatory reporting statutes and adult protective services, and then looks at ideas for changes in the paradigm adopted by the states in dealing with elder abuse.

An initial criticism of reporting laws is that they have had no impact. The assumption behind reporting laws is that the elderly will not self-report, either because they are incompetent and unable to do so, or fear retaliation by their their caretakers and will not do so (a third source of reluctance is that of fear of institutionalization, which cuts against involuntary protective services).[43] However, reporting statutes have not caused an increase in the number of cases of elder abuse being reported: 95 percent of reports are by the elderly victim.[44] Other reporting is done by nonprofessionals—friends. relatives, neighbors—not designated professionals.[45]

The lack of efficacy of reporting laws may be due in part to the lack of funding for protective services following up on reports of abuse. In 1984. approximately $2.90 per elderly person was spend on protective services.[46]

Like child abuse reporting laws, mandatory reporting laws for elderly abuse may be characterized as "sake of appearance" legislation.[47] Given the absence of commitment of the state (beyond passing a cosmetic law), there is likely to be little compliance with the law. One early advocate of adult protective services, James Bergman, has commented that reporting laws without adequate funding for follow up services are of no help and may do much harm.[48]

As was noted above, the elderly may have their own reasons for not reporting abuse. Fear of forced removal from their homes or loss of independence through appointment of guardians may cause the elderly to tolerate at least some level of abusive treatment.[49] One critic has even suggested that knowledge that medical personnel are required to report suspected cases of abuse may discourage the elderly from seeking medical treatment.[50]

In addition to being of no effect, mandatory reporting laws have been criticized on two separate grounds, that they contribute to ageism, and that they preclude more effective measures against elder abuse. As discussed above, ageism is a cause of elder abuse, stereotyped beliefs about the elderly dehumanizing them and permitting rationalization or justification of the victimizer. Ironically, mandatory reporting laws are argued to contribute to such stereotyping. Age-based definitions in reporting laws confirm stereotypes about the elderly being incompetent.[51] Some states make protective services available to inform adults, regardless of age, avoiding the age-based definition problem. However, this groups the infirm elderly with the disabled and the mentally ill. It is an open question whether society will discriminate between the infirm elderly and other persons of advanced years in its stereotyping, especially if such laws are used primarily with regard to the elderly.

The second criticism of reporting laws is that they preclude more effective measures against elder abuse. This is consistent with the view that reporting laws are only "sake of appearance" legislation. Reporting laws by themselves require no additional expenditures by the state. Of course, as originally envisioned by advocates for the aged, reporting laws were to be only part of a system of dealing with elder abuse.[52] The reality is that states passed elder abuse reporting laws and, in most cases, have done little else, unless prodded by a large senior citizen constituency. A reporting law on the books can be pointed to as evidence that the legislature has responded to the problem.

An opportunity costs theory of legislative decision-making posits that politicians have a finite amount of political and social as well as economic capital available: acting in response to a particular problem subtracts from capital available to deal with remaining social concerns. In the case of elder abuse, advocates were successful in gaining passage of mandatory reporting laws. Having caused political and social costs in this regard, advocates are unlikely to gain passage of additional measures within the same area of social concern. While reporting laws identify the problem, they have tended to preclude the development of services to combat the problem.[53] To some extent, programs to deal with elder abuse are also affected by state government budget cuts, responding to the loss of federal revenue under the Reagan Administration, with social service positions being likely candidates for elimination.

Adult protective services have been criticized on several grounds as well, including contributing to ageism. As alluded to above, the chief areas of concern are those of due process and privacy rights of alleged victimizers being reported and of the rights of personal independence and self-determination of the aged being ignored by involuntary protective services and civil commitment procedures.

Modification of adult protective services brings into focus two separate but related debates about legislativemodels for dealing with elder abuse: 1) whether the model for elder abuse statutes should be the child abuse or domestic violence-spousal abuse statutes; and 2) whether the focus of elder abuse statutes should be on the victim or the victimizer.

As discussed above, the initial model for elder abuse statutes was child abuse legislation. Outside of convenience for legislators, who had just passed child protection legislation in the previous year or two, the analogy between elder abuse and child abuse has at least some surface merit: like children, it was argued, elders are often incapable of reporting abuse and are at the mercy of their caretakers. In addition, legislatures have been receptive to the position that society has a protectible interest in its children: it can be argued that it has a similar interest in its retired adults. Of course, highlighting such similarities has been argued to promote ageism, infantilizing the elderly.[54]

The position that the proper analogy should be between elder abuse and spousal abuse, not child abuse, stems from the attack on the presumption of incompetency which attaches to the victim in child abuse, but not to the victim in spousal abuse. Like child abuse laws (and elder abuse laws) spousal abuse laws focus on the vulnerability of the victim, noting his or her dependency on others for care. However, spousal abuse laws make no presumptions about the competency of the victim, nor do they render services involuntarily. Social responses, through shelters, counseling, and crises intervention, emphasize self-sufficiency for the victim and respect for the victim's civil rights. Critics of the child abuse analogy argue that elder abuse laws should emulate domestic violence legislation in avoiding independence and respect for the rights of the victim.[55]

The spousal abuse analogy is not without its problems however. Laws patterned on domestic violence statutes could still contribute to ageism (even though domestic violence laws generally are sex-neutral in terminology. they are generally thought of as "battered women" laws). It should be noted that the principal weapon in the arsenal of domestic abuse laws is the order of protection, which can be entered on an ex parte basis. Finally, it should also be noted that the support services for victims of spousal abuse—shelters, counseling, crises intervention—have generally been privately funded and operated, and have only recently developed liaison with law enforcement officials. While there are private foundations which provide guardianship services for the elderly,[56] care of the elderly victim has most often been provided by public social services agencies.

Whether elder abuse legislation should focus on the victim or the victimizer is also a concern. Involuntary protective services legislation tends to focus on the victim of abuse or neglect, especially as the elderly person may be the "victim" of his or her own conduct.[57] Remedies modeled on domestic violence statutes focus instead on caretakers alleged to have victimized the elderly.[58]

The argument for focusing on aid to victims is based on two interrelated positions. First, elder abuse laws are primarily social welfare-directed laws, not criminal laws. Their goal is improving the situation of the victim: penalizing the victimizer is ancillary to this purpose. It can be responded that this is not entirely true, particularly if the alleged abuser is a nursing home employee. Second, it is argued that prosecuting abusers worsens the problem, as they may retaliate against the victim. If the abuser has been the victim's sole means of support, prosecution means the victim will be institutionalized.[59]

The argument for focusing on the victimizer rather than the victim stems from the position that the adult protective services agency's role should be that of surrogate for the victim. The agency, acting for the victim, should center its attention on the conduct of the person allegedly responsible for abuse, not that person's victim. Again, this is consistent with domestic violence laws, which focus on the conduct of the spouse who has been abusive, not the spouse who has been abused.

The difficult question that remains is of appropriate remedies. Jail terms and fines are appropriate if it can be assumed that elder abuse is subject to deterrence. A study by the Benjamin Rose Institute found that adult protective services do not prevent or slow deterioration or death.[60] Emergency intervention amounts to the equivalent of women's shelters for victims of domestic abuse. Where the victim is being abused by a caretaker relative, the difficult choice is between institutionalization (usually resisted by the victim) or of counseling the abuser and paying for monitoring to insure that abuse does not resume. In this sense, elder abuse can be analogized to child abuse, as it faces the same dilemma, placing the victim in foster homes or counseling the abusive parent and monitoring as a follow up measure.

Two final comments need to be made about dealing with elder abuse. First, adult protective services are a relatively recent adjunct to public guardianship agencies. In handling the problem of the physically and mentally infirm and elderly, such agencies have at best a mixed record. Most jurisdictions view public guardianship as fee-generating, funding agencies through fees charged to the elderly. This is also true of adult protective services: 22 of the 34 states with such services charge fees and fund their agencies through collection of fees.[61] In fact, through public guardianship agencies, the public sector has developed a near monopoly on the seizure, control, and management of the property and assets of the incapacitated elderly.[62] Public guardians have been accused of mishandling and converting the funds of the elderly.[63] The other major criticism of public guardianship services is that they are vastly underfunded (an explanation for permitting them to collect fees): as a result they tend to avoid providing new services or benefits which conflict with cost-containment goals. On the other hand, public guardians have been accused of a tendency to overuse involuntary protection machinery, "streamlining" the process used in that regard.[64]

A final comment also needs to be made about involuntarily-mandated protective services. One advocate of the Model Protective Services, John Regan, first changed his position to that of placing a moratorium on involuntary orders for emergency and protective services and guardianships, then to a "minimal intervention" position between having protective services and abolishing them.[65] In part, the fear is that overworked social services agencies tend to do that which is most expedient: counseling and monitoring are time-intensive, institutionalizing the elderly is not. The risk posed by public agencies with great latitude and little accountability for their actions is that they themselves will become the victimizers of the elderly.[66]

B. Age Discrimination

In 1967, Congress passed the Age Discrimination in Employment Act ("ADEA"), which parallels Title VII of the 1964 Civil Rights Act in prohibiting discrimination on the basis of age in the hiring, firing, or promotion of employees.[67] Under Section 631 (a), the ADEA originally applied to all employees age 40 to 65. The Act was amended in 1974 to include government employees. In 1978, it was amended to prohibit mandatory early retirement of employees, as well as to extend the upper limits of the Act to age 70.[68] In 1986, the upper age limit was eliminated.

In adopting the ADEA, Congress responded to what it perceived as a high rate of involuntary unemployment among persons over age 45.[69] This was ascribed to misconceptions about the ability of older workers to perform in the workplace.[70]

Despite the ADEA, the proportion of older adults who are employed has continued to decline.[71] The percentage of older adults who do not work for health reasons is declining, while the number who list "economic reasons" (that they are unable to obtain employment) is increasing.[72] Meanwhile, the number of persons applying for Title II Social Security benefits earlier than age 65 has increased.[73]

The Social Security Administration is an interested party for another reason, the reduced contributions of persons between ages 45 and 65, which might otherwise be the most highly paid years of their lives. Persons who are terminated or who reach early retirement agreements within this time frame may not work at all, work for reduced salary or wages, or work part-time,[74] cutting the amount of taxes paid in to the Social Security trust fund. It is probably not the case that there is a one-for-one replacement of older workers with younger workers. This is because the U.S. economy at most times is closer to full employment, so the job market is more reflective of the labor demand than of a finite number of jobs being transferred from one generation to another.[75]

The remainder of this Section addresses these topics: 1) causes of age discrimination or disemployment of older workers; 2) remedies available under the ADEA; and 3) problems posed by two growing business practices, contractual waivers of ADEA rights and early retirement agreements.

1. Causes of the Problem

Several causes can be given for reduced employment among older workers. Conservative economists have argued that Social Security itself is a cause, as it reduces incentives to work and save. This is probably a more persuasive argument as to persons age 65 and older. Persons who work past age 65 can receive their Social Security entitlements but will have their income above a moderate amount taxed at a fifty percent rate.[76] As a result, there is a reduced economic incentive for such persons to work, even when not limited from doing so for health reasons. The argument is different for workers between the ages of 45 and 60, who are not eligible for benefits under Social Security until age 62. At best, the existence of future benefits might reduce the impetus to save, but there would still be economic reasons for most such workers to be employed.[77] It could also be argued that the existence of Social Security benefits operates as an encouragement to employees to offer early retirement to older workers: any guilt or reluctance about asking persons to end their careers early would be assuaged by the knowledge that those persons will be eligible for benefits in a few years.

A better argument can be made that private pension benefits for white-collar workers encourage early retirement. Between 1976 and 1979, 20 percent of the persons who retired with pensions did so before age 60, and 58 percent did so by age 63.[78]

Another reason for reduced employment among older workers is work dissatisfaction or burnout. Although many of the persons who cite poor health as a reason for early retirement are indeed too ill to work, this can also mask boredom or frustration with work.[79] The economic rewards of continuing to work for a few years at an unpleasant job may not exceed the emotional and physical costs of doing so. Of course, the availability of Social Security benefits and pensions influences this choice. It can also be argued that job dissatisfaction among older workers may reflect not unintentional conduct by their employers, who may hope to encourage "voluntary" retirement decisions which will save them labor and pension contribution costs. Such workers find early retirement offers attractive.[80]

Other reasons for decreased employment among older workers are the subjects of age discrimination litigation. These are: 1) stereotypic beliefs about the productivity of older workers ("ageism"); and 2) economic motives for terminations, i.e., savings in employee labor costs and pension contributions through discharge of persons at the high end of the wage or salary scale.

The ADEA's proponents presumed that ageism differed from racism in that it reflected ignorance or misconceptions about older workers, rather than animosity or hatred toward them. Section 622(a) of the ADEA provided for research and educational programs to inform employers and the public about the problems of older workers and the advantages of hiring them. That ageism and resultant discrimination are produced by ignorance and not animus is open to question. Older persons, those approaching age 65 as well as those exceeding it, are subject to demeaning beliefs about their mental and physical capabilities.[81] If education was to remedy ignorance, it has been ineffective, given the record since 1967. As is discussed in the next Section age discrimination is treated in a different manner than sex or race discrimination, suggesting a more lenient attitude toward ageist treatment of older employees.[82]

The other cause, economic benefit to the employer, is more pernicious. Even if an employer (who might himself or herself be elderly) held no stereotypic beliefs about older employees, they would still engage in discriminatory behavior if this made sense from a profit-and-loss standpoint. Simply put, a senior employee with high salary is replaced by a younger or entry-level employee at much lower salary. Although the new employee may in fact not be as productive, the net reduction in salary outweighs the reduction in productivity. In practice, it may be hard to separate this cause of discrimination from ageism. For example, in replacing an older sales representative with a younger one, an employer could be reflecting both a desire to cut costs and a stereotypic belief that older persons are less aggressive or have less stamina. In addition to savings in salaries, employers may also seek reduced rates of pension contributions or to avoid pension liability altogether, if an employee has not been with a company long enough for his or her pension to have vested. Employers may also seek to avoid higher health insurance rates or increased amounts of absenteeism associated with poor health correlated with age: again, one can argue whether this reflects actuarial tables or stereotypes.

In any event, age discrimination does not appear to be on the wane. As education appears not to have ameliorated the problem, the alternative is litigation under the ADEA, either by the employees or by the Equal Employment Opportunity Commission ("EEOC") on their behalf. The next Section examines age discrimination suits as a remedy.

2. Litigation Under the ADEA

Bringing suit under the ADEA is similar to Title VII employment discrimination actions, although there are important differences. There has been a significant increase in ADEA claims in the last few years, coinciding with the increasing use of reduction in force ("RIF") programs by employers.[83]

Persons who have been the target of discrimination can file claims with the EEOC. In addition, they can file complaints with a state human rights commission: such commissions perform administrative reviews of complaints and can order relief under state statutes, which generally provide the same remedies as the ADEA.[84] There are arguments to be made for preferring either the EEOC or state commissions.[85] The purpose of filing with either group is to have the commission conduct an investigation of the employer's practices. If there is a finding of substantial evidence of discrimination, settlement procedures are encouraged. Claimants, at their option, can sue the employer following absence of a finding of discrimination, failure to reach conciliation, or failure of the EEOC to sue within 180 days of the filing of the claim of discrimination.[86] This is one factor which has a major impact on the victims of age discrimination: the process is very lengthy. Although this has its effects on the victims of race, sex, and handicap discrimination as well, the effects may be more marked on older workers, whose employability and health and pension benefits are affected by delay in the outcome of the litigation. That there can be intervals of several years between the filing of a claim and the resolution of a suit is reflected in the remedies available to discriminatees under the ADEA.

Four types of relief are provided to victims of age discrimination: back pay, front pay, liquidated damages and fringe benefits. In interpreting the ADEA, the courts have refused to award damages for emotional injury and have refused to assess punitive damages against employers.[87] Although the ADEA covers discrimination in hiring and promotion, most suits have been about terminations.

"Back pay," a standard remedy in employment discrimination cases, provides the employee with compensation from the date of the act of discrimination. This can be the rate of pay the claimant was receiving at the time of termination, or it can be the increment between what the claimant was actually paid and the amount they would have been paid, had they not been denied a promotion for unlawful reasons. A discharged employee is required to show reasonable diligence on his or her part in attempting to find substitute employment: income from employment and unemployment compensation is deducted from awards of back pay.[88]

"Front pay" is of special importance to age discrimination cases. It consists of the back pay rates of payment extended to some post-trial date, typically age 70.[89] Front pay is not expressly authorized by the ADEA: it is inferred from the "catch-all" provision of Section 626(b), which authorizes "such ... relief as may be appropriate to effectuate the purposes of this Act." Not all courts award front pay: they are more likely to do so where the claimant is close to age 70.[90] Front pay is important to victims of age discrimination as an alternative to reinstatement. Typically, successful employment discrimination plaintiffs are given back pay and reinstatement in the first available opening for their old job. Since age discrimination often involves reductions in force, their old job may no longer be in existence.[91]

Liquidated damages (chiefly, unpaid wages and overtime pay) are provided for under ADEA, but on a much more limited basis than under the Fair Labor Standards Act ("FLSA"), after which the ADEA's enforcement provisions are patterned. To receive liquidated damages under the ADEA, claimants must show willful misconduct by the employer. Under FLSA, such damages are provided for every proven violation, and claimants receive double damages as a remedy. Hence, it can be argued that the ADEA has less of a deterrent effect against discrimination than does the FLSA.[92]

Fringe benefits, including pension rights and health benefits, are a significant issue in ADEA damage awards. The cutting off of pension rights can be the discriminatory motive of the employer.[93] A leading court case in this area is *Loeb v. Textron,* in which the court treated pension rights as part of compensation, to be awarded as back pay.[94] In *Loeb,* the plaintiff was discharged before his pension rights vested: however, the period for which the court awarded back pay made him eligible for a pension.[95] Without doing so, the plaintiff would not be "made whole" by the remedy, and the employer would be permitted to benefit from his discrimination.[96]

To make out a successful age discrimination claim, plaintiffs must follow the same general procedures as other employment discrimination claimants. There are some differences in the way in which proof is evaluated and some additional defenses which make ADEA claims more difficult to establish.[97] This may be due to the Supreme Court's view that age is not a suspect class and regulations affecting it are not therefore deserving of special scrutiny; it may also reflect a less urgent attitude toward age discrimination as opposed to race and sex discrimination.[98] There is also the fact that older employees generally have the protection of seniority systems, which frequently work to the disadvantage of minorities and women, as older employees are more often white and male.

All employment discrimination cases follow a three-step process outlined by the Supreme Court in interpreting Title VII of the Civil Rights Act.[99] The first two steps are seldom, if ever, controversial. In step one, the plaintiff makes out a prima facie case by proving that: 1) he or she is a member of a protected class under the Act (i.e., black, female); and 2) if the case involves hiring, shows that he or she was qualified for a job, applied, was not hired, but the job remained open and the employer continued to interview applicants after his or her rejection; or 3) if the case involves termination, that the claimant was an employee and was discharged, raising an inference of discrimination. In step two, the employer articulates a legitimate, nondiscriminatory reason for its refusal to hire (better-qualified applicants) or decision to terminate (poor job performance). The third step is critical: the plaintiff must establish that the reasons offered by the employer are "pretextual," i.e., that they are a disguise for the real motivation for the employer's conduct, which was discrimination.

ADEA cases are differnt in the following respects. Not all the federal circuit courts are as liberal as step one with ADEA plaintiffs. This is because the "nonprotected class" consists of workers under age 40, who could be expected to be hired and employed in workplaces which were not discriminatory as well as ones which are.[100]

More importantly, employers have broader defenses available under the ADEA than under Title VII. Under Title VII, there is a limited defense to proof of sex discrimination where the employer can prove that preference for males over females is the result of a "bona fide occupational disqualification" ("BFOQ") necessary to the normal operation of the business. The Supreme Court held this to be an extremely narrow exception to Title VII in a case involving a female prison employee excluded from being a correctional counselor at an all-male maximum security prison.[101] In contrast, the ADEA includes three exceptions which excuse an employer's noncompliance with the statute: 1) discipline for good cause; 2) age-based differential treatment due to "reasonable factors other than age" ("RFOA"); and 3) the BFOQ defense to Title VII.

Courts appear willing to accept as RFOAs "business judgment" defenses. Hence, they are likely to find nondiscriminatory the elimination of positions held by ADEA plaintiffs where the employer can articulate plausible business-related reasons for having done so.[102] The court need not agree with the business judgment reached: the function of the business judgment defense or rule is to argue that the court should not second-guess such judgments, even where they are erroneous.[103]

The BFOQ defense is applied more broadly to the ADEA as well. The courts have required that the BFOQ defense for sex discrimination requires a demonstration that the essence of a business will be undermined if the defense is not allowed. [104] In contrast, the courts have required only a minimal showing that age-based employment practices were not arbitrary or intentionally discriminatory, even where the employer lacked convincing statistical evidence linking age to job performance: one court ruled that employers need only show a "good faith belief" as to the BFOQ.[105]

As with all discrimination cases, age discrimination cases present proof problems for plaintiffs. Discrimination can be shown by individual disparate treatment, where a "smoking gun" in the form of statements by the employer can be found establishing discriminatory conduct.[106] It can also be shown through evidence of systemic disparate treatment of a group by an employer[107], or through the differential treatment of a group by an employer[107], or through the disparate impact on a group of facially neutral policies imposed by an employer.[108] Age discrimination cases have tended to be individual disparate treatment cases. Three explanations can be offered: 1) time lag—the ADEA is simply catching up with Title VII where the cases also were initially individual cases, then became systemic cases; 2) hesitancy of older workers (particularly blue-collar) to sue; and 3) fewer discriminatory systems (as opposed to treatment of targeted individuals) adversely affect older workers—to the contrary, seniority systems aid them.[109] Therefore, although there have been systemic disparate treatment and systemic disparate impact cases under ADEA[110], the tendency has been for litigation to be one individual at a time. The typical ADEA claimant is a relatively well-paid male managerial employee in his 50s, not a member of a union, who has been terminated.[111] The result is that ADEA litigation has been burdensome and time-consuming for employers, as white-collar employees challenge reductions in force.[112] This has led employers to use the tactics discussed in the next section to avoid litigation.

3. Waivers and Early Retirement Agreements

Employers have responded to growth in ADEA claims by white-collar employees through the use of private contracts or waivers. A waiver agreement is a privately executed contract between an employee and an employer under which the employee agrees to forego his or her right to sue under the ADEA in exchange for valuable consideration.[113] Such consideration may include severance pay or fringe benefits.

Viewed positively, waivers are a nonadversarial, speedy legal device for disposing of age discrimination claims.[114] From the perspective of the employer, a comprehensive release forecloses future liability and litigation, with attendant "expenses, risk, and lost management time."[115] From the standpoint of employees, severance pay and benefits (such as vesting of a pension or an employer agreement to maintain health insurance coverage) provide guaranteed rewards up front, as opposed to a risk of recovery after several years of litigation. And, from the perspective of the government, waivers are judicially and administratively efficient, resolving private disputes which would otherwise utilize many hours of EEOC time and court time.

Viewed negatively, waivers rob victims of age discrimination of their ability to receive redress. Where waivers are requested of persons not being terminated (for possible future use by the employer), they not only rob the employee of civil rights, they also encourage the employer to violate the law, knowing that it will be able to find refuge in the waiver agreement. This can also be argued to be a classic case of "unequal bargaining power." Particularly for the older employee whose job is being terminated, the certainty of the benefits offered by the employer may be too attractive to resist signing the agreement.

While it would appear that, from this perspective, the employer gains considerably more than the employee, opponents of age discrimination would argue that the employer is harmed in a subtle, indirect way. This occurs through the purposeful self-deprivation by the employer of the resources that can be provided by older employees. When the ADEA was enacted, the legislative history suggested that Congress was motivated not only by the effects of discrimination on older workers, but by the effects on the economy of cutting off a supply of talented, experienced employees.[116] This problem will be intensified as, given demographic trends, older workers become a larger proportion of the labor force over the next few decades.[117]

It can also be argued that waivers damage the national interest, to the extent that they condone possible age discrimination. The purpose of damage provisions under the ADEA is to provide deterrence to future acts of discrimination, as well as to provide redress to the employee. Since punitive damages are not awarded under the ADEA, actions which minimize the number of persons claiming actual damages further weakens an already limited deterrent.

Whether waivers will be upheld by the courts is complicated to some extent by whether those courts will look to the Fair Labor Standards Act ("FLSA") or to Title VII of the Civil Rights Act of 1964 for guidance. The ADEA takes much of its substantive language from Title VII, but borrows its enforcement provisions (with important modifications) from the FLSA.[118] Under the FLSA, which prescribes mandatory minimum wages, overtime wages, and maximum hour requirements for businesses in interstate commerce, the courts have consistently held that employees cannot waive their rights by agreement.[119] Under Title VII, private waivers have been upheld, given certain conditions.

Title VII encourages the voluntary resolution of discrimination claims, and includes conciliation machinery within its enforcement clauses. Hence, where private settlement agreements are entered into voluntarily and knowingly, courts uphold them, extinguishing employees' rights to sue under Title VII.[120] Courts look to whether the employees have some degree of sophistication and had the benefit of legal advice before signing the agreement: if so, absent proof of fraud or duress, a clear and unambiguous agreement will be upheld.[121] Other courts have refused to uphold agreements where the settlement agreement was intricate and workers were less educated.[122]

Several courts have applied Title VII precedent in dealing with waiver agreements in ADEA cases.[123] While the result would appear to be the opposite where FLSA precedent is applied, the Sixth Circuit has upheld a waiver agreement while relying on the FLSA. It did so on the basis that the FLSA did not exclude private settlement of factual disputes, only ones involving legal issues (i.e., whether the employer was covered by the Act). The Court also commented that the FLSA was meant to protect less educated workers in minimum wage jobs, while the ADEA deals with workers who are more highly paid and capable of securing legal advice.[124] The case therefore attempts to carve out an exception to the rule in FLSA cases, where the Supreme Court has held on two occasions that private waivers of rights are not effective.[125]

The EEOC currently favors following Title VII instead of LSA as precedent, and has proposed a regulation allowing private releases of ADEA claims, so long as the waiver of rights is voluntary and knowing.[126] The EEOC, following the Sixth Circuit reasoning, takes the position that although under the FLSA there is an absolute presumption that waivers of minimum wage rights are based on unequal bargaining power and duress, this reasoning does not apply to the ADEA.[127]

Two final points to consider concerning waivers have to do with the stereotype of ADEA claimants. As indicated above, ADEA claimants tend to be white-collar employees, highly paid and well-educated. Does this mean that waivers should be enforced? While waivers are enforced with regard to Title VII, an argument can be made that permitting waivers at all prioritizes the government's interest in conciliation over the interest in deterring discrimination. That ADEA claimants are aware of what they are doing justifies upholding waivers from a contract theory perspective, but not from a prohibition of discrimination perspective.

Second, does higher pay change the bargaining position of the ADEA claimant? The argument in favor says that this gives him or her greater access to legal representation. The argument against says that the ADEA claimant is still in an unequal bargaining position because of the degree of unemployment and underemployment of workers above the age of 40, which would make the benefits associated with signing a release attractive. In essence, this is a "hidden coercion" or duress agreement.

A different reduction-in-force employment strategy with ADEA ramifications is early retirement. This is most commonly used by public employers, especially secondary school systems.[128] A typical early retirement plan would be to offer $10,000 to any employee who has reached the age of 55, has at least ten years of service, and who agrees to retire immediately; after age 55, the incentive is either withdrawn or substantially reduced in increments for age.[129] This is done by contract: some states have statutes governing early retirement provisions for public employers.[130]

As mentioned at the start of this section, mandatory early retirements were common before 1978, when Congress amended the ADEA to explicitly outlaw them. At present, early retirement plans, to be permissible, must be shown to be voluntary.[131] The courts have routinely upheld early retirement plans stated to be voluntary. These have included plans in which age 55 was specified as a retirement age and extra-contractual benefits were extended to employees terminated under the plan[132] and in which the "sliding scale of diminishing benefits" was used as a carrot to encourage early retirement.[133] Another decision upheld early retirement incentives as bona fide retirement plans and therefore protected employer activity under the ADEA.[134]

It is not necessarily true that early retirement plans are favored by employers and resisted by employees. Early retirement plans are resisted by some companies as more costly than alternative force-reduction strategies.[135] And, as mentioned earlier, early retirement is attractive to some workers. There have been unsuccessful suits by younger workers who argued they were discriminated against by the restriction of early retirement options to persons 55 and older.[136] Finally, as discussed in Chapter Three, early retirement plans have a negative effect on the Social Security trust fund, decreasing contributions and increasing pre-65 benefit claims: the 1983 Social Security Act amendments are aimed at higher retirement ages, not lower ones. Since public school systems are often the employer encouraging early retirement, different levels of government are working at cross purposes.

The legal argument against early retirement plans is that they are violative of the ADEA: this requires that it be established that they are not a bona fide benefit plan, and are instead an illegal discriminatory tactic. The Supreme Court has not heard a case where this was at issue: the Circuit Courts of Appeal which have heard the issue have rejected this argument.[137]

The policy-based arguments against early retirement consider the purpose of the ADEA, combatting ageism, rather than its specific language and provisions. Five such arguments can be made. First, early retirement plans foster ageist stereotypes, reducing participation of older adults in the workforce. Second, persons taking advantage of early retirement are harmed: although initally benefitting employees, the length and quality of their lives may be diminished, particularly if they do not obtain substitute employment. Third, early retirement incentives, despite being labelled voluntary, are coercive in nature. This is both because of the bargaining context and because of the ability of employers to withdraw or reduce the benefits offered if not accepted at age 55. Fourth, younger employees, including those between ages 40 and 54 protected under the ADEA, are discriminated against on the basis of age by early retirement incentives. Finally, employees older than 55 are discriminated against. Typically, employees very close to 65 are not offered the retirement incentive, or receive it at a considerably reduced rate.[138]

As the labor force becomes older in the next few decades, more employees may face what are arguably age discrimination situations. Two factors are of importance in this regard. First, what will be the attitude of employers toward older workers? Ageist stereotypes may explain employer behavior which is not always economically justified. Second, is the U.S. economy entering a prolonged period of stagnation and limited growth? There is a rough correlation between discriminatory practices and a weak economy, although this is usually more the case for racial discrimination than for other forms of discrimination. However, reductions in force and early retirement plans tend to be options used by employees in some financial difficulty. To the extent that the economy achieves growth in productivity, the employment security of older workers will also be affected.[139]

C. HOUSING AND THE ELDERLY

The housing situation of the elderly has an impact on a number of other topics. First, for those persons over age 65 who own their own homes, that asset has a major effect on their ability to obtain nursing home care and to receive Medicaid assistance in receiving such care. Second, the proportion of income spent on housing competes with the amount available to be spent on other basic needs. Food and medical care, including prescription drugs, are the two items which most often are sacrificed. This, combined with problems in paying for heat, as well as health and sanitation problems in substandard housing, explains why poor housing has an impact on health among the elderly.

Housing problems among the elderly take on different forms, depending on the type of housing and the income level of the persons at issue. This section of this chapter examines four major housing-related matters: 1) problems facing elderly homeowners; 2) conversion of rental apartments into condominiums; 3) public and subsidized housing for the elderly; and 4) heating assistance and the low-income elderly.

1. Home Ownership Problems

Persons who acquired housing in the construction boom of the 1950s are now reaching retirement age: contrary to stereotypes about retirees moving to Arizona and Florida, most remain in their homes.[140] They will be added to the current generation of retirees, which also contains a high percentage of homeowners. Over 70 percent of the elderly now live in their own homes, over 80 percent of them debt-free.[141]

The problem for the current group of retirees, especially "the oldest old," is that they often are "house poor." Their houses are relatively old (more than half were built before 1939) and in need of repairs, which their owners are unable to make personally.[142] Yet the elderly retain these homes instead of moving to other houses or changing to renting rather than owning even where this has become impractical for them to do so.[143]

A difficulty in dealing with this problem is that these elderly homeowners are rarely low-income persons; in addition, what is being asked for is not preservation of minimum shelter needs, but home ownership, something which under-65 persons who cannot afford to purchase homes are unlikely to see as an urgent social priority.[144] The suggestions listed below could be undertaken through governmental action, but could also be accomplished through private sector initiatives. Many of the elderly now retiring live in suburbia,[145] in locations which are attractive to both lenders and to younger home-buyers, so the options discussed below could be achieved without government involvement.

Two types of private sector initiatives would be of assistance, those which would permit the elderly to stay in their current homes and those which would require relocation. Options permitting the elderly to remain in their current homes consist of home financing strategies and assume that the elderly own their home debt-free, and that the home has some reasonable market value. One option is reverse annuity mortgages and reverse debt mortgages, under which the homeowner borrows against accumulated equity to generate needed income for major repairs.[146] This has been unattractive to the elderly because of the disparity in interest rates at which they obtained home loans decades ago and the current market interest rates. The second approach is sale-lease backs, under which the financial institution purchases the home from the elderly homeowner, and then executes a long-term lease of the newly acquired property back to the seller/lessee. This provides the elderly homeowner with cash for repairs, uninterrupted possession, and a favorable rental arrangement, while the lender receives tax benefits from the purchase, a cash flow from the lease, and (ultimately), marketable property.[147]

The second set of options involves relocation. One approach involves exchanging a home currently owned for a condominium of smaller size which is "purpose-built," i.e., is adapted to the needs of the elderly, such as wheelchair access and congregate dining facilities to be shared with adjacent condominiums.[148] An assumption of this idea is that elderly homeowners are "over housed," living in a home with excess space; this permits the financial institution to underwrite their relocation to a newer facility, as well as to be able to market their previous home.[149] The second option is a shared equity plan under which the elderly homeowner sells his or her house and uses the proceeds to purchase a different location in combination with a financial institution, paying back the co-equity holder on a rental basis.[150] While relocating is not preferred by the elderly homeowner, the options discussed above would permit them to relocate to housing conditions adapted to their needs and with lesser maintenance and repair demands.

All of the above options could also be engaged in using funds or loan guarantees through the federal secondary mortgage market or through state housing development authorities. The impetus of the Reagan Administration, which has not been successful to date, has been to get the federal government out of the home-lending market.[151] The attractiveness of the options above to private lender institutions will be determined in part by prevailing interest rates. Currently, they are at a rate which would make the options viable; if driven higher by interest rates on the national debt and other factors, they could make these options impractical for lenders and the elderly. At that point, government loan guaranteed or subsidized at a lower rate would be necessary to make these options workable. As mentioned above, there is some question as to whether federal expenditures on loans for elderly homeowners would be politically possible, given attitudes toward them and current constraints.

2. Condominium Conversions and the Elderly

This is a different matter altogether than the condominium option described above. Apartment buildings in urban areas in which middle-income and low middle-income elderly have lived in for years are now being converted to condominium ownership. Absent liquid assets to make down payments, this effectively forces the elderly individuals and couples to relocate, typically to lower quality housing.[152] The effect of disruption of lifestyle patterns on the elderly is also not to be underestimated.

The elderly who have traditionally lived in urban areas are caught between two trends. First, there is gentrification of urban areas, as upper middle-income persons are attracted to rehabilitated buildings closer to workplaces. Second, there is the continuation of the exclusionary zoning of the 1970s in suburban areas, excluding multi-family housing and setting minimum lot size or housing cost minimums which effectively keep out low income and low middle income persons.[153]

The Reagan Administration has favored a policy decentralization, leaving land-use regulations to local communities.[154] Efforts to preserve affordable rental housing, including that for the elderly, have taken place at a state level. Several states have provided for "inclusionary zoning," requiring counties to include a mix of lower-cost housing within area-wide development plans. A leader in this area is New Jersey, which passed a Fair Housing Act in 1985 which requires that municipalities use their zoning powers to ensure that affordable housing would be built. These efforts to create "spatial deconcentration" of low-income persons were taken in response to state court litigation against exclusionary zoning regulations.[155] Other states and county governments have also taken inclusionary zoning actions, which indirectly provide benefits to low-income and low-middle income elderly persons.[156]

New Jersey also has taken action directly pertinent to the effects of condominium conversions on the elderly. In 1983, the New Jersey legislature enacted the Senior Citizens and Disabled Protected Tenancy Act, which grants low-income elderly and disabled tenants residing in buildings slated for conversion a forty-year protective tenancy.[157] Although the law was challenged by a developer, a federal court of appeal upheld the law's constitutionality.[158] Other states and municipalities have protected the elderly from conversion-related evictions by granting them extended tenancy periods or by passing ordinances regulating conversions.[159]

3. Public and Subsidized Housing for the Elderly

The sections above largely concern the non-poor elderly, although condominium conversion does affect some low-income persons.[160] Low-income elderly, such as those subsisting on SSI, have been affected by cutbacks and policy changes toward public and subsidized housing for the elderly under the Reagan Administration. The last Carter Administration budget proposal for housing assistance was for $27.6 billion, while the first Reagan Administration proposal was for $18.2 billion, a figure which has continued to decline.[161] The Reagan Administration has placed a lower social priority on housing assistance than previous administrations, and has de-emphasized new construction and substantial rehabilitation, shifting support to the use of existing housing instead.[162]

The elderly have fared somewhat better than the non-elderly poor insofar as construction programs under the Reagan Administration is concerned. Under Section 202 of the Housing and Community Development Act of 1974, the Reagan Administration has continued to build approximately 14,000 housing units per year for the elderly and handicapped.[163] However, low-income elderly persons still have serious unmet housing needs. In 1982, 1.35 milion elderly singles and 800,000 elderly couples were classified as eligible but received no support from federal housing assistance programs.[164] Since that time, new construction other than Section 202 units has been limited to completion of pre-Reagan contracts. The Reagan Administration has made it clear that it sees housing as a "limited entitlement," and that there will be fewer slots than persons eligible to receive aid under federal programs.[165] The Housing and Community Development Act of 1987, signed by President Reagan in February, 1988 authorized $7.17 billion in aggregate budget authority for housing assistance in fiscal 1988 and $7.3 billion in fiscal 1989.[165] Included in the 1988 budget is authorization for $1.68 billion for new Section 202 elderly housing units.[167]

In addition to housing specifically for the low-income elderly under Section 202, the elderly can participate in the low or moderate income subsidy programs available regardless of age, primarily under Sections 8 and 236 of the 1974 Act, as updated by the 1987 Act. Both programs subsidize rent of tenants: tenants pay 30 percent of their income and the Department of Housing and Urban Development ("HUD") pays the balance to the landlord.[168] One study estimated that one-third of all public housing tenants were elderly, while 35 percent of all Section 236 benefits went to persons over age 65, and 40 percent of all Section 8 housing units were occupied by the elderly.[169]

Under the Section 8 and 236 programs HUD must approve participation by both the tenant and the landlord: the landlord's building must meet federal quality standards and the landlord is responsible for overseeing the building, unlike public housing.

A controversy has emerged concerning Section 8 building owners who received HUD construction assistance, under which they agreed to continue to rent to Section 8-eligible persons for stated periods of time, usually 20 to 40 years. Once this time period has expired, landlords are no longer required to rent apartments to persons in the Section 8 program. Prior to the 1987 Act, owners were also permitted to prepay the balance of loans to HUD and exit the program early. The 1987 Act placed substantial restrictions on prepayment.[170] Even without prepayment, these buildings will eventually leave the program: while some will continue to rent at relatively low market rates to low-middle income persons, others (in gentrifying areas) will obtain market level rents from middle income tenants.[171]

The approach favored by the Reagan Administration is having vouchers, under which low-income persons would receive a flat amount to be used in paying for housing obtained on the private market.[172] The Reagan Administration's view is that the housing problem facing low-income persons is affordability, not quality (something with which critics would disagree)[173]: hence, more money solves the problem. Use of existent private housing is more desirable than constructing housing with public funds, since it is twice as expensive to provide one month of housing in a newly built federal unit than it is to lease a private unit.[174]

Congress initially reacted unenthusiastically to vouchers.[175] The objections to vouchers are that they provide no regulation of the quality of housing and that they would simply result in an increase in housing costs. Vouchers were used in Pittsburgh, Phoenix, South Bend, and Green Bay in the 1970s under an Experimental Housing Assistance Plan with good results: housing costs were not increased artificially by the presence of vouchers.[176] The voucher program operated on a demonstration basis until the 1987 law, when the "demonstration" label was removed.[177]

Government assistance for low-income housing is a casualty of budget politics. Housing is part of the 20 percent which the Reagan Administration has viewed as "controllable," i.e., it is not a social entitlement, interest on debt, or defense spending.[178] Housing expenditures have been cut back but would have been reduced even further had the Reagan Administration been able to secure Congressional approval.[179]

4. Heating Assistance

Heating assistance is a program accessible to low income persons of all ages but of special importance to the elderly. The greater susceptibility of the elderly to pneumonia and hypothermia makes adequate home heating critical to their health.

The federal government has provided money to the states for distribution under the Low-income Home Energy Assistance Program ("LIHEAP"). The program was begun in the late 1970s in response to the huge increase in energy costs of that decade. Persons on fixed incomes, including the elderly on Social Security, were ravaged as housing-related energy costs increased 293 percent as a nationwide average between 1972 and 1979.[180] At its peak in 1985, LIHEAP received $2.1 billion, yet that was the same year that the gap between fuel costs for the poor and the amount of federal assistance available reached its widest point.[181] The program mainly provides heating assistance funds, but also pays for weatherization to increase energy efficiency.[182] Between 1980 and 1986, LIHEAP funds declined from paying 40 percent of eligible households' energy bills to less than 20 percent.[183] The program serves only about 39 percent of eligible households.[184]

LIHEAP has suffered cuts for reasons unrelated to the efficacy of the program. As oil costs have been reduced, so has Congressional support for energy assistance, even though few of the elderly or poor have oil-heated furnaces. Those persons with low incomes pay four times the rest of the population in percentage of income for energy costs.[185] LIHEAP has been a vulnerable target for Gramm-Rudman-Hillings deficit reductions, being cut from $2.009 billion in fiscal 1986 to $1.825 billion in fiscal 1986 to $1.825 billion in fiscal 1987.[186] This figure was cut still further to $1.53 billion in fiscal 1988 and the White House's proposal for fiscal 1989 was to cut it even more, to $1.19 billion.[187] As of late March, 1988, the House had rejected this proposal, keeping the 1988 amount with a full inflation increase.[188]

LIHEAP funding has also been affected by the availability of funds from settlements of two major lawsuits in which oil companies were ordered to pay back fuel overcharges to customers.[189] The Department of Energy, which oversees state uses of overcharge money, has required states to use their share of overcharge funds to supplant, rather than supplement, previous heating assistance commitments.[190] In addition, the oil overcharge distribution formula tends to favor Southern and Western states, which had been losing less LIHEAP money than "frost belt" states, as "sunbelt" states got less LIHEAP money to begin with.[191] Hence, oil overcharge funds have a net negative effect on LIHEAP in Northern and Midwestern states.

Another approach to heating assistance was suggested by the House version of the 1987 Housing and Community Development Act. This legislation would have guaranteed public housing and Section 8 tenants a reasonable utility allowance. The Senate-House conferees removed this provision, replacing it with a requirement that the General Accounting Office do a study on allowances and make recommendations to Congress by October 30, 1988.[192]

Unless there is some dramatic turn of events, such as another round of increases in oil prices, energy assistance is likely to continue to decline.[193] Like Section 8 housing, energy assistance has become a limited entitlement, with eligible persons receiving aid on a first come-first serve basis and the bulk of eligible applicants receiving no aid at all.

Overall, the elderly face serious problems in securing and retaining adequate housing. Although a high percentage of persons over age 65 own their homes, they lack funds to maintain them. Those who live in multi-family dwellings face condominium conversion efforts and the prospect of being tossed into a rental market with low availability rates. Although the elderly poor have received more assistance in public and subsidized housing than have their younger cohorts, Reagan Administration policies have nevertheless had a negative effect on them. The question which remains is whether the Administration's successors will continue its privatization efforts and its reduction in importance of adequate housing as a social priority.

NOTES TO CHAPTER SEVEN

1. U.S. House of Representatives, Select Committee on Aging, *Elder Abuse: An Examination of a Hidden Problem*, 97th Congress, 1st Session (Hearings, 12981). (Hereinafter, "House Select Committee on Aging, 1981")

2. Katheryn Katz, "Elder Abuse," *Journal of Family Law* (1980), v. 18, pp. 695-722.

3. Marilyn Block and Jan D. Sinnott, *The Battered Elder Syndrome: An Explanatory Study* (1979).

4. Christine A. Metcalf, "A Response to the Problem of Elder Abuse: Florida's Revised Adult Protective Services Act," *Florida State University Law Review* (1986), v. 14, pp. 746-747.

5. House Select Committee on Aging, 1981, p. xix.

6. Metcalf, p. 747.

7. Metcalf, p. 747.

8. Metcalf, p. 747.

9. Katz, p. 700.

10. Metcalf, p. 747.

11. Metcalf, pp. 747-748.

12. Block and Sinnott, p. 57. See also Marshall B. Kapp, "Health Care Delivery and the Elderly: Teaching Old Patients New Tricks," *Cumberland Law Review* (1987), v. 17, p. 442.

13. Lawerence R. Faulkner, "Mandating the Reporting of Suspected Cases of Elder Abuse: An Inappropriate, Ineffective and Ageist Response to the Abuse of Older Adults," *Family Law Quarterly* (1982), v. 16, p. 76.

14. Faulkner, p. 87.

15. Winsor C. Schmidt, "Adult Protective Services and the Therapeutic State," *Law and Psychology Review* (1986), v. 10. p. 101.

16. Schmidt, pp. 102-103; and Metcalf, pp. 745-746.

17. Katz, p. 710.

18. Dyana Lee, "Mandatory Reporting of Elder Abuse: A Cheap But Ineffective Solution to the Problem," *Fordham Urban Law Journal* (1986), v. 14, p. 724.

19. Lee, p. 725.

20. Lee, p. 739.

21. Lee, pp. 741-742.

22. Metcalf, p. 747.

23. Lee, pp. 730-731.

24. Metcalf, p. 775.

25. Lee, p. 739.

26. Lee, pp. 740-741.

27. Metcalf, p. 749.

28. Lee, pp. 750-751.

29. Lee, pp. 744-746.

30. Lee, p. 747.

31. Lee, pp. 748-749.

32. Schmidt, p. 102.

33. Schmidt, pp. 105-106.

34. Schmidt, p. 104.

35. Metcalf, p. 760; and Schmidt, p. 105.

36. Schmidt, p. 115.

37. Schmidt, p. 104.

38. Schmidt, pp. 103-104.

39. Dalend, et al., "Elder Abuse Reporting: Limitations of Statutes," *Gerontologist* (1984), v. 24, p. 66.

40. Metcalf, p. 755.

41. 424 U.S. 319 (1976).

42. Schmidt, p. 120.

43. Lee, pp. 731-732; and Metcalf, p. 754. Another reason is embarrassment or social stigma attached to having to admit having raised an abusive child. Lee p. 731.

44. National Senior Citizens Law Center, *Elder Abuse: Public Policy Options Other Than Direct Service Delivery* (1983), p. 74.

45. Lee, p. 740.

46. U.S. House of Representatives, Select Committee on Aging, *Elder Abuse: A National Disgrace*, 99th Congress, 1st Session (Hearings, 1985), p. 5. (Hereinafter, "House Select Committee on Aging, 1985") While 40 percent of all reported abuse cases involved adults (spousal abuse as well as elder abuse), only 4.7 percent of state protective service budgets are committed to elderly protective services.

47. Lee, p. 734.

48. Cited in Schmidt, pp. 118-119.

49. Metcalf, p. 754; and Lee, pp. 731-732.

50. Faulkner, p. 69.

51. Lee, p. 731, n. 46 and accompanying text.

52. Lee, p. 734; and Schmidt, pp. 117-118.

53. Lee, pp. 733-734.

54. Lee, pp. 730-731; and Faulkner, p. 87.

55. Metcalf, p. 775.

56. Robert M. Gordon and Simon N. Verdun-Jones, "Privatization and Protective Services for the Elderly: Some Observations on the Economics of the Aging Process," *International Journal of Law and Psychiatry* (1986), v. 8, pp. 316-323.

57. Schmidt, pp. 111-112.

58. Schmidt, pp. 111-112.

59. Metcalf, p. 774.

60. Cited by Schmidt, p. 119.

61. Gordon and Verdun-Jones, pp. 318-319.

62. Gordon and Verdun-Jones, p. 323.

63. Gordon and Verdun-Jones, pp. 317-318.

64. Gordon and Verdun-Jones, p. 323.

65. See Schmidt, pp. 117-118.

66. Schmidt, pp. 120-121.

67. The ADEA is codified at 29 U.S. Sections 621-634.

68. The amended Section is 623(f)(2). The amendment was in response to a Supreme Court case, *United Airlines v. McMann*, 434 U.S. 192 (1978), which permitted this practice.

69. See Amy Wax, "Waiver of Rights Under the Age Discrimination in Employment Act of 1967," *Columbia Law Review* (1986), v. 86, pp. 1067-1068.

70. Wax, pp. 1067-1068, n. 8 and accompanying text.

71. Michael J. Boskin, *Too Many Promises: The Uncertain Future of Social Security* (Homewood: Dow Jones-Irwin, 1986), pp. 22, 51.

72. Boskin, p. 51.

73. Richard G. Kass, "Early Retirement Incentives and the Age Discrimination in Employment Act," *Hofstra Labor Law Journal* (1986), v. 4, p. 63, n. 2.

74. W. Andrew Achenbaum, *Social Security: Visions and Revisions* (New York: Cambridge, 1986), p. 118.

75. Boskin, pp. 47-48.

76. Boskin, p. 60. This will be changes to a 33 percent rate in 1990. Achenbaum, p. 103.

77. A possible exception would be federal, military, and municipal workforce retirees. In 1980, the average age of federal civil service retirees was 56. Police and fire department retirees are clustered in the age 48.53 range. Boskin, p. 59. Such "retirees," however, frequently become "double dippers," working in a new career and earning a second pension.

78. Achenbaum, p. 117.

79. Achenbaum, pp. 119-120.

80. Wax, p. 1088, n. 118 and accompanying text.

81. For an argument that age discrimination resembles sex and race discrimination in all pertinent respects, see Kass, pp. 74-75.

82. Support for this view comes from the Supreme Court's determination that age was not a suspect classification (and therefore not subject to strict scrutiny) in *Massachusetts Board of Retirement v. Murgia:*

> While treatment of the aged in this section has not been wholly free of discrimination, such persons, unlike, say, those who have been discriminated against on the basis of race or national origin, have not experienced a "history of purposeful unequal treatment" or been subjected to unique disabilities on the basis of stereotyped characteristics not truly indicative of their abilities ... (O)ld age does not define a "discrete and insular" group ... in need of "extraordinary protection from the majoritarian process." Instead, it marks a stage that each of us will reach if we live out our normal span.

427 U.S. 307, 313 (1976). In *Murgia,* the Court upheld a mandatory retirement

age of 50 for state highway troopers as being reasonably related to the state's interest in the physical fitness of state troopers.
83. Wax, pp. 1068-1069, 1086, n. 115.
84. In Illinois, for example, the Illinois Human Rights Act, ch. 68 Ill. Rev. Stat Sections 1-101 et. seq. provides remedies for age discrimination as well as other forms of discrimination. State hearings follow state procedure and precedent and state case law cannot be inconsistent with Supreme Court rulings.
85. The EEOC and federal courts can be more hospitable forums to discriminatees than are their state counterparts, although this tends to be more the case with race discrimination. State commissions also vary widely in the degree of budgetary support provided. However, it is also true that the EEOC is greatly overburdened, particularly by age discrimination claims: see note 83, above. 15,000 ADEA claims were filed with EEOC in fiscal 1983, up 66 percent over 1982, leading to long waiting periods. While state human rights commissions hear nothing but discrimination cases, AEDA claims wind up in federal district court, competing with other federal civil and criminal cases for the time and attention of the judge.
86. Michael J. Zimmer, Charles A. Sullivan, and Richard F. Richards, *Cases and Materials on Employment Discrimination* (Boston: Little, Brown, 1982) pp. 363-366, 712-713.
87. Albert F. Kuhl, "Remedies Under the Age Discrimination in Employment Act," *Labor Lawyer* (1986), v. 2, p. 229.
88. Kuhl, pp. 232-233.
89. Kuhl, pp. 241-242.
90. Kuhl, pp. 242-243.
91. Kuhl, pp. 245-246.
92. Kuhl, p. 236.
93. See Chapter Three, note 164, discussing *Folz v. Marriott Corp.*, 594 F. Supp. 1097 (W.D. Mo. 1984).
94. 60 F.2d 1003, 1021 (1st Cir. 1979).
95. 600 F.2d 1003, 1021 (1st Cir. 1979).
96. Kuhl, pp. 247-248.
97. Wax, pp. 1086-1087.
98. Wax, pp. 0186-1087; see also note 82 above.
99. See *McDonnell Douglas Corp. v. Green*, 411 U.S. 792 (1973); and *Texas Department of Community Affairs v. Burdine*, 450 U.S. 248 (1981).
100. Wax, pp. 1087-1088, n. 117.
101. *Dothard v. Rawlinson*, 433 U.S. 321 (1977).
102. N. Thomas Powers, "Reductions in Force Under the Age Discrimination in Employment Act," *Labor Lawyer* (1986), v. 2, pp. 199-200.
103. Powers, pp. 200, 202-203.
104. Wax, p. 1087, n. 117, citing *Diaz v. Pan American World Airways, Inc.*, 442 F.2d 385 (5th Cir. 1974), in which being a female was found not to be a BFOQ for being an airline cabin attendant.
105. Wax, p. 1087, citing *EEOC v. City of Janesville*, 630 F.2d 1254 (7th Cir. 1980) and *Hodgson v. Greyhound Lines*, 499 F.2d 859 (7th Cir. 1974). A different result was reached in *Usery v. Tamiami Trail Tours, Inc.*, 531 F.2d 224 (5th Cir. 1976), where the court held that the employee needed to show that "all or substantially all" persons over age 40 would be unsafe bus drivers.
106. See, for example, *Schulz v. Hickok Manufacturing Co.*, 358 F. Supp. 1208 (N.D. Ga. 1973), where a supervisor told the plaintiff that the company "wanted younger people." See also, *Buchholz v. Symons Manufacturing Co.*, 445 F. Supp. 706 (E.D. Wis. 1978), where the plaintiff responded to a "choice" between early

retirement and termination that this was "nothing but age discrimination," to which his supervisor replied, "You're damned right it is."

107. See, *Teamsters v. United States*, 431 U.S. 324 (1977) (race discrimination); and *Hazelwood School District v. United States*, 433 U.S. 299 (1977) (use of statistical analysis in disparate treatment).

108. See, *Griggs v. Duke Power Co.*, 401 U.S. 424 (1971) (high school diploma requirement held to discriminate against blacks).

109. Zimmer, et al., p. 685.

110. See, *Mistretta v. Sandia Corp.*, 15 EPD Paragraph 7902 (D.N.M. 1977), *aff'd sub. nom.: EEOC v. Sandia*, 639 F.2d 600 (10th Cir. 1980); and *Geller v. Markham*, 635 F.2d 1027 (2d Cir. 1980)

111. Wax, pp. 1089-1090, n. 22 and accompanying text.

112. Powers, p. 197.

113. Wax, p. 1069.

114. Wax, p. 1067.

115. Wax, p. 1069, citing "How Using Releases Helps Avoid Age Discrimination Litigation," *National Law Journal* (June 17, 1985), pp. 28-29.

116. Kass, p. 69.

117. Achenbaum, p. 115. By 2000, that part of the labor force aged 20 to 34 is predicted to drop from the current 45 percent to 35 percent.

118. Wax, p. 1070. Unlike the FLSA, the ADEA includes within its enforcement provisions for conciliation, conference, and persuasion borrowed from Title VII. Wax, pp. 1078-1079, nn. 82-83.

119. Wax, pp. 1074-1075, n. 53 and accompanying text.

120. Wax, pp. 1071-1072. The principal case in this regard is *Alexander v. Gardner Denver Co.*, 415 U.S. 36 (1974).

121. Eax, pp. 1071-1072.

122. Wax, pp. 1071-1072.

123. Wax, pp. 1071-1072.

124. Wax, pp. 1074-1077. The case discussed was *Runyan v. National Cash Register Corp.* 787 F.2d 1039 (6th Cir. 1986). The plaintiff was an experienced labor lawyer, who had discussed the possibility of age discrimination before he signed a release.

125. The cases are *Brooklyn Savings Bank v. O'Neil*, 324 U.S. 697 (1945); and *D.A. Schulte, Inc., v Gangi*, 328 U.S. 108 (1946).

126. Powers, p. 226.

127. Powers, p. 226, citing comments by the EEOC accompanying the proposed regulation in the Federal Register.

128. Kass, p. 65.

129. Kass, pp. 64-65.

130. See, for example, Minnesota's law, at Minnesota Statutes Section 125.61.

131. Powers, p. 218. The section of the ADEA in question is Section 623(f)(2), which states:

> (f) It shall not be unlawful for an employer, employment agency, or labor organization:
>   (2) to observe the terms of a bona fide seniority system or any bona fide employee benefit plan such as a retirement, pension, or insurance plan, which is not a subterfuge to evade the purposes of this chapter, except that no such employee benefit plan shall require or permit the involuntary retirement of any individual specified by section 631(a) of this title because of the age of such individual:

132. *Sutton v. Atlantic Richfield Co.*, 646 F.2d 407 (9th Cir. 1981). See, Powers, p. 218, n. 135 and accompanying text.

133. *Patterson v. Independent School District No. 709*, 742 F.2d 465 (8th Cir. 1984). See, Powers, pp. 218, 224. See also, Kass, pp. 97-99.

134. *Cipriano v. Board of Education*, 785 F.2d 51 (2nd Cir. 1984). See, Kass, pp. 97, 99-101.

135. Powers, pp. 217-218.

136. *Rock v. Massachusetts Commission Against Discrimination*, 424 N.E.2d 244 (Mass. 1981). See, Kass, pp. 85-86.

137. Kass, pp. 97-101.

138. Kass, p. 65.

139. It should also be noted that the United States does very little in the way of targeting job creation or retraining programs toward older workers, unlike Western European nations. See, Achenbaum, p. 113-114.

140. Katherine Warner, Demographics and Housing," in *Housing for a Maturing Population* (Washington: Urban Land Institute 1983), p. 5.

141. M.H. Hoeflich, "Housing the Elderly in a Changing America: Innovation Through Private Sector Initiative," *University of Illinois Law Review* (1985), v. 1985, p. 3.

142. Hoeflich, p. 4.

143. Hoeflich, p. 5.

144. Hoeflich, pp. 5-6.

145. Warner, p. 5. See also, Hoeflich, p. 2.

146. Hoeflich, p. 9.

147. Hoeflich, p. 9.

148. Hoeflich, p. 10.

149. Hoeflich, p. 10.

150. Hoeflich, p. 11.

151. Raymond J. Struyk, Neil Meyer, and John A. Tuccillo, *Federal Housing Policy at Reagan's Midterm* (Washington: Urban Institute, 1983), p. 4. (Hereinafter, "Struyk, et al.")

152. The elderly faced with relocation by condominium conversion may suddenly be faced with the prospect of coping with tight rental markets, particularly if they attempt to stay near where they have previously been relocated. For example, the state of New Jersey has one of the worst rental vacancy rates in the nation at 4.8 percent. Springfield Township, the location of an important anti-conversion ruling, has a vacancy rate of 1.2 percent. See, Jerilynn D. Troxell, "Protecting the Elderly from Displacement by Condominium Conversion: Troy, Ltd. v. Renna," *Journal of Urban and Contemporary Law* (1986), v. 30, p. 277, n. 13.

153. See, Alan Mallach, "The Fallacy of Laissez-Faire: Land Use Deregulation, Housing Affordability, and the Poor," *Journal of Urban and Contemporary Law* (1986), v. 30, pp. 35-72. The elderly are unintentional victims of exclusionary zoning. The motives behind exclusionary zoning are primarily aesthetic (preventing high density population) and economic (low-cost housing does not generate property tax revenues sufficient to cover the municipal expenses created by such housing). A major concern of suburban towns and villages is school financing, which explains their aversion to low-cost, multi-family dwellings: more school children would be added than would be supported by the property tax revenues generated. One slogan describing exclusionary zoning efforts is that suburbs prefer new residents to be "newly wed or nearly dead," i.e., producing tax revenues without school-related costs. The elderly (who also generate above-average emergency medical service costs) are attractive to suburbia, however, only if they can afford single-family dwellings or condominiums.

154. See, Struyk, et al., p. 3. See also, Mallach, pp. 36-37, 40-42. Mallach argues that although the Reagan Administration was ideologically committed to deregulation in general, it gave only tepid support to deregulation in zoning and land-use, as it conflicted with conservative Republican support of exclusionary zoning by localities.

155. See, Harold A. McDougall, "From Litigation to Legislation in Exclusionary

Zoning Law," *Harvard Civil Rights-Civil Liberties Law Review* (1987), v. 22, pp. 627, 635. The court cases were *Southern Burlington County NAACP v. Township of Mount Laurel*, 336 A.2d 715 (N.J. 1975) (*Mount Laurel I*) and *"Mt. Laurel II*," with the same parties, 465 A.2d 390 (N.J. 1983).

156. See, Mallach, pp. 67-72. A different approach has been taken by large cities through what are termed "exactions." Under a city ordinance, a developer in obtaining a permit to construct a building, typically for office space, must contribute to a fund for the construction of low-income housing. This is meant to compensate for the loss of low-income housing stock and increased rents resulting from a net reduction in apartments when office buildings are constructed. Such construction usually involves the demolition of apartment buildings. Jerold S. Kayden and Robert Pollard, "Linkage Ordinances and Traditional Exactions Analysis: The Connection Between Office Development and Housing," *Law and Contemporary Problems* (1987), v. 50, pp. 127-137.

157. Troxell, pp. 277-278.

158. Troxell, pp. 276, 278. *Troy, Ltd. v. Renna*, 727 F.2d 287 (3rd Cir. 1984).

159. Troxell, p. 276, n. 6.

160. This is the result of a two-step process in which low-income persons are forced to leave through extreme increases in rent, trumped-up "for cause" eviction charges, and other forms of harassment, after which an empty or nearly-empty building is converted to condominiums. The elderly are more affected than other low-income persons because they tend to be long-term residents of buildings which are fundamentally sound and are the targets of conversion.

161. Jill Khadduri and Raymond J. Struyk, "Housing Vouchers for the Poor," *Policy Studies Review Annual* (1982), v. 6, p. 550.

162. Struyk, et al., pp. 4, 69-70.

163. Struyk, et al., pp. 69-70.

164. Khadduri and Struyk, p. 559. To be eligible for federal housing assistance, a household must have 50 percent or less of the median family income for a metropolitan area.

165. Struyk, et al., p. 60. See also, Mallach, p. 52; and McDougall, p. 625.

166. National Housing Law Project, "Summary of the 1987 Federal Housing Legislation," *Clearinghouse Review* (March, 1988), v. 21, p. 1183. (Hereinafter, "1987 Legislation")

167. 1987 Legislation, p. 1183.

168. Struyk, et al., p. 65. The percentage of income to bepaid was originally a variable amount between 15 and 25 percent of income, with the poorest members of the program paying 15 percent. This was increased to a minimum of 20 percent, then to 25 percent, and finally to 30 percent in 1981. It is estimated this last increase reduced the benefit of the housing subsidy to elderly individuals by 15 percent and to elderly couples by 19 percent. Struyk, et al., pp. 14, 73.

169. Cited in Hoeflich, p. 6.

170. See, 1987 Legislation, pp. 1189-1190.

171. See, "Major Threats Imperil Subsidized Projects," *Housing Law Bulletin* (July/August, 1986), v. 16, p. 1.

172. Struyk, et al., pp. 4-5.

173. Struyk, et al., p. 71.

174. Struyk, et al., p. 70.

175. Struyk, et al., p. 70.

176. Khadduri and Struyk, pp. 551-552.

177. 1987 Legislation, p. 1186.

178. Struyk, pp. 1-2.

179. Struyk, p. 3.

180. Hoeflich, p. 4.

181. *Congressional Quarterly Weekly Report* (March 12, 1988), p. 630. (Hereinafter, "*CQWR*")

182. *Clearinghouse Review* (July, 1986), v. 20, p. 255.

183. *CQWR* (March 12, 1988), p. 630.

184. *CQWR* (March 12, 1988), p. 630.

185. "Consumer and Energy Law Developments," *Clearinghouse Review* (January, 1987), v. 20, p. 1222; and *CQWR* (March 12, 1988), p. 630, citing Helen Gonzalez, National Consumer Law Center.

1986. "Consumer and Energy Law Developments," *Clearinghouse Review* (January, 1987), v. 20, p. 1223.

187. *CQWR* (March 12, 1988), p. 630.

188. *CQWR* (March 26, 1988), p. 771.

189. *CQWR* (March 12, 1988), p. 630.

190. *CQWR* (March 12, 1988), p. 630.

191. *CQWR* (March 12, 1988), p. 630.

192. 1987 Legislation, p. 1184.

193. Although another jolt in oil prices might increase Congressional support for LIHEAP. This would be a disaster for the poor, since any increase in assistance would be unlikely to cover the entire amount of the increase, and would not be available to all persons eligible to receive aid.

Bibliography

PERIODICALS

Adamache, Killard W., and Louis F. Rossiter. "The Entry of HMOs Into the Medicare Market: Implications for TEFRA's Mandate." *Inquiry*, 23 (Winter 1986), 349-364.

Applebaum, Eileen, and Cherlyn Skromme Granrose. "Hospital Employment Under Revised Medicare Payment Schedules." *Monthly Labor Review*, Aug. 1986, pp. 37-45.

Barakat, Sami Jamil, and Thomas E. Mulinazi. "Elderly Drivers: Problems and Needs for Research." *Transportation Quarterly*, 41, No. 2 (April 1987). 189-206.

Bayer, R. and D. Callahan. "Medicare Reform: Social and Ethical Perspectives." *Journal of Health Politics, Policy, and Law*, 10 (1985), 553-547.

Boskin, Michael J., and Michael D. Hurd. "Indexing Social Security Benefits: A Separate Price Index for the Elderly?" *Public Finance Quarterly*, 13, No. 4 (Oct. 1985), 436-449.

Brecher, Charles, and James Knickman. "A Reconsideration of Long-Term-Care Policy." *Journal of Health Politics, Policy and Law*, 10, No. 2 (Summer 1985), 245-273.

Cafferata, Gail L. "Knowledge of Their Medicare Coverage by the Elderly." *Medical Care*, 22 (1984), 835-847.

Chambers, Donald E. "The Reagan Administration's Welfare Entrenchment Policy: Terminating Social Security Benefits for the Disabled." *Policy Studies Review*, 5 (1985), 230-240.

Charles, Edgar Davidson, and William Willard Higdon. "Medicare: The Prospective Payment System." *Cumberland Law Review*, 17 (1987), 417-436.

Cofer, Donna Price. "The Question of Independence Continues: Administrative Law Judges Within the Social Security Administration." *Judicature*, 69 (1986), 228-235.

Cotterill, Phillip G. "Testing a Diagnosis-Related Group Index for Skilled Nursing Facilities." Health Care *Financing Review*, 7 (Summer 1986), 75-85.

Couney, Lee M., Jr., and Brant E. Fries. "Validation and Use of Resource Utilization Groups as a Case Mix Measure for Long-Term Care." *Medical Care*, 23 (February 1985), 123-132.

Culler, Steven, and David Ehrenfried. "On the Feasibility and Usefulness of Physician DRGs." *Inquiry,* 23 (Spring 1986), 40-55.

Dallek, Geraldine, "Health Care for America's Poor: Separate and Unequal." *Clearinghouse Review,* 20 (Summer 1986), 361-371.

Davidson, Stephen M., Jerry Cromwell, and Rachel Schurman. "Medicaid Myths: Trends in Medicaid Expenditures and the Prospects for Reform." *Journal of Health Politics, Policy, and Law,* 10, N. 4 (Winter 1986), 699-728.

Delaney, Meg. "Who Will Pay for Retiree Health Care?" *Personnel Journal* (March 1987), 82-91.

Doty, Pamela, Korbin Liv, and Joshua Wiener. "An Overview of Long-Term Care." *Health Care Financing Review,* 6 (1985), 69-78.

Dowell, Michael A. "Hill-Burton: The Unfulfilled Promise." *Journal of Health Politics, Policy, and Law,* 12, No. 1 (Spring 1987), 153-174.

Dumont, J.P. "The Evolution of Social Security During the Recession." *International Labor Review,* 126, No. 1 (Jan.-Feb. 1987), 1-19.

Easterlin, Richard A. "The New Age Structure of Poverty in America: Permanent or Transient?" *Population and Development Review,* 13, No. 2 (June 1987), 195-207.

Edelman, Toby. "Discrimination by Nursing Homes Against Medicaid Recipients: Improving Access to Institutional Long-Term Care for Poor People." *Clearinghouse Review,* 20 (Summer 1986), 339-350.

Elrod, Linda Henry. "Housing Alternatives for the Elderly." *Journal of Family Law,* 18 (1980), 723-759.

Faulkner, Lawrence R. "Mandating the Reporting of Suspected Cases of Elder Abuse: An Inappropriate, Ineffective and Ageist Response to the Abuse of Older Adults." *Family Law Quarterly,* 16 (1982), 69-91.

Feder, Judith, and William Scanlon. "The Underused Benefit: Medicare's Coverage of Nursing Home Care." *Milbank Memorial Fund quarterly,* 60 (1982), 604-632.

Feldblum, Chai R. "Home Health Care for the Elderly: Programs, Problems, and Potentials." *Harvard Journal on Legislation,* 22 (1985), 193-254.

Fisher, William B. "Continuing Care Retirement Communities: A Promise Falling Short." *George Mason University Law Review,* 8, No. 1 (1985), 47-81.

Frazier, Shervert H., M.D. "Responding to the Needs of the Homeless Mentally Ill." *Public Health Reports,* 100, No. 5 (Sept.-Oct. 1985), 462-469.

Fries, Brant E., and Leo M. Cooney, Jr. "Resource Utilization Groups: A Patient Classification System for Long-Term Care." *Medical Care,* 23 (February 1985), 110-122.

Gabel, J.R., and T.H. Ria. "Reducing Public Expenditures for Physician Services: The Price of Paying Less." *Journal of Health Politics, Policy, and Law,* 9 (1985), 595-609.

Gegelman, Randy L. "The ERISA Trustee: Saying 'No' To a Tender Offer." *Washington University Law Quarterly,* 64 (1986), 953-965.

Ginzberg, Eli, and Miriam Ostow. "The Community Health Care Center: Current Status and Future Directions." *Journal of Health Politics, Policy, and Law,* 10 (1985), 283-298.

Gordon, Robert M. and Simon N. Verdun-Jones. "Privatization and Protective Services for the Elderly: Some Observations on the Economics of the Aging Process." *International Journal of Law and Psychiatry,* 8, (1986), 311-325.

Grady, Thomas J. "Liability for Unpaid Pension Contributions: Are Corporate Officers or Shareholders 'Employers' Under ERISA?" *Labor Lawyer,* 4 (1988), 1-20.

Harrington, Charlene, and James H. Swan. "The Impact of the State Medicaid Nursing Policies on Utilization and Expenditures." *Inquiry,* 24 (Summer 1987), 157-172.

Hill, Bette S., C. Jean Blaser, and Pamela W. Balmer. "Oversight and Competition in Profit vs. Nonprofit Contracts for Home Care." *Policy Studies Review*, 5, No. 3 (Feb. 1986), 588-597.

Hoeflich, M.H. "Housing the Elderly in a Changing America: Innovation Through Private Sector Initiative." *University of Illinois Law Review*, 1985 (1985), 1-38.

Holahan, John. "State-Rate-Setting and Its Effect On the Cost of Nursing Home Care." *Journal of Health Politics, Policy, and Law*, 9 (1985), 647-667.

Holahan, John, and Joel Cohen. "Nursing Home Reimbursement: Implications for Cost Containment, Access, and Quality." *The Milbank Quarterly*, 65, No. 1 (1987), 112-147.

Horvath, Diane, and Patricia Nemore. "Nursing Home Abuses as Unfair Trade Practices." *Clearinghouse Review*, 20 (Nov. 1986), 801-810.

Ikenberry, G. John, and Theda Skocpol. "Expanding Social Benefits: The Role of Social Security." *Political Science Quarterly*, 102, No. 3 (Fall 1987), 389-416.

Jacobs, B. "The National Potential of Home Equity Conversion." *Gerontologist*, 26 (1986), 496-504.

Jacobs, Bruce, and William Weissert. "Using Home Equity To Finance Long-Term Care." *Journal of Health Politics, Policy, and Law*, 12, No. 1 (Spring 1987), 77-95.

Kapp, Marshall B. "Health Care Delivery and the Elderly: Teaching Old Patients New Tricks." *Cumberland Law Review*, 17 (1987), 437-467.

Kass, Richard G. "Early Retirement Incentives and the Age Discrimination in Employment Act." *Hofstra Labor Law Journal*, 4 (1986), 63-109.

Katz, Katheryn. "Elder Abuse." *Journal of Family Law*, 18 (1980), 695-722.

Kayden, Jerold S., and Robert Pollard. "Linkage Ordinances and Traditional Exactions Analysis: The Connection Between Office Development and Housing." *Law and Contemporary Problems*, 50 (1987), 127-137.

Khadduri, Jill, and Raymond J. Struyk. "Housing Vouchers for the Poor." *Policy Studies Review Annual*, 6 (1982), 550-562.

King, Joe, Jr. "Adequacy of Transportation in Minority Communities for Handicapped, Low Income and Elderly Groups." *Transportation Quarterly*, 41, No. 2 (April 1987), 247-261.

Kinney, Eleanor D. "Making Hard Choices Under the Medicare Prospective Payment System: One Administrative Model for Allocating Medical Resources Under a Government Health Insurance Program." *Indiana Law Review*, 19 (1986), 1151-1197.

Kosterlitz, Julie. "Costly Miracle Machines." *National Journal*, 4 (May 1986), 823-826.

Kosterlitz, Julie. "Prescribing Pain." *National Journal*, 18 (July 1987), 1845-1848.

Kosterlitz, Julie. "Protecting the Elderly." *National Journal*, 24 (May 1986), 1254-1258.

Kosterlitz, Julie. "They're Everywhere." *National Journal*, 28 (Feb. 1987), 492-494.

Kuhl, Albert F. "Remedies Under the Age Discrimination in Employment Act." *Labor Lawyer*, 2 (1986), 229-249.

Lave, Judith R. "Cost Containment Policies in Long-Term Care." *Inquiry*, 22 (Spring 1985), 7-23.

Lee, Dyana. "Mandatory Reporting of Elder Abuse: A Cheap But Ineffective Solution to the Problem." *Fordham Urban Law Journal*, 14 (1986), 723-765.

Lingle, Earle W., Jr., Kenneth W. Kirk, and William R. Kelly. "The Impact of Outpatient Drug Benefits on the Use and Costs of Health Care Services for the Elderly." *Inquiry*, 24 (Fall 1987), 203-211.

Liu, Korbin, and Yuko Palesch. "The Nursing Home Population: Different Perspectives and Implications for Policy." *Health Care Financing Review*, 3 (1981), 15-23.

Liu, Korbin et al. "The Feasibility of Using Case Mix and Prospective Payment for Medicare Skilled Nursing Facilities." *Inquiry,* 23 (Winter 1986), 365-370.

Logue, Barbara J. "Public Transportation Disability and the Elderly: An Assessment Based on 1980 Census Data." *Population Research and Policy Review,* 6 (1987), 177-193.

Mallach, Alan. "The Fallacy of Laissez-Faire: Land Use Deregulation, Housing Affordability, and the Poor." *Journal of Urban and Contemporary Law,* 30 (1986), 35-72.

Mariner, Wendy K. "Prospective Payment for Hospital Services: Social Responsibility and the Limits of Legal Standards." *Cumberland Law Review,* 17 (1987), 379-415.

Martucci, William C., and John L. Utz. "Unlawful Interference With Protected Rights Under ERISA." *Labor Lawyer,* 2 (1986), 251-266.

McCall, Nelda, Thomas Rice, and Arden Hall. "The Effect of State Regulations on the Quality and Sale of Insurance Policies to Medicare Beneficiaries." *Journal of Health Politics, Policy, and Law,* 12, No. 1 (Spring 1987), 53-76.

McDougall, Harold A. "From Litigation to Legislation in Exclusionary Zoning Law." *Harvard Civil Rights-Civil Liberties Law Review,* 22 (1987), 623-663.

McMath, Sandy. "The Nursing Home Maltreatment Case: Tips for Plaintiffs' Attorneys." *Trial,* 21 (Sept. 1985), 52-53.

Meiners, Mark R. "The Case for Long-Term Care Insurance." *Health Affairs,* 2 (1983), 55-79.

Metcalf, Christine A. "A Response to the Problem of Elder Abuse: Florida's Revised Adult Protective Services Act." Florida State University Law Review, 14 (1986), 745-777.

Mitchell, Eugenie Denise. "Spousal Impoverishment: Medicaid Burdens on the At-Home Spouse of a Nursing Home Resident." *Clearinghouse Review,* 20 (Summer 1986), 358-360.

Muldonado, Kirk F. "Fiduciary Responsibilities Under ERISA." *Labor Lawyer,* 2 (1986), 819-837.

Munnell, Alicia H. "The Current Status of Our Social Welfare System." *New England Economic Review* (July-Aug. 1987), 3-12.

Munnell, Alicia H. "Paying for the Medicare Program." *Journal of Health Politics, Policy, and Law,* 10, No. 3 (Fall 1985), 489-511.

Muse, Donald N. "States Not Protected from Medicaid Growth." *State Government News* (Feb. 1986), 12-14.

Myrtle, Robert C., William W. Lammers, and David Klingman. "Long Term Care Regulation in the States: A Systematic Perspective." *Policy Studies Review,* 5, No. 2 (Nov. 1985), 337-347.

National Health Law Program. "The Omnibus Budget Reconciliation Act of 1987: Legislative Changes in Medicaid, Medicare, and Related Programs." *Health Advocate* (Feb. 1988), 1-48.

National Housing Law Project. "Summary of the 1987 Federal Housing Legislation." *Clearinghouse Review,* 21 (March 1988), 1183-1198.

Newcomer, Robert, Juanita Wood, and Andrea Sankar. "Medicare Prospective Payment: Anticipated Effect on Hospitals, Other Community Agencies, and Families." *Journal of Health Politics, Policy, and Law,* 10, No. 2 (Summer 1985), 275-282.

O'Brien, J., B.O. Saxberg, and H.L. Smith. "For Profit or Not-for-Profit Nursing Homes: Does It Matter?" *Gerontologist,* 23 (1983), 341-348.

Patrick, Renne R. "Honor Thy Father and Mother: Paying the Medical Bills of Elderly Parents." *University of Richmond Law Review,* 19 (1984), 69-83.

"Pension Plans as a Spur to Labor Force Withdrawal." *Monthly Labor Review,* 107 (Dec. 1984), 39.

Peterson, Wallace C. "The U.S. 'Welfare State' and the Conservative Counterrevolution." *Journal of Economic Issues,* 19, No. 3 (Sept. 1985), 601-641.

Perkins, Jane. "The Effects of Health Care Cost Containment on the Poor: An Overview." *Clearinghouse Review,* 19 (Dec. 1985), 831-848.

Powers, N. Thompson. "Reductions in Force Under the Age Discrimination in Employment Act." *Labor Lawyer,* 2 (1986), 197-228.

Rango, Nicholas. "The Social Epidemiology of Accidental Hypothermia Among the Aged." *Gerontologist,* 25 (Aug. 1985), 424-430.

Regan, John J. "Protecting the Elderly: The New Paternalism." *Hastings Law Journal,* 32 (1981), 1111-1132.

Reichstein, K.S., and L. Berqofsky. "Domiciliary Care Facilities for Adults: An Analysis of State Regulations." *Research on Aging,* 5 (1983), 25-43.

Roos, Noralou P., Patrick Montgomery, and Leslie L. Roos. "Health Care Utilization in the Years Prior to Death." *The Milbank Quarterly,* 65, No. 2 (1987), 231-253.

Rosko, Michael D., Robert W. Broyles, and William E. Aaronson. "Prospective Payment Based on Case Mix: Will It Work in Nursing Homes?" *Journal of Health Politics, Policy, and Law,* 12, No. 4 (Winter 1987), 683-701.

Ruben, Ann. "Preserving the Judicial Independence of Federal Administrative Law Judges: Are Existing Protections Sufficient?" *Journal of Law and Politics,* 4 (1987), 207-232.

Ruben, Ann. "Social Security Administration in Crises: Non-Acquiescence and Social Insecurity." *Brooklyn Law Review,* 52 (1986), 89-133.

Sabatino, Charles P. "An Advocate's Primer on Long-Term Care Insurance." *Clearinghouse Review* (Summer 1986), 351-357.

Sapolsky, Harvey M. "Prospective Payment in Perspective." *Journal of Health Politics, Policy, and Law,* 11, No. 4 (1986), 633-645.

Schlenker, Robert E. "Case Mix Reimbursement for Nursing Homes." *Journal of Health Politics, Policy, and Law,* 11, No. 3 (Fall 1986), 445-461.

Schmidt, Winsor C. "Adult Protective Services and the Therapeutic State." *Law and Psychology Review,* 10 (1986), 101-121.

Schwartz, Roger, and Jane Perkins. "The Omnibus Budget Reconciliation Act of 1987: Legislative Changes in Medicaid." *Clearinghouse Review,* 21 (April 1988), 1295-1304.

Scogin, Forrest, and James Perry. "Guardianship Proceedings with Older Adults: The Role of Functional Assessment and Gerontologists." *Law and Psychology Review,* 10 (1986), 123-128.

Shaughnessy, Peter, et al. "Nursing Home Case-Mix Differences Between Medicare and Non-Medicare and Between Hospital-Based and Freestanding Patients." *Inquiry,* 22 (Summer 1985), 162-177.

Sheingold, Steven, and Thomas Buchberger. "Implications of Medicare's Prospective Payment System for the Provision of Uncompensated Hospital Care." *Inquiry,* 23 (Winter 1986), 371-381.

Sisk, Jane E. et al. "An Analysis of Methods to Reform Medicare Payment for Physician Services." *Inquiry,* 24 (Spring 1987), 36-47.

Smeeding, Timothy M., and Lavonne Straub. "Health Care Financing Among the Elderly: Who Really Pays the Bills?" *Journal of Health Politics, Policy, and Law,* 12, No. 1 (Spring 1987), 35-51.

Smits, Helen, Judith Feder and William Scanlon. "Medicare's Nursing Home Benefit: Variations in Interpretation." *New England Journal of Medicine,* 307 (Sept. 30, 1982), 855-862.

Stein, Norman P. "Raiders of the Corporate Pension Plan: The Reversion of Excess Plan Assets to the Employer." *American Journal of Tax Policy,* 5 (1986), 433-508.

Sulvetta, M.B., and J. Holahan. "Cost and Case Mix Differences Between Hospital-Based and Freestanding Nursing Homes." *Health Care Financing Review,* 7 (Spring 1986), 75-84.

Suzman, R., and M.W. Riley. "Introducing the 'Oldest Old.'" *Milbank Memorial Fund Quarterly/Health and Society,* 63 (1985), 177-186. (Special issue on the 'Oldest Old.')

Tamburi, Giovanni, and Pierre Mouton. "The Uncertain Frontier Between Private and Public Pension Schemes." *International Labour Review,* 125, No. 2 (March-April 1986), 127-140.

Tedesco, Theresa, and Ann Walmsley. "Profits in Health Care." *Maclean's,* 8 (June 1987), 26-27.

Thorpe, Kenneth E., and Charles Brecher. "Improved Access to Care for the Uninsured Poor in Large Cities: Do Public Hospitals Make a Difference?" *Journal of Health Politics, Policy, and Law,* 12, No. 2 (Summer 1987), 313-324.

Troxell, Jerilynn D. "Protecting the Elderly from Displacement by Condominium Conversions: *Troy, Ltd. v. Renna.*" *Journal of Urban and Contemporary Law,* 30 (1986), 275-292.

Turner, Margery A. "Building Housing for the Low-Income Elderly: Cost Containment in the Section 202 Program." *Gerontologist,* 25 (June 1985), 271-277.

Warren, David G. "Serving the Health Needs of Aging Americans: Market Opportunities and Legal Permissiveness." *Cumberland Law Review,* 17 (1987), 469-484.

Wax, Amy. "Waiver of Rights Under the Age Discrimination in Employment Act of 1967." *Columbia Law Review,* 86 (1986), 1067-1092.

Waxman, Howard M. "Community Mental Health Care for the Elderly—a Look at the Obstacles." *Public Health Reports,* 101, No. 3 (May-June 1986), 294-299.

Weissert, William G. "Hard Choices: Targeting Long-Term Care to the 'At Risk' Aged." *Journal of Health Politics, Policy, and Law,* 11, No. 3 (Fall 1986), 463-481.

Weissert, William G., and William J. Scanlon. "Determinants of Nursing Home Discharge Status." *Medical Care,* 23, (1985), 333-343.

Wilson, Christine J. "Health Law—CPR Training Brings Life Support Issues to California Nursing Homes—California Administrative Code Title 22 Section 72517(b)." *Whittier Law Review,* 7 (1985), 591-611.

GOVERNMENT DOCUMENTS

The Continuum of Health Care for Indian Elders: Hearings Before the Senate Special Comm. on Aging, 99th Cong., 2nd Sess. (1986).

Delays in Medicare Payments: Hearings Before the Subcomm. on Health and Long-Term Care of the House Select Comm. on Aging, 99th Cong., 2nd Sess. (1986).

DRG's: The New York Experience: Hearings before the Subcomm. on Human Services of the House Select Comm. on Aging, 99th Cong., 2nd Sess. (1986).

Elder Abuse: A National Disgrace: Hearings before the House Select Committee on Aging, 99th Cong., 1st Sess. (1985).

Elder Abuse: An Examination of a Hidden Problem: Hearings before the House Select Committee on Aging, 97th Cong., 1st Sess. (1981).

General Accounting Office, U.S. Congress. *Reimbursing Physicians Under Medicare On the Basis of Their Specialty.* Washington, D.C.: Government Printing Office, Sept. 1984.

Health Care Financing Administration. *Study of the Skilled Nursing Facility Benefit Under Medicare.* Washington, D.C.: Department of Health and Human Services, 1985.

Health Care Problems of the Black Aged: Hearings Before the House Select Comm. on Aging, 99th Cong., 2nd Sess. (1986).

High Drug Costs and Older Americans: A Prescription for the Future: Hearings Before the Subcomm. on Housing and Consumer Interests of the House Select Comm. on Aging, 99th Cong., 2nd Sess. (1986).

Home Equity Conversion: Issues and Options for the Elderly Homeowner: Hearings Before the House Select Committee on Aging, 99th Cong., 1st Sess. (1985).

Impact of the Gramm-Rudman-Hollings Law: Hearings Before a Subcomm. of the House Comm. on Government Operations, 99th Cong., 2nd Sess. (1986).

Medicare: Oversight on Payment Delays: Hearings Before the Senate Special Comm. on Aging, 99th Cong., 2nd Sess. (1986).

Office of Technology Assessment, U.S. Congress. *Payment for Physician Services: Strategies for Medicare.* Washington, D.C.: Government Printing Office, Feb. 1986.

The Older Americans Act and Its Application to Native Americans: Hearings Before the Senate Special Comm. on Aging, 99th Cong., 2nd Sess. (1986).

Quality of Care Under Medicare's Prospective Payment System: Hearings Before the Senate Special Comm. on Aging, 99th Cong., 1st Sess. (1985).

Quality of Life In Nursing: Hearings Before the Subcomm. on Human Services of the House Select Comm. on Aging, 99th Cong., 2nd Sess. (1986).

Retiree Health Benefits: The Fair-Weather Promise: Hearings Before the Senate Special Comm. on Aging, 99th Cong., 2nd Sess. (1986).

Staff of Subcomm. on Health and Long-Term Care of the House Select Comm. on Aging, 99th Cong., 2nd Sess., *Report on The Attempted Dismantling of the Medicare Home Care Benefit* (Comm. Print 1986).

Staff of Subcomm. on Health and Long-Term Care of the House Select Comm. on Aging, 99th Cong., 2nd Sess., *Report on Catastrophic Health Insurance: The "Medicare" Crisis* (Comm. Print 1986).

BOOKS

Aaron, Henry, and William Schwartz. *The Painful Prescription: Rating Hospital Care.* Washington, D.C.: Brookings, 1984.

Achenbaum, W. Andrew. *Social Security: Visions and Revisions.* New York: Cambridge University Press, 1986.

American Bar Association Commission on Legal Problems of the Elderly. *Model Recommendations: Intermediate Sanctions for Enforcement of Quality of Care in Nursing Homes.* Washington, D.C.: American Bar Association, 1981.

American Enterprise Institute. *Proposals to Deal With the Social Security Notch Problem: 1985, 99th Congress,* 1st Session. Washington, D.C.: American Enterprise Institute, 1985.

Berkowitz, Edward, and Kim Quaid. *Creating the Welfare State: The Political Economy of Twentieth Century Reform.* New York: Praeger, 1980.

Cofer, Donna Price. *Judges, Bureaucrats, and the Question Independence: A Study of the Social Security Administration Hearing Process.* Westport: Greenwood, 1985.

Committee on Nursing Home Regulation, Institute of Medicine. *Improving the Quality of Care in Nursing Homes.* Washington, D.C.: National Academy Press, 1986.

Crystal, Stephen. *America's Old Age Crisis: Public Policy and the Two Worlds of Aging.* New York: Basic Books, 1982.

Davidson, Stephen M., and Theodore R. Marmor. *The Cost of Living Longer: National Health Insurance and the Elderly.* Lexington: Lexington Books, 1980.

Dobelstein, A.W., and A.B. Johnson. *Serving Older Adults: Policy, Programs, and Professional Activities.* Englewood Cliffs: Prentice-Hall, 1985.

Ferrara, Peter J. *Social Security: Prospects for Real Reform.* Washington, D.C.: Cato Institute, 1985.

Grimaldi, Paul L. *Medicaid Reimbursement of Nursing Home Care.* Washington, D.C.: American Enterprise Institute, 1982.

Haighthurst, Clark C. *Deregulating the Health Care Industry.* Cambridge: Ballinger Publishing Company, 1982.

Hombs, M.E. and Mitch Snyder. *Homelessness in America: A Forced March to Nowhere.* Washington, D.C.: Community for Creative Non-Violence, 1982.

Johnson, Colleen L., and Leslie A. Grant. *The Nursing Home in American Society.* Baltimore: Johns Hopkins, 1985.

Kane, R.L., et al. *Outcome-Based Reimbursement for Nursing Home Care.* Santa Monica: Rand Corporation, 1984.

Kapp, Marshall B. *Preventing Malpractice in Long-Term Care: Strategies for Risk Management.* New York: Springer, 1987.

Kittrie, Nicholas N. *The Right to be Different: Deviance and Enforced Therapy.* Baltimore: Johns Hopkins, 1971.

Krause, Daniel. *Home, Bittersweet Home: Old Age Institutions in America.* Springfield: Charles C. Thomas, 1982.

Lieberman, Lance. *Disability Appeals in Social Security Programs.* Washington, D.C.: Federal JusticeCenter, 1985.

Light, Paul C. *Artful Work: The Politics of Social Security Reform.* New York: Random House, 1985.

Long-Term Care: Perspectives from Research and Demonstrations. Ed. Ronald J. Vogel and Hans C. Palmer. Rockville: Aspen Systems Corporation, 1985.

Lopata, Helena Z., and Henry P. Brehm. *Widows and Dependent Wives: From Special Problem to Federal Program.* New York: Praeger, 1986.

Marmor, Theodore B. *Political Analysis and American Medical Care: Essays.* New York: Cambridge University Press, 1983.

Marmor, Theodore B., and Jon B. Christianson. *Health Care Policy: A Political Economy Approach.* Beverly Hills: Sage, 1982.

Mashaw, Jerry. *Bureaucratic Justice.* New Haven: Yale University Press, 1983.

McCormick, Harvey L. *Social Security Claims and Procedures.* 3rd ed. St. Paul: West Publishing, 1983.

Monk, Abraham, Lenard W. Kaye, and Howard Litwin. *Resolving Grievances in the Nursing Home: A Study of the Ombudsman Program.* New York: Columbia University Press, 1984.

Myers, Robert J. *Social Security.* Homewood: R.D. Irwin, 1985.

Oberg, Charles N., and Cynthia L. Polich. *Medicaid—Entering the Third Decade.* Excelsior: Interstudy, 1986.

Office of Technology Assessment. *Medicare's Prospective Payment System.* New York: Springer, 1986.

Piven, Frances Fox, and Richard A. Cloward. *The New Class War.* New York: Pantheon Books, 1982.

The Reagan Experiment: An Examination of Economic and Social Policies Under the Reagan Administration. Ed. John Palmer and Isabel Sawhill. Washington, D.C.: Urban Institute, 1982.

The Reagan Record: An Assessment of America's Changing Domestic Priorities. Ed. John Palmer and Isabel Sawhill. Cambridge: Ballinger Press, 1984.

Rosenwaike, I., and Barbara Logue. *The Extreme Aged in America: A Portrait of an Expanding Population.* Westport: Greenwood Press, 1985.

Schultz, James H. *The Economics of Aging.* Belmont: Wadsworth, 1985.

Sinnott, Jan D. *Sex Roles and Aging: Theory and Research from a Systems Approach.* New York: Karger, 1986.

Smith, D.B. *Long-Term Care in Transition: The Regulation of Nursing Homes.* Ann Arbor: Health Administration Press, 1982.

Social Security: A Critique of Radical Reform Proposals. Ed. Charles Meyer. Lexington: Lexington Books, 1987.

Social Security after Fifty: Successes and Failures. Ed. Edward D. Berkowitz. New York: Greenwood Press, 1987.

Social Security: Beyond the Rhetoric of Crisis. Ed. Theodore R. Marmor and Jerry L. Mashaw. Princeton: Princeton University Press, 1988.

Stone, Charles, and Isabel Sawhill. *Economic Policy and the Reagan Years.* Washington, D.C.: Urban Institute, 1984.

Winkleross, Henry E., and Alwyn V. Powell. *Continuing Care Retirement Communities: An Empirical, Financial and Legal Analysis.* Homewood: R.D. Irwin, 1984.

Wolff, Nancy, *Income Redistribution and the Social Security Program.* Ann Arbor: University of Michigan Press, 1987.

Work, Health, and Income Among the Elderly. Ed. Gary Burtless. Washington, D.C.: Brookings, 1987.

NTC Debate Books

1988/89 Topic
Enhancing the Quality of Life For Aging
Citizens, *Goodnight, Gander, Palczewski*
Securing the Future for Americans Over
Sixty-Five, *Flaningam*
The Problems Of Aging Americans, *Hynes*

Debate Theory and Practice
Advanced Debate, *ed. Thomas and Hart*
Basic Debate, *Fryar, Thomas, & Goodnight*
Coaching and Directing Forensics, *Klopf*
Cross-Examination in Debate, *Copeland*
Forensic Tournaments: Planning and Administration,
Goodnight & Zarefsky
Getting Started in Debate, *Goodnight*
Judging Academic Debate, *Ulrich*
Modern Debate Case Techniques, *Terry, et al.*
Strategic Debate, *Wood & Goodnight*
Student Congress & Lincoln-Douglas Debate,
Giertz & Mezzera

Debate Aids
Debate Award Certifictes
Debate Lectern
Debate Pins
Debate Timer
Case Arguments Flow Charts
Plan Arguments Flow Charts
Lincoln-Douglas Debate Cassette Tape

 For a current catalog and information about our complete line
of language arts books, write:
National Textbook Company,
a division of NTC Publishing Group
4255 West Touhy Avenue
Lincolnwood (Chicago), Illinois 60646-1975 U.S.A.